HARDPRESS.NET
HOME OF HARD-TO-FIND BOOKS

Letters Addressed to the Right Hon. Lord Alvanley, on His Pamphlet Entitled the State of Ireland Considered, and Measures Proposed for Restoring Tranquillity to That Country
by Hugh Charles Clifford (Baron Clifford of Chudleigh)

Address:
HardPress
8345 NW 66TH ST #2561
MIAMI FL 33166-2626
USA
Email: info@hardpress.net

126 · F.

The Lord Stanley
with Ld Cs respects
July 24. 1845.

O'Connell — pp. 25 - 39

301

LETTERS

ADDRESSED TO

THE RIGHT HON. LORD ALVANLEY,

ON HIS PAMPHLET ENTITLED

THE STATE OF IRELAND CONSIDERED,

AND MEASURES PROPOSED FOR RESTORING
TRANQUILLITY TO THAT COUNTRY.

BY

HUGH CHARLES LORD CLIFFORD.

PART I.

Part II |

PRINTED FOR
T. JONES, 63, PATERNOSTER ROW;
FOR THE BENEFIT OF THE ROMAN CATHOLIC SCHOOL AT THE GERMAN
CHAPEL, ST. BONIFACE'S, GREAT ST. THOMAS APOSTLE, LONDON.

1841.

Price One Shilling.

W. Davy, Printer, 8, Gilbert-street, Oxford-street,

INDEX AND CONTENTS.

PART I.

PART II.

A 2

same in 1830, on the opportunity which the Emancipation Act of 1829 gave to the Catholic Clergy in Ireland, to retire from political agitation, pages 171 to 176—(C.) Twelfth resolution of the Catholic Prelates of the Province of Connaught on the same subject, page 176—(D.) Resolution extracted from the proceedings of the Catholic Archbishops and Bishops in Ireland assembled, on the 28th January, 1834, confirming the Pastoral Address of 1830, pages 177 and 178.

Appendix V.—Letter of Patrick Flannelly, P. P., and Archdeacon of Easky, to the Right Rev. Dr. O'Finan, p. 179.

Letter V. pages 181 to 294.—Alarm which would be excited in Ireland by the publication of the two first of these letters, foreseen by Lord Clifford—Difference of opinion between Lord Alvanley and Lord Clifford, as to the mode of securing tranquillity to Ireland—Opinion of the Rt. Hon. C. Grant, now Lord Glenelg, Secretary for Ireland in 1819, upon the influence of the Catholic Hierarchy in Ireland, upon public tranquillity in that country—Note. Opinion of Sir Henry Parnell on the same point in 1819—Extract from the Pastoral Letter of Right Rev. Dr. Poynter, Vicar Apostolic of the London District in 1813—Extract from the Pastoral Letter of the Right Rev. Dr. Baines, Vicar Apostolic of the Western District of England, in 1840—Opinion of Earl Roden—Conduct of Archbishop Murray, a refutation of that opinion—Real Security, by which Earl Roden holds his estates in Ireland, rather than by his title-deeds—Principles of the great Catholic Seminary of Ireland, the College of Maynooth—Difference of opinion between Earl Roden and the late Mr. Burke, on the utility of severe discipline in a Catholic Seminary—Violation of the statutes of that Seminary by Archbishop M'Hale—Earl Roden and the late Bishop Doyle at variance—Consequence of the Law of Elizabeth prohibiting " open " communication with the Holy See, on the mission of Sir Henry Seymour to Rome in 1831—Consequences of it, in the promotion of Archbishop M'Hale in 1835 to his present station in the Catholic Church in Ireland—Duty of every Legislator, in either House of Parliament, respecting the Law of Elizabeth—Opinion of Lord Clifford, that Lord Alvanley has written nothing, in his " Measures Proposed for Restoring Tranquillity to Ireland," of which his Lordship has any reason to be ashamed—Letter signed " ✠ Archbishop of Tuam," in the *Freeman's Journal* of December 20, 1841—Observations of Lord Clifford on that Letter—Characters of the late Archbishop Kelly, of Bishop O'Finan, and of Archbishop Murray—Great cause of mischief, in the affair of the suspension of Bishop O'Finan—The attempt of Archbishop M'Hale to enslave the Public Press in Ireland, the real cause of his disgrace—Declaration of Lord Clifford, disclaiming any wish to fetter the Catholic Hierarchy of Ireland—Reflections on the Sligo trial of 1837—Repeal of the Legislative Union—Opinion of the late Mr. Burke, as to the expediency of its enactment—Lord Clifford's opinion, as to the *certain* consequences of its repeal—His opinion, as to the *possible* consequences of its maintenance—Report, printed in Ireland, of proceedings in Court, on a trial in a Civil Suit for Libel, brought by the Rev. Michael Gallagher, Roman Catholic Curate of Islandeady in Ireland, against the Hon. Frederick Cavendish, Proprietor of the *Telegraph* newspaper, in August, 1841—Opening speech of Mr. O'Dowd, Counsel for the Plaintiff—Do. of Mr. O'Malley, do. pages 220 to 228—Evidence of Martin Quin—Of Archbishop M'Hale—Of Christopher Birmingham—Of Rev. Richard Henry, Roman Catholic Parish Priest of Islandeady—Effect of Speech of Richard Keating, Esq. Q.C. Counsel for Defendant—Evidence of Richard O'Grady, Esq.—Of Mrs. R. O'Grady—Of Joseph Burke, Esq.—Of Mr. James Nolan—Of John Burke, Esq.

LETTERS,

&c. &c.

LETTER I.

London, Oct. 25th, 1841.

My Lord,

Mr. O'Connell, as I am told, has declared that he is the best abused man in the Empire. Perhaps that may be true of him as an *individual;* but I maintain most decidedly, and am prepared to prove most demonstratively, that the Peer's House of Parliament is the best abused *body* in the Empire. It has been called a house of pigs. Never was accusation less founded on truth, in my humble opinion at least. Virgil says :

" Immundi meminere sues jactare maniplos."

Georgics, B. i. l. 400.

Pigs can foretell a storm, and it is said can smell the wind. It is admitted by the very parties who cry out loudest against the House of Lords that it can do neither. Pigs if you pull them back by the tail are sure to go forward. Perhaps the House of Lords has no such tail as Mr. O'Connell is said to have; but pull, push, attempt to drag in any pos-

sible direction the House of Lords, it will not
move. If, since Mr. O'Connell began his system of agitation, Ireland be an example of perpetual motion, the House of Lords is fixity itself.
In this sense it is certainly conservative, that it
keeps inflexibly in the same position, and will
not stir an inch. " This much is certain," said
the Right Hon. Wm. Elliot, M.P., in the House
of Commons, in a debate on Catholic Emancipation, (a) on the 21st of May, 1816, formerly known
among his friends by the name of the Castle
Spectre, and one of the best of men and truest
friends of Ireland that ever breathed—" our pre-
" sent position is untenable. Backwards or for-
" wards we must go........Stop where we are and
" close the question—close the question! Sir,
" you might as well attempt to stop the tides."
Nevertheless, my Lord, the House of Peers did
stop the question, till in 1829 the great Duke
made it move, *nolens volens*, with as much quick-
ness as he made Bonaparte move at Waterloo;
but it has remained stationary as to advance
almost ever since that time, though kicking
out every now and then, and putting back
its ears. Now all this resembles in nothing
at all a pig, whatever other animal it may
resemble. No! my Lord, the House of Peers
is not a house of pigs; neither you nor I believe
it to be so, or you would not have written,

(a) See Hansard's Parliamentary Debates, Vol. XXXIV., p. 653.

nor should I now offer my reflections on " The State of Ireland considered."

But if the House of Peers is not, what I am told, some persons have dared to call it, what I hope I have shown with some plausibility at least it certainly is not, a house of pigs, is there any more truth in calling it a public nuisance, which unquestionably it would be by the regulations of the metropolis, if the appellation to which I demur were just?—for your Lordship is no doubt aware that pigs are not allowed to go at large in the streets of London. Now my answer to this question will be quite as decided as my denial of the first charge; but more brief. I say then, that the House of Peers is not a public nuisance; and further I say, that as long as it contains members like your Lordship,—and I believe that it contains several such members,— the House of Peers is a very great public benefit, and never can be deserving of the appellation of a public nuisance.

As long as the House of Peers contains several members, say ten, the number of honest men which would have been sufficient to save two well-known cities of old, mentioned by name, with some others whose names are not mentioned, in Holy Writ, from an awful destruction; as long as it shall furnish men, like your Lordship, descending, if I may so express myself, from their Parliamentary privilege, and entering the lists

with a bold front and high bearing, as champions
in our political arena of the press " from disin-
" terested motives, and with the firm conviction
" of the policy of the measures which they advo-
" cate and the benefit that the adoption of them
" would confer on the Empire at large,"(*b*)—your
Lordship will see by this quotation that I have
read your " State of Ireland considered " to the
very end, or at least read the end of it,—the
House of Peers *ought to be* held in esteem by
the People of an UNITED Empire. I do honestly
believe that *it is* so held, and long may it continue to remain so to be held.

Observe, my Lord, that I do not rest my
claim for esteem on the part of the People of
Great Britain and Ireland for *their* House of
Lords, on the circumstance of any one of its members coming away *victorious* in every respect from
the arena of our Political Press, after having
broken every lance, unhorsed every courteous
adversary who in " free and gentle passage "
gives him a stomach ache for a week with a
blunted lance, or every adversary " a toute
outrance " who may choose to strike the point
of a sharp lance against his emblazoned shield.
—By no means.—It is sufficient, in my humble
opinion, that the champion should bear himself
as a true and gallant knight. I will wish him

(*b*) State of Ireland considered, p. 36.

scatheless in the shock, and rewarded with the smiles of his "Queen of Beauty" after he has distributed "largesse" to the trusty squire who brought him his charger for the lists, and his equally perhaps welcome palfrey to return from them — the noble champion perhaps saying to him at the time, "Now mind I do not give you " this gold for having accompanied me *to* the " field, but for having accompanied me *back* " again."

Your Lordship and myself have both travelled and have met in foreign climes. Wise and holy and amiable men, who have been charmed with the cultivated mind and fascinating manners of your Lordship, have also deigned to admit him who now presumes to enter the lists in what he intends to be no bloody fray, but a determined trial of skill with your Lordship, to their friend- ship also ; and beautiful eyes which have beamed with usual, if not unusual radiance upon your Lordship on the Citorian mount, have looked also upon the stricken deer of St. Marcellus, at least with the benevolence of pity.

We have returned to our mutually loved country, both anxious for a similar though not precisely the same object. Your Lordship has THREE remedies for the deep wounds which the Sassenagh, still more than the No Popery savage has inflicted on the bleeding bosom of that lovely girl, who would have done honor to Great Britain as her wedded wife in 1800, if her guilty suitor had had honorable intentions in her regard; and who even now rejects or struggles against the unhallowed embrace, ONLY because that suitor, whose happiness must essentially consist in an honorable and intimate connexion with that "first flower of the earth," wickedly, basely, and foolishly in reference to the interests of Great Britain, would make Ireland a degraded handmaid, instead of a partner in Empire, as Heaven intended her to be, and as her merits entitle her to be.

I, my Lord, have but ONE remedy to propose for the deep wounds of Ireland. It is very like in appearance to the second of yours, though it is essentially different. I propose to myself to examine, one by one, the three remedies of your Lordship, and to lay before you, in presence of the public, my reasons for thinking, that you are totally wrong in your first, wrong in your second as you have compounded your remedy, and if not totally, at least greatly wrong in your third.

I am anxious to blow my bugle and throw down my glove as soon as possible. There will be time enough before the meeting of the next session of Parliament for me to run my three courses. Let the People of Great Britain and Ireland be umpires between us—our respective printers will, I am sure, have no objection to say, " *Laissez aller ;*" and I believe both of us are equally ready to say Amen to the cry of " God defend the Right," and " God save the " Queen."

I have the honor to be,

MY LORD,

Very respectfully and in all Knightly courtesy,

Yours, &c.

CLIFFORD.

LETTER II.

London, Oct. 26th, 1841.

My Lord,

In this letter I propose to make a cursory review of the statement which you present to your readers, of the deplorable case of the interesting sufferer whom you wish to befriend, in the first twenty-four pages of " The State of Ireland considered." We will, if you please, discuss this state, rather with the gravity which becomes hereditary statesmen, than with the flaunting feathers of knight-errantry waving over our crested helmets; and the Norman dragon of Duke Rollo shall lay down quietly, if your Lordship will give him leave, in the shade of the Saxon plumes of Allwyn de Ardern.(c) We will only remember, that it becomes neither of us to use language, of which our ancestors would have been ashamed. We are both Christians; and if both of us have not an equal wish that Great Britain and Ireland should profess the faith of the " good king Edward," (d) the

(c) High Sheriff of Warwickshire in the time of Edward the Confessor.—See Debrett.

(d) See in Wilkin's Leges in Angliâ conditæ, copied into Canciani's Leges Barbarorum—Leges boni Regis Edouardi quas Guglielmus Bastardus postea confirmavit.

Confessor, neither of us, I am quite sure, have any community of feeling with that detestable race of men, the disgrace alike of Christianity and of the United Empire of Great Britain and Ireland, of whom the late Rt. Hon. Edmund Burke says, in his printed letter to an Irish Peer on the penal laws against Irish Catholics, dated Feb. 21, 1782:——" I have known men, to whom I am not " uncharitable in saying (though they are dead) " that they would have become papists in order " to oppress protestants; if being protestants, it " was not in their power to oppress papists."

I too have known men who, while they were loud upon the hustings in declaring that their conscience (!!!) would not permit them to consent to the Relief Bill of 1829, in favor of persons who, as those noisy and false-tongued loyalists asserted, were by the tenets of their religion rendered incapable of bearing full and undivided allegiance towards their Sovereign, have slunk from the gaze of their deluded hearers into the dark recesses of an Orange den, and sworn to bear allegiance to King William, or to his successor, Queen Victoria, (although that God to whom they impiously appealed had, by His own act, imposed upon them that allegiance as a duty at their birth, prior and paramount to any obligation which they might think fit to impose, or to attempt to impose, by any act of their own, upon themselves) so long only as King William, or Queen Victoria, should support Orange ascendancy, and the moral, civil, and political degradation of seven millions of their fellow-subjects.

But your Lordship must also allow me, who have lived so long in Rome that I am claimed as a Roman citizen there, to adopt in writing to your Lordship, who have also brought back with you from that centre of Christianity fond recollections of it, the phraseology of its admirable Sovereign and Pastor, Gregory XVI., who has eliminated, in his addresses to the Prussian government, from the language of the Vatican, the odious term *heretic*, and even the less offensive term *protestant;* wisely, as your Lordship observes, p. 31, " modelling " (not the " *doctrines* " of the Church of Rome, for they, like " the prin- " ciples on which that Church was founded, are " immutable," pp. 30, 31) its expressions, " and " particularly those which apply to persons pro- " fessing another form of worship, in a spirit " more accordant to the age in which we live."

In return I have to request of your Lordship, and not only of your Lordship but of all who may read these lines, that they will consider these letters, not as addressed by a papist to a heretic, or even to a protestant, in the Orange acceptation of that term at least, but as addressed by a British Christian in communion with the See of Rome, to a British Christian not in communion with the See of Rome, yet holding equally with himself, full and undivided allegiance to Her Majesty Queen Victoria, her heirs and successors; and believing, equally with himself, that it is the duty of *every* Peer, spiritual or temporal, of Great Britain and Ireland, to exert himself, in the station of life in which God has placed him, for the speedy abrogation of every law still existing on the Statute Book, which interferes with the rights and prerogatives and interests of Queen Victoria, and with the birthrights and interests of her subjects.

This being premised, I will commence with the first page of the subject-matter of your Lordship's pamphlet, that is to say p. 3, and agree with your Lordship at the onset, that "some " *new* and *more efficient* line of policy must be " adopted, which shall repress and put under " control *irresponsible* power."

I understand your Lordship, I think I do not *misunderstand* you, to mean, that the power now wielded in Ireland by Mr. O'Connell, and by a certain portion of the Irish Catholic clergy, which refuses to make the wise and unanimous declaration of *all* the Roman Catholic bishops in Ireland, assembled together in 1830 and 1834, the rule of its conduct, should be repressed and put under control. In other words, that Ireland should keep the peace of Queen Victoria, not of Mr. O'Connell or of Archbishop M'Hale.

I must beg leave to observe to your Lordship,

that it is absolutely necessary, in order to prevent
not only gross misconception but gross injustice,
to make a broad and wide distinction between
the power now wielded by Mr. O'Connell, and
the power now wielded by Archbishop M'Hale
and the clerical party, which met together at
the celebrated Galway dinner, where Bishop
Brown, of Galway, the chairman, introduced or
announced Archbishop M'Hale as the " brightest
ornament and lustre " of the Catholic Clergy of
Ireland, and about to speak to them the sentiments
of the Roman Catholic Hierarchy of Ireland. (e)
I mean no disrespect to the Rt. Rev. Chairman
by saying, that a most incorrect assertion was in
these words, supposing them to be truly reported,
palmed on the credulity of the assembly, if I
am to judge from the Report given of the Speech
of Archbishop M'Hale in the *Freeman's Journal*.
Certainly, as far as the circumstances in which
I myself have been placed since 1831, when
Gregory XVI. was elected to the exalted station
which He now holds (and may He long continue to hold it) with such honor to Himself
and advantage to Christianity, enable me to
form an opinion ; never perhaps was there an
occasion, in which a Catholic Archbishop spoke
so mischievously at variance with the sentiments
of the Head of his Church, as Archbishop M'Hale
spoke, at variance with the sentiments and feelings

(e) See Report in the Freeman's Journal of Nov. 26, 1838, of the proceedings at the dinner at Kirdy's Hotel, in the town of Galway, Nov. 20, 1838.
" He will speak to you the sentiments which we all entertain." See also
p. 120 of these letters.

towards England of Gregory XVI. at the Galway dinner, where he flew in the face of the unanimous resolutions and of the published Exhortation of *all* the Roman Catholic Bishops in Ireland, *himself included,* (though your Lordship may perhaps think it an *Irishism* to say that a man *flew in his own face*) to the Roman Catholic Clergy in Ireland in 1830 and 1834. I think that if Gregory XVI. had suspected in the most remote degree, that the sentiments of Archbishop M'Hale would have been so widely different from the sentiments of Hierophilos, Dr. M'Hale would never have been coadjutor bishop or afterwards Bishop of Killala, still less would he ever have been Roman Catholic Archbishop of Tuam.

But as to Mr. O'Connell, if your Lordship or any one who may read this letter, wishes to know *my* opinion of that great man, you and they must *not* take it from the pages of " a pamphlet just " written by a Roman Catholic Nobleman of " high birth and ancient family, in which senti- " ments of sound and liberal patriotism (in your " Lordship's opinion), and, at the same time, devo- " tion to his religion, are put forward in a manner " that does him the greatest credit," (State of Ireland considered, p. 35); but you and they may take in hand the second volume of a work entitled, " Ireland, Social, Political, and Religious, by Gustave de Beaumont, *(f)* translated

---

(f) See Appendix No. II.

from the French, and edited by W. C. Taylor
LL.D., of Trinity College, Dublin, printed
by Richard Bentley, New Burlington Street,
London, publisher in Ordinary to Her Majesty,
1839, and there you and they may read from p.
68 to p. 84, what, to a great degree at least, I
myself, and what, to the best of my knowledge
and belief, *by far the greater part* of the Roman
Catholics of Great Britain and Ireland think of
Mr. O'Connell. (*g*) A man would hardly deserve, in my humble opinion, the appellation of
a British or Irish Catholic who did not think
thus of Mr. O'Connell.

The virtues of Mr. O'Connell are his own. To
Lord Liverpool, not to Mr. O'Connell, must be
imputed whatever of inconvenience, rather than
of danger to public tranquillity, arises from the
wonderful career of that extraordinary man,
who holds in his hands the destinies, not only of
Ireland but of Great Britain and her Colonies;
but I do not believe there is one man in all that
vast extent of Empire, who more sincerely desires that throughout the whole of that vast extent, and in every part of it, the peace of Queen
Victoria and not the peace of Mr. O'Connell
should be kept, than Mr. O'Connell himself. It
is because Mr. O'Connell is intimately and pain-

(*g*) I must except however the opinion expressed p. 81, that
" if Mr. O'Connell thought that a fair open revolt would succeed,
" he would become a revolutionist," especially if he thought such
a revolt would be attended by *bloodshed.*—The expression, *fair*
revolt, is an awkward one.

fully convinced, that the measures hitherto pursued towards Ireland and towards the brave and loyal sons of Ireland in every quarter of the globe, are not and cannot be calculated to preserve the peace of Queen Victoria, that he prefers and promotes the constitutional agitation of Mr. O'Connell to the tyranny of the Sassenagh and the No Popery Orangeman, as a sad but inevitable alternative, until that Justice is done to Ireland and to the best interests of Great Britain, which it is evidently the wish of your Lordship, and the intention of your Lordship's pamphlet, to promote.

With reference to " the Roman Catholic No-" bleman of high birth and ancient family," to whom your Lordship alludes, p. 35, I beg leave to say, that I esteem him for his many excellent qualities. I have known him, I may say, from his childhood; and I can bear willing testimony to his sincere wish to be of service to Ireland, and to the assiduity with which he has applied himself, even to the injury of his health, to the study of her grievances, which as your Lordship justly observes, p. 28, lines 6 and 7, are " real and onerous." I have not the least doubt that the publication to which your Lordship alludes, and which I must be permitted to term, most unfortunate, especially at the present crisis of Ireland's fate, has been edited under a conscientious conviction, that it was an act of duty. I

B

do not believe that it is the production either wholly or in part of any other person; *certainly not of any clergyman.* But it is one thing to have a well stored druggist's shop, full of most excellent decoctions and powerful agents on the human constitution, another thing to be gifted with that medicinal skill, which assisted by regular professional education and much experience, can alone enable the physician to pronounce decisively upon the true nature of the disease, to calculate the forces of the patient and to prescribe unhesitatingly the appropriate remedy. The very best gargle is a bad remedy for a sore leg; and quinine will not do in an intermittent fever with a pulse at a hundred and twenty, nor sweet spirits of nitre with a pulse at sixty: of the use of the lancet I say nothing; for in talking of Ireland I abhor the very mention of shedding blood! Poor girl! one honest kiss from Great Britain, would do her more good than twenty venesections from Welch fencibles. Hitherto it would seem, at least till very lately, that the only part of Plowden's History of Ireland which has been read by those who have been entrusted with the government of Ireland, is the page which records the horrible boast, that "the " bayonet generally removed all sqeamishness." These thoughts take away my night's rest, and make my blood, which is beginning to grow old, boil, when I see it put in doubt whether Ireland

may not perhaps think herself happy, if Mr
O'Connell does not tell her to the contrary, so
long as the Orangeman has power in Ireland, to
call over the Sassenagh to keep down the mere
Irish, or even thinks he may have that power
soon. But I have detained your Lordship so
long upon merely the third page of your valuable
pamphlet, that I know not how to apologise,
except by promising to confine all that I think
it necessary further to observe upon the first
twenty-four pages, to a single question upon
these words of p. 8.

" The secular clergy of Ireland was composed
" of a superior class of men, to what might have
" been expected from the semi-barbarous state
" of the country." I presume that the Invaders
formed the barbarous half, the courageous and
suffering flocks, and their exemplary and well-
educated priests who sustained that courage, the
civilized, and, as an Irishman would say, the
bigger half, for your Lordship immediately
adds: " They were generally Irishmen educated
" at the universities in Spain, or native Spaniards,
" who, from motives of piety, had devoted them-
" selves to the priesthood there; and the manner
" in which they sustained the courage, and
" shared the sufferings of their flocks, has meri-
" ted and obtained the suffrage of the contempo-
" rary writers of the day."

It is, I confess, new to me, that native

B 2

Spaniards ever formed any considerable portion of the Catholic clergy in Ireland. I am curious to know who gave your Lordship this information. I know that Ireland has greatly contributed to christianize Europe; but I have yet to learn, that any country in Europe ever sent foreign priests into Ireland in any considerable quantity, sufficient to take from the native Irish priest the *almost exclusive* merit of preserving Catholicity in Ireland. The difficulty of the language was *prima facie* a great obstacle to any such undertaking. That the educational establishments in Spain did certainly contribute, perhaps more than those of France, Portugal, or Italy, to the formation of the young Irish ecclesiastic, is I believe the truth; but I am unwilling, and your Lordship will see why later, to admit, that Ireland has been indebted, in any great degree, to any other than her native priesthood, for her unrivalled position in the Christian world.

I have the honor to be respectfully,

My Lord,

Your obedient humble Servant,

CLIFFORD.

APPENDIX.

No I.

LETTER II. OF HIEROPHILOS TO THE ENGLISH PEOPLE ON THE MORAL AND POLITICAL STATE OF IRELAND.

" Non equidem hoc dubites, amborum fœdere certo
" Consentire dies, et ab uno sidere duci."   PERSIUS.

" Sure on both nations the same star hath shone,
" Joint are their fates, their destinies are one."

WHATEVER may be the visions of some romantic lovers of country, it is one of the soundest and most incontestible maxims of political science, that there are some countries whose fortunes must ever be obedient to the destinies of others.* This principle, which experience has confirmed in the example of other countries, seems peculiarly applicable to the condition of Ireland. To the strength and abundance of her natural resources I feel proud in bearing ample testimony; but as these must be estimated in relation to the surrounding countries, it must be confessed that she seems to have been destined to be an appendage of the English nation. Though this reflection may be mortifying to our national vanity, we should still be consoled with the consciousness that we may securely repose under the pro-

---

* See Grotius, Des différentes Sortes de Guerre, et de la Souverainete, L. I, c. 3 ; with the notes of his interpreter, Barbeyrac.

tection of the British empire, instead of being placed in the doubtful position of Anactorium, which, if we are to credit the account of Thucydides, was disputed by the contending claims of Corinth and Corcyra.

This obvious principle has taken deep root in the Irish mind. The people are too sensible of the advantage of British connexion to wish for a separation. They would consider as their worst enemies those who would entertain the chimerical project of divorcing that connexion, and the only object they sigh for is to draw closer its relations, by a fuller participation of its benefits. We know that it is the dispensation of Providence, that one kingdom should be swayed by the wisdom and subject to the authority of another. We know that our fate is connected with that of England, and that in " the peace thereof shall our peace be ; " and, therefore, that he who would attempt to seduce the people from their allegiance, would be realizing the language which Jeremias held to the false prophet Hananias, " Thou hast broken chains of wood, and thou hast made for them chains of iron."

The principle of dependance on the English government, which nature seems to suggest, and a sense of self-interest must confirm, derives from the Catholic faith a still stronger influence. The attachment of the Catholic to the person of his Sovereign is derived from a nobler source than those yet alluded to; and the loyalty he must feel, in common with every other subject, is hallowed by the peculiar instruction of his religion. It is a well known truth, that the relative duties of sovereigns and of subjects have been discussed in the sister country with a bold, and, perhaps, dangerous freedom of opinion. We know that some of its most eminent political writers have ventured to fix the boundaries where obedience would cease to be an obligation, and resistance would become a duty. These are discussions which, in the Catholic church, are consider edas questions of a delicate and dangerous tendency; nay, they have even startled the impiety of Hume.* Seldom are these extreme cases agitated by its professors, and never proposed to its followers as maxims of practical adoption. We hold with Mr. Burke, that the speculative line of demarcation, where obedience ought to end and resistance must begin, is faint, obscure, and not easily definable, and that, with or without a right, a revolution will be the very last resource of the thinking and the good. Far, therefore, from entertaining the dangerous theory that would fix the bounds of suffering, which would justify resistance, we are reproached with extending our doctrine of obedience beyond what human nature can endure. Through the vicissitudes of eighteen centuries, the doctrine of the Catholic has remained the same that was preached by St. Paul,† and

---

* " Besides we must consider that as obedience is our duty, in the common course of things, it ought chiefly to be inculcated; nor can any thing be more preposterous than an anxious care and solicitude in stating all the cases in which resistance may be allowed. In like manner, though a philosopher reasonably acknowledges, in the course of an argument, that the rules of justice may be dispensed with in cases of urgent necessity, what should we think of a preacher or casuist, who should make it his chief study to find out such cases, and enforce them with all the vehemence of argument and eloquence ? Would he not be better employed in inculcating the general doctrine, than in displaying the particular exceptions, which we are, perhaps, but too much inclined of ourselves to embrace and to extend !"—*Hume, Essay 13th, on Passive Obedience.*

† " Let every soul be subject to higher powers; for there is no power but from God: and those that are, are ordained of God. Therefore, he that resisteth the power, resisteth the ordinance of God. And they that resist, purchase to themselves damnation. Wherefore be subject of necessity, not only for wrath, but also for conscience sake."—*Romans*, c. xiii.

" Christians are aware who has conferred their power on the Emperors;—they know it is God: after whom they are first in rank, and second to none other. From the same source which imparts life they also derive their

illustrated by the commentaries of Tertullian; and it shall (*Query* will) ever be the reproach, or the glory of our religion, that it shall (*Query* will) ever be inaccessible to the wisdom or the folly of modern maxims of allegiance. For the loyalty of those* which rests on so firm a basis there is little room for apprehension. It is not that fluctuating loyalty which may shift with times and circumstances, and which is measured by the calculating standard of interest or convenience; ours is a loyalty depending on an eternal principle——the dispensation of a ruling Providence; and of which the calls of a capricious self-interest can never annul the obligation.

---

power. We Christians invoke on all the Emperors the blessings of a long life, a prosperous reign, domestic security, a brave army, a devoted senate, and a moral people.''—*Tertullian Apologeticus adversus Gentes*, c. 30.

" Such was the practical Commentary of Tertullian on the words of St. Paul, when the Christians suffered from the cruelty of Severus. I know that Paley applies a more accommodating interpretation to the doctrine of the Apostle.''—See *Moral Philosophy*, b. 6, c. 4.

* " For the loyalty of those which"—*Melius*. For that loyalty which. This observation and the two queries, are here made, in justification of the opinion expressed by the writer of these letters, upon the proof sheets of Hierophilos when sent to him in 1822 for his sentiments upon the work. They were expressed in these words, written in perfect ignorance of the highly talented clergyman, who disguised himself under the signature, Hierophilos :—" It is " an admirable and highly useful work ; and, perhaps, with the exception of " the works of the late Mr. Burke, the finest specimen of the Anglo-Irish " style I have ever read. I would not alter a single word.'' The *Irishcisms* were to me like the Scotch *lilt* on the lips of a beautiful Scotch girl.—C.

No. II.

IRELAND; SOCIAL, POLITICAL, AND RELIGIOUS.
BY GUSTAVE DE BEAUMONT. Cap. vii. Sec. II.

The movement of the association is that of all Ireland ; but this great work of the nation has special agents, and it possesses one so eminent and so celebrated, that I cannot pass him over in silence : I mean O'Connell. If the association guides Ireland, O'Connell rules the association. O'Connell exercises so extraordinary an influence over his country, and over England itself, that to omit him would be to neglect something more than a man, and almost a principle.* It seems necessary, therefore, in order to give some details respecting him, that I should digress for an instant from the regular course of ideas with which I am engaged, but to which I shall be naturally brought back by this subject.

Every day, in our age, great men become more scarce ; not because less great things are effected than of old time ; but whatever great deed is now effected by the people, is the work not of one man, but of several, and in proportion as many agents contribute to a work, the glory of each individual agent is diminished. When in any country I do not find any single man elevated above his fellows, I do not conclude that all the men of this country are mean ; I should rather infer, that they have all a certain degree of greatness. Nowhere are great individualities more rare than in a country of general equality. Look at the United States ; where will you find the common level so high with so few individual prominences ? Ireland, with its immense

---

* If Ireland has, as I think she has, a peculiar merit to herself in the Anglo-Irish style, America may be said to have a peculiar merit to herself in the Anglo-French style. These words of Mr. G. de Beaumont are a beautiful specimen of this style.—C.

miseries, its contrasts of luxury and indigence, with its large masses animated by homogeneous passions, was perhaps the soil best prepared to nurture the glory of a single man.

Is not the power of O'Connell one of the most extraordinary that can be conceived? Here is a man who exercises a sort of dictatorship over seven millions; he directs the affairs of his country almost alone; he gives advice which is obeyed as a command, and this man has never been invested with any civil authority or military power. I do not know if, in the history of nations, a single example of such a destiny could be found: examine, from Cæsar to Napoleon, the men who have ruled over nations by their genius or their virtue, how many will you find who, to establish their power, did not first possess the majesty of civil station, or the glory of arms? Would the name of Washington have reached us if that great man had not been a warrior before he became a legislator? What would Mirabeau have been without the *tribune* of the constituent assembly; or Burke, Pitt, and Fox, without their seat in the British parliament? O'Connell is, indeed, a member of the British parliament, but his great power goes back to a time when he was not so—it dates from the famous election of Clare; it is not parliament that has given him strength; it is on account of his strength that he is in parliament.

What, then, is the secret of this power obtained without any of the means which are usually its only source? To comprehend the singular fortune of this man, it is necessary to go back to the political situation which was its starting point, and which is still its foundation.

After the fatal catastrophe of 1798, Ireland, cloven down, expiring under the feet of England, who crushed her without mercy, believed that henceforward she should renounce all hope of obtaining by arms the blessings, for the conquest of which she had so fatally revolted. She was then in the strange position of a nation, which, possessing some political rights, is menaced with their loss for having attempted to obtain by force those rights which were wanting; which, by an imprudent zeal to obtain complete independence, risks falling into complete slavery, and which, for the future, had no chance of obtaining new liberties, save contenting itself with those it possessed, and no longer disputing the rights of its master. Finally, after the union in 1800, it was more closely linked to England, which, holding Ireland as a rebellious slave, was greatly tempted to punish her, but could not do so without violating the engagements and guarantees, respect for which is so strongly inculcated by the British constitution.

In this conjuncture, what was necessary to Ireland? It wanted not a general fit to lead an army, but a citizen capable of directing a people; it wanted a man whose ascendancy could be established by peaceable means, fit to gain the confidence of Ireland, without, in the first instance, giving alarm to England; who, deeply impressed with the state of the country, comprehending equally its necessities and its perils, would have the great art of devoting himself entirely to the one, and incessantly avoid the other; a lawyer sufficiently skilful to distinguish what had been repealed in the code of tyranny, and what still remained in force—an orator sufficiently powerful to excite the ardent passions of the people against, and sufficiently wise to check their zeal when it verged on insurrection—a clever pleader, as well as a fiery tribune, employed in keeping awake at the same time the anger and the prudence of the people; impetuous enough to excite, strong enough to restrain, capable of managing at will a public assembly, stimulating or soothing popular passion; and who, having taught the people to hate the laws without violating them, was also able, when excesses were committed, to defend them at law, to excuse the authors, and to fascinate a jury as if it were a popular assembly. Ireland wanted a man who, while he bestowed his whole heart on her, did not cease to keep his eyes fixed on England, knew how to behave with the master as well as the slave, to stimulate the one without alarming the other, to press forward the progress of the former without troubling the security of the latter; who, strong in existing institutions, made them his shield for defence, and his sword for attack; showed how one right summoned another right, one liberty another liberty; imprinted on the heart of every Irishman the deep conviction, that his want of independence exposed him to the severest tyranny, but was sufficient to conquer his complete emancipation; and after having thus disciplined Ireland, could one day present her to England as a nation *constitutionally insurgent*, agitated but not rebellious, standing up as one man, resolved not to sit down again until justice had been done. This man, for whom Ireland called, was revealed to her in 1810; it was Daniel O'Connell.* He could not appear sooner or later; for his production a country was required already free, and yet still a slave: there was wanting sufficient oppression to render authority odious, and sufficient liberty for the tribune of the people to be heard; there was wanting that singular accident of a tyranny supported by law, to give such empire to a man familiar with the laws, and who, from their skilful interpretation, could derive the liberty of the people and the independence of his country. Had O'Connell come fifty years before, he would probably have perished on the scaffold; half a century later, his voice would not be listened to in a country that had become more free and more prosperous.

---

* O'Connell succeeded Keogh.

Doubtless a providential interference assured to Ireland some great interpreter for her great misfortunes; but it was a fortunate accident for her that she met one so extraordinary as O'Connell. I am not one of those who believe that Ireland owes her being roused from slavery to O'Connell alone. No; the passions, the inclinations, the destiny of an entire people, do not belong to a single man. No; it is not granted to a single individual, whatever may be his genius and his power, to be everything for his country. The great men who seem to conduct the age very often only give it expression; it is believed that they lead the world, they only comprehend it; they have perceived the necessities of which they constitute themselves the defenders, and divined the passions of which they make themselves the organs. We are astonished, when they speak, that their voice sounds so loud, and do not reflect that their voice is not that of a man, but of a people. If O'Connell and the secret of his power be studied closely, it will be seen that his principal merit is having undertaken the defence of seven millions who were suffering, and whose misery was an injustice. It is pleasant to think that resistance to iniquity is so noble a source of glory. But if O'Connell has not created emancipated Catholic Ireland, what other person could so well have represented it? If he has not alone imprinted on Ireland the great movement which has stirred it so deeply, and still agitates it, how can it be denied that he has prodigiously hastened and developed it? He has not, it is true, forged the weapons of liberty that Ireland possesses, but who could have wielded them so well has he has done? Who, in the presence of the necessities of Ireland, would have studied them so wisely, embraced with such profound intelligence, and employed in their service such vast powers of mind?

I have said that the interests of Ireland required a *con-*

stitutional war, a peace incessantly agitated, an intermediate state between the rule of the laws and insurrection.

Consider with what art O'Connell organised the plan of this association, which was to become the mistress of Ireland, and had to be formed in the midst of laws designed to prevent its birth. It is at present confessed by all, that the Irish association owed its life and its daily preservation only to the sagacity of O'Connell, who having preserved it in the cradle from the attacks of the laws then in force, protected it subsequently from the new laws by which it was incessantly menaced, and finally extorted from his adversaries the confession, that " it was very easy to talk about arresting Mr. O'Connell, and bringing him to trial, but the difficulty was to catch him tripping, and to find a law which he could be formally accused of violating."* Finally, the association triumphed over all attacks; it was predominant; O'Connell became its leader;† and what a leader !—what zeal ! — what prudence ! — what impetuous wisdom !—what fertility of expedients !—what variety of means !

Look at O'Connell when he appeared in 1825 before a committee of the House of Commons for investigating the state of Ireland ; you must admire the lucid simplicity, the ingenuous candour, with which he explained the rigours that then pressed upon Catholic Ireland ; not mingling a single word of bitterness with his recitals, speaking only of peace, union, and harmony, assuring his hearers that when

---

* This was said by Mr. Plunkett, then Attorney-General, now Lord Plunkett.

† It may not be useless, if indeed injustice and oppression can be expected to improve themselves by reflection, to observe, that if the late Lord Fingall had not been arrested in the chair of the association, the present Lord Mayor of Dublin might never have proposed the Repeal of the Union at the Corn Exchange.—C.

when once parliamentary emancipation had been granted, Protestants and Catholics, hitherto divided amongst themselves, but not enemies, would love each other like brethren; answering all objections, declaring all grievances, indicating a remedy for all evils, not leaving a single one of the miseries of Ireland in obscurity, nor one of its persecutions, and pronouncing, in the midst of a thousand designed snares and a thousand inevitable interruptions, if not the finest, at least the most useful appeal that was ever made on the part of an oppressed people.*

But this timid and modest man, who held such conciliating language before a committee of the English parliament, was the same whose formidable voice echoed through the county of Clare, and said to the people,† "The law forbids you to send a Catholic to parliament! Well, I am a Catholic—nominate me." This man, so recently moderate and calm, appeals to all the passions of the people, rouses all their sympathies, excites their most ardent enthusiasm, breaks with one blow the bonds by which the aristocracy held their dependents in subjection, separates Catholic from Protestant, tenant from landlord, servant from master, procures every vote, and leaves in profound and unforeseen isolation this aristocracy, quite stupified by the audacity and success of its enemy.‡

The principal arms used by O'Connell in this constitutional war, of which he is the leader, are his speeches in parliament, the association, and meetings, his election addresses, and his letters in the newspapers. His parliamentary labours engage him half of the year; he speaks on

---

* See Parliamentary Report on the State of Ireland, 1825.

† This step was suggested by the late Mr. Leader.

‡ The representation of the Irish counties has been almost wholly wrested from the landlords.

almost every occasion of public importance; when parliament is closed, he opens the sessions of the association, and supports the principal toil of debate; and yet these are not sufficient aliment for his inconceivable activity. Meetings, which, in Ireland as in England, are held for almost every purpose, and in which O'Connell rules, because he excels there, cannot satiate the thirst for action by which he is consumed. He never allows an opportunity to escape of declaring his opinion to the people, and exercising his power. Is there a general election? O'Connell directs it almost as a sovereign. He says to a constituency, " Vote for such a candidate; " to another, " Do not return such a one," and he is always obeyed. Informed that an election is doubtful in the north, he hastes thither, raises his voice, all-powerful with the Irish multitude, and ensures the triumph of the candidate he has supported; thence, without a moment's repose, he speeds to the south, where he has learned that another election is perilled; he facinates and binds his hearers with a spell, procures the election of his son, his son-in-law, or some of his friends, and, resuming his journey as he steps down from the hustings, he arrives in Dublin precisely at the hour the association is sitting, in the midst of which his voice is heard more fresh and sonorous than ever. O'Connell is endowed with indefatigable ardour; when he has not occasion to act, he speaks; if he does not speak, he writes; his acts, words, and writings, are all directed to one common object — the people, and attain their end by the same way — publicity. There is scarcely a single day in the whole year that the press does not publish a resolution, a speech, or a letter, from O'Connell.

What distinguishes O'Connell is not the splendour of any particular quality; it is rather the assemblage of several common qualities, whose union is singularly rare.

It would not be difficult to find a more eloquent orator, a more skilful man of business, or a more distinguished writer ; but the more brilliant orator could not manage public affairs ; the man of business could not write ; the superior writer could neither speak nor act. O'Connell, who probably would never have become distinguished by his writings, his speeches, or his political actions, taken separately, is at present the most illustrious of his contemporaries, because he is capable, though in a secondary degree, of all three at the same time. It is, however, only just to say that O'Connell was superior at the bar, and that in popular assemblies he is without a rival.

There is in O'Connell's fortune something still more surprising than its origin, and the means by which it was established,—that is, the duration of his power, a power entirely founded on the frail base of popular favour. Men may be seen who are great for a day, the heroes of a brilliant deed, the expression of some considerable event accomplished by them, or by the nation whose efforts they direct, and whose power usually vanishes with the great circumstance of which they are the representative ; but what we find nowhere else is the continued empire of a single man, who during twenty years has reigned over his country without any title, save popular assent, every day required, and every day given. This is, perhaps, the greatest and most glorious of all existences, but it is also the most laborious. The life of O'Connell is one perpetual enterprise, a never ending combat. Were he to abstain from writing, speaking, or acting, for a single day, his power would instantly crumble into dust. The man, whom his country has invested with the supreme magistracy, continues strong, and is obeyed ; after he has become president or king, he may remain so in complete inactivity. But O'Connell at rest is nothing ; his power is only main-tained on the condition of incessant action; hence that feverish agitation by which he is distinguished, and which, it must be said, is the source of his happiness as well as his glory, for repose is inconsistent with his indefatigable nature.

If it be easy to conceive how continuous efforts are necessary to perpetuate this power, which dies and is born again every day, it is far less easy to comprehend how the person, to whom the necessity of incessant action is imperatively prescribed, should always find abundant elements of action ready to his hand. O'Connell excells as much in their discovery as in their management. Scarcely is one grievance of Ireland removed, when his vigilant eye discovers a new grievance, which is to become the text of his complaints; his tact in divining and anticipating the popular passions is quite marvellous; it is not that he forms thought differently from the rest of the world, but he thinks quicker, and he says what every body was going to say. Of all his faculties, the most eminent, no doubt, is the good sense with which he is endowed, by the aid of which he measures a difficulty at a glance, sees at once the best course to adopt, and judges so surely of the present, that no one is so close to the future. Such profound intelligence is clearly genius, and, of all forms of genius, the most beneficial to the people, when selfishness does not corrupt it at its source.

Many represent O'Connell in the character of an ardent and devout Catholic, excited by fanaticism to the defence of liberty. To judge how far this opinion is true, we should be able to read the interior of hearts, a power that belongs to God alone. Still, if it were permitted to hazard a judgment on the most impenetrable secrets of the soul, I would say that in this respect O'Connell displays more good sense than passion, more intelligence than faith.

O'Connell speaks to Ireland the only language that Ireland comprehends; he judges Ireland too well not to know that nothing can be done except by the influence of Catholicism; and he would probably be an ardent Catholic from calculation, were he not so from religious faith.

Others, who only regard O'Connell in his political life, ask whether he plays a part, or acts from conviction. It is a doubt that seems very difficult to be admitted. There is not a mere hired advocate who, after having pleaded for some hours, well or ill, the worst of causes for the worst of clients, does not become almost convinced of the sanctity of his cause, and is roused to zeal, and sometimes even to disinterestedness; and is it asked, if there be good faith and sincere devotedness in a man who for thirty years has defended the same cause—the cause of an entire people of a country which is his own,—a cause to which he has devoted all his life, and to which he owes all his glory,— the most equitable cause that has ever existed, and which he would believe just, even if it were not really so?

O'Connell is exposed to attacks which, if not better merited, are more easily understood. The declared partisans of passive obedience cannot pardon his liberal proceedings and his revolutionary tendencies; and those who regard an armed insurrection as the only remedy for the misery of the people, impute to him all the evils of Ireland, which suffers without revolting. It is plain that O'Connell's conduct cannot satisfy these classes. There is in the political principle which serves him as a guide in that intermediate doctrine between respect for the laws and aggression, a mixture that renders his character difficult of explanation, making O'Connell at one time a loyal subject, at another a factious partisan; one day humbled before the sovereign, the next, sovereign himself in some public meeting, half demagogue, half priest. To understand O'Connell, his character must be examined in this double point of view at the same time. O'Connell is neither a member of a pure parliamentary opposition, nor a revolutionist; he is one or the other in turn, according to circumstances. His principle in this matter is formed by events; all consists in obeying or resisting with discernment. O'Connell, whose good sense always masters his passions, never aims but at that which is possible. Does he find public opinion cold on the subject of reform, he will pursue parliamentary reform with no weapons but those of pure logic and reason. On the contrary, if a subject be agitated which excites popular passions, and in which the nation feels a deep interest, O'Connell no longer limits him-self to reasoning; he acts. He no longer simply invokes a principle; he makes an appeal to physical strength. Thus, in the time preceding emancipation in 1829, he had all Ireland on foot; thus, in 1831, he raised the entire country against the payment of tithes; observe, he raised, but did not arm it; he displayed menacing preparations,* and waited until irritated power, by attacking him, would give him the privileges and advantages of defence. O'Connell knows wondrously the advantage to be derived from the shelter of law, and how far violence may be pushed without passing its limits; he deems it a folly for a people possessing liber-ties to abandon those potent arms, whose usage is legal and exempt from danger, to have recourse to insurrection, whose employment is so dangerous, and whose result is so uncertain. If O'Connell thought that a fair, open revolt†

---

* The power of the people is not when they strike, but when they keep in awe: it is when they can overthrow every thing, that they never need to move; and Manlius included all in four words, when he said to the people of Rome, " Ostendite bellum pacem habebitis."—*The Constitution of England*, by J. L. De Lolme, *Chap.* xiv., *last words.*—C.

† See note (*g*).—C.

would succeed, and render Ireland free and happy, he
would assuredly become a revolutionist. He would have
applauded the movement of the volunteers in 1778; but I
doubt whether, in 1792,* he would have engaged in the
more national movement of the United Irishmen. O'Connell has his soul and his memory stored with all the miseries that violent efforts for independence have brought upon
Ireland; hence his constant effort to create what he calls
constitutional agitation; that undecided system between
peace and war, between submission and revolt, between
legal opposition and revolt,—a system which, without doubt,
does not confer on the people the benefits of a sudden and
prosperous revolution, but which also does not expose the
country to the awful responsibilities of an unsucessful
insurrection.

But whether O'Connell be considered as an ardent
sectary or as the great leader of a party, a politician or an
enthusiast, a parliamentary orator or a revolutionist, in
every case we are obliged to recognise his extraordinary
power; and what is especially remarkable in this power
is, that it is essentially democratic. O'Connell is naturally, and by the mere fact of his political position in
Ireland, the enemy of the aristocracy; he could not be the
man of the Irish and Catholic people without being the adversary of the Anglican oligarchy. Perhaps in no country
is the representative of popular interests and passions so

---

* Mr. Burke wrote his celebrated letter to Sir Hercules Langrishe in
January, 1792. In it he says, " The true revolution to you, that which most
" intrinsically and substantially resembled the English revolution of 1688,
" was the Irish revolution of 1782." I fear that the "national movement" of
1792, reduced the English Cabinet to *nearly the necessity of wishing* for the
insurrection of 1798, as an awful alternative—even if it did not make the executive power in Ireland conceive, as has been said, the horrible idea of ex-
citing it.—C.

necessarily the fierce enemy of the upper classes as O'Connell, because there is not perhaps a country in the world where the separation between the aristocracy and the people is so open and complete as in Ireland.

We must not then be astonished if O'Connell wages an eternal war against the aristocracy of Ireland. Nothing can restrain him in those attacks which his passions suggest, and which his interests do not forbid. Nor must we be astonished if O'Connell, the idol of the people, provokes the bitter hostility of the higher ranks of society. There is not perhaps another man so much loved and so much hated. The resentment of the aristocracy against him is very natural; but woe to the Irish nobleman who, unable to disguise his hatred, provokes this formidable enemy!

Once at a public dinner, a noble lord, alluding to the tribute which O'Connell receives from Ireland,* called him " the big beggarman; " the next day O'Connell, at the association, spoke to the following effect: " I have to tell you of a new attack made upon me by the Marquis of ——, who has dared to call me a mendicant. I should like to know what right he has to treat me in this way? Is it because I have sacrificed an income equal at least to the best of his estates, in order to devote myself more completely to the defence of my countrymen, and defend them better against an aristocracy whose only desire is to trample them in the dust? My fortune, perhaps, is different from that of any other man, and Ireland has done for me what no other nation has ever done for a private individual. Yes, it is true that I receive a tribute and high wages for my feeble services. I am proud of it. I reject with disdain, as I hear with contempt, the insults of this cowardly aristocracy, which would

---

* The notion has been abandoned.

march over the body of the people, if it did not find me on the road. What are the claims of this Marquis of —— to public consideration? How did he get the large estates he possesses in Scotland? I will tell you. His ancestor was Lord ——, abbot of ——, in the time of Knox. Betraying the trust reposed in him, he surrendered the vast possessions dependant on his abbey, after having first secured for himself a grant of two-thirds. Let us look at the origin of his estates in Ireland. How did they get into his family? Why, by the usual way in those times—by perjury, robbery, and murder. And here is a man, inheriting the fruit of such crimes, who dares to attack a person whose only crime is, that he has been chosen the defender of his country against the monsters who have crushed it for ages beneath the weight of their tyranny."

It is not merely by bitter sarcasms, invectives, and violent declamations, that O'Connell attacks the upper classes in Ireland, and upsets their authority; he overthrows their empire by the ascendancy he has acquired over those who owe them obedience; he destroys their power by the dominion that he personally exercises over Ireland. By placing the people under a single central influence, derived from the assent of each, O'Connell has taught them to count as nothing the legal and traditional privileges which in an aristocratic government are supposed to be attached to name, birth, and social condition.

LETTERS

ADDRESSED TO

THE RIGHT HON. LORD ALVANLEY,

ON HIS PAMPHLET ENTITLED

THE STATE OF IRELAND CONSIDERED,

AND MEASURES PROPOSED FOR RESTORING
TRANQUILLITY TO THAT COUNTRY.

BY

HUGH CHARLES LORD CLIFFORD.

PART II.

PRINTED FOR

T. JONES, 63, PATERNOSTER ROW;

~~FOR THE BENEFIT OF THE ROMAN CATHOLIC SCHOOL AT THE GERMAN
CHAPEL, ST. BONIFACE'S, GREAT ST. THOMAS APOSTLE, LONDON.~~

1841.

~~Price Six Shillings.~~

LETTERS,

&c. &c.

LETTER III.

London, December 1st, 1841.

My Lord,

Upon the three remedies which your Lordship has proposed for restoring tranquillity to Ireland, I have ventured in my last letter to you to intimate this opinion,—that your Lordship is totally wrong as to the first, namely, the payment of the Roman Catholic Clergy; partially wrong in your second, namely, the restoration of communication with the Holy See; and totally wrong in your third, namely, "the reformation," as your Lordship expresses yourself, p. 32, "of the college of Maynooth." Before I commence the series of observations which I wish to be permitted publicly to address to your Lordship upon each of your three remedies, or to submit to your Lordship's consideration and to that of the People of Great Britain and Ireland, the adoption of *one single* legislative measure from which, should it be adopted by public

A 2

consent, public tranquillity would, I think, necessarily and as it were spontaneously result, I must beg leave to explain, in a few words, why I have allowed so great a length of time to elapse between the date of this letter and of my last. For some may perhaps think that I have kept back from the fulfilment of my pledge, on account of some misgivings in my own mind, that I had rashly engaged in a bad cause; while others may suppose, that I have yielded to the advice of persons more prudent than myself, who may have suggested to me, that my interference in a career, in which your Lordship was not likely to have engaged without having to encounter far more able adversaries than myself, might much more probably do injury to the cause in which I had volunteered my services, than be productive of credit to myself. I assure your Lordship, therefore, that I have had no misgivings in my own mind, since I had the honor of last addressing you, as to the propriety of the step which I have taken, in announcing myself to the public on the 26th of last October as your Lordship's antagonist; nor has any one suggested to me that which, nevertheless, if it had been suggested to me, ought not perhaps to have occasioned in me any surprise, still less any displeasure. (a)

(a) I must except, from this general observation, the following

It was not with any, even the most remote, view of doing credit to myself, that I addressed your Lordship last October my two last letters; and my sole reason for not addressing to your

---

entertaining communication from an hon. and learned barrister, who, after due consultation with several brother-critics, lay and clerical, as he informs me, wrote to me as follows, Nov. 12, with double and single interlinings :

" I hope you will not think me IMPERTINENT, though *candid.*
" I have no wish to be the *former*, but always anxious to be the
" *latter* in your regard : now allow me to convey to you my
" *opinion* and *others*, *Rev.* as well as *Laymen*, upon your late
" letters to Lord Alvanley, which I have read with MUCH AT-
" TENTION. I must say, that *I* agree with all who I have con-
" versed with upon them, *who have read them*, in thinking, that
" they are written in very *bad style* and *taste*, and, I fear, in
" *language* which will do no credit to the writer, or the cause
" you mean to advocate. They are not written in the language
" adapted to a Peer of the realm, or in such language as, in my
" opinion and others, ought to be addressed by one Peer to
" another. Pardon these remarks ; they are written with the
" best intentions, for I well know the ways of the world, and
" that many may praise the letters to your face, and condemn
" them behind your back ;—such shall *never be my case.*"

Had it not been for this single exception, I should be under the necessity of admitting, that my vanity must have been as much mortified during the last month, as that of Mr. Gibbon, who, after the publication of one of his works, sent out daily his servant to the different news-rooms and publishers in the vicinity, to learn what answers to his essay, or criticisms upon it, had appeared ; but regularly received, until he was tired of making enquiry, the same stoical answer,—" None at all, Sir ! "— " Pshaw ! " exclaimed, as regularly, the disappointed Essayist.

Lordship this letter a month ago was, that I considered my last letter to you sufficient for the
purposes which I had principally in view in
publishing it. I wished it to be known publicly,
as speedily as possible after the appearance of
your Lordship's pamphlet, not indeed that I laid
claim to be numbered (for I do not) among the
most distinguished and influential Catholics to
whom your Lordship alludes, p 31 ; but that I
had no reason for thinking that Pope Gregory
XVI., or any distinguished and influential Catholics, whom I have had opportunities of meeting
in Rome, since 1829, when I accompanied
thither the late Cardinal Weld, my lamented
father-in-law, entertain, or had ever entertained,
such sentiments as those which are attributed to
the present head of the Roman Catholic Church,
and to them in the following words of your
Lordship's pamphlet, pp. 28, 29, and 31.

" The next step to be taken towards the reali-
" zation of the great object in view, ought to be
" the repeal of the enactments forbidding *open*
" communication with the Court of Rome, and
" the appointment of a minister to that Court,
" *after the example of Russia and Prussia.* . . .
" Enlightened men have modelled its *doctrines,*
" and particularly those which apply to persons
" professing another form of worship, in a spirit
" more accordant to the age in which we live.
" *The relations existing with Russia, Prussia,* and

" other Greek and Protestant States, are the
" best proof that such is the case ; and it is cer-
" tain, *that the Pope and the most distinguished*
" *and influential Catholics anxiously desire that*
" *similar relations should be established in this*
" *country.*"

I felt anxious, my Lord, from the first moment
that I read this assurance, thus confidently given
to the people of Great Britain and Ireland by
your Lordship, who had been at Rome, and
might be supposed to have good grounds for
making it, to declare, that *I know of no such
grounds;* but whether I have grounds for believing *the contrary to be the case,* is a question
into which I do not intend to enter in this letter.

It appeared to me last October, that it would
be, after the public expression I then made of my
opinion upon the accuracy of your Lordship's
information, quite time enough, at any period
before the next Session of Parliament, to enter
into the examination of your Lordship's grounds
for believing, that Pope Gregory XVI., or any
one whom his Holiness may very naturally be
supposed to have consulted on such a subject, if
it were ever proposed to his Holiness, " anxiously
" desired that relations with the Holy See,
" *similar* to those now existing between that See
" and the Governments of *Russia and Prussia,*
" should be established in this country." I also
wished last October, that it should be publicly

known, as soon as possible, after the appearance
of your Lordship's pamphlet, that, while I cordially agreed with your Lordship that "the Ro-
" man Catholic Nobleman of high and ancient
" family," to whom your Lordship alludes in p.
35, is actuated " by sentiments of " sincere " and
" liberal patriotism, and, at the same time, de-
" votion to his religion," I considered the appearance of his publication at that moment most
unfortunate, though I considered the appearance
of your Lordship's pamphlet rather fortunate
than otherwise. I feared that the publication of
the noble Earl, to which your Lordship alludes,
would produce an immediate re-action, which
would be more detrimental to the cause which
that noble Earl and yourself wish, both of you
doubtless most sincerely, to serve, than the public expression of his sentiments, as set forth in
that publication, would, or perhaps could, benefit that cause ; nevertheless, I am far from condemning entirely many of those sentiments ; and
some of them I highly approve ;—as, for example, when the noble Earl says, p. 8,—
" O'Connell is undoubtedly the man whom
" Providence has employed as the dispenser of
" many blessings both to Ireland and TO US."
(Here, I presume, the noble Earl writes as an
English Catholic.) And when again he says,—
" Ireland progressed in strength and *health*
" under this new reign." But I had little hope

that such sentiments, as I have just quoted, would, in such a publication, have the due weight which I wish such sentiments from the noble Earl may yet have with his readers *in his own favour*.

Such were my reasons for wishing to appear before the public in October last as an antagonist, though not an enemy, of your Lordship; but there seemed to me to be no immediate hurry for the appearance of this letter. I considered, that with the public task which I had already undertaken in reference to India, it was only by physical and mental exertions to which I felt myself unequal, that I could, at an earlier period than the present, redeem my pledge to your Lordship and to the public. That pledge was, in fact, to prove satisfactorily to the people of Great Britain and Ireland, that the measures proposed by your Lordship for restoring tranquillity to Ireland were not, however well intentioned, such as would or could effect the proposed purpose; but were, on the contrary, such as might very probably increase the present agitated state of public opinion in the United Empire, even by the *attempt* to bring those measures into operation, however impossible it might be really to establish any one of them in practice. As, however, there was not in last October any likelihood that any such attempt would be made, even if it were ever to be made, before the next

Session of Parliament, I have consequently thought it lawful to devote my time, during the last month, to the promotion of measures which appear to me indispensable, and of immediate necessity for obtaining justice to India ; and have had the satisfaction of finding myself supported in my endeavours to direct public attention to India, by one of its truest and ablest friends, the Lord Mayor of Dublin. I felt quite confident, that the cause of justice to Ireland would meanwhile be advocated by much abler champions than myself, and by none more so than the chief magistrate of its capital city ; and I now willingly return to offer my humble services to that sacred cause, in the shape of remarks to your Lordship on the last twelve pages of " The state of Ireland considered, and mea-" sures proposed for restoring tranquillity to that " country."

In offering these remarks, I trust I am actuated by feelings towards your Lordship far different from those which seem to have dictated two very disgraceful articles inserted, the first, in the Dublin University Magazine for November 1841, pages 635 to 642, and entitled " Lords " Shrewsbury and Alvanley on Ireland ;" the second, in the same Magazine for December 1841, pp. 765 to 776, entitled " Recent Pamph-" lets on Ireland. Alvanley, Shrewsbury, and " Meyler." It is foreign to the object of these pages, and it would be a very nauseous task for me, to criticise in detail, either the scurrility, introduced into those articles upon the perfectly erroneous supposition, that a distinguished Prelate, whose great talents and amiable manners and style of writing are equally the theme of general admiration, is the real author of the Earl of Shrewsbury's pamphlet, with which that Prelate had *nothing whatsoever to do ;* or the total absence of historical information and of good breeding which the writer of those two articles has shamelessly displayed in his abuse of your Lordship's Essay,—I shall content myself with saying, in reference especially to the second of those articles, in the very words of the author of it, as I find them printed towards the bottom of the first column of page 766, that " it is very " difficult to comment upon " that article " with- " out using disagreeable language," and that the whole of the remainder of the paragraph from the commencement of which I have quoted the above words, appears to me, and I think must appear also to every unprejudiced reader of your Lordship's Essay and of the two articles in which it is reviewed in the Dublin University Magazine, which they disgrace, a much more accurate description of those two articles, than of your Lordship's Essay, or even of any part of it.

There is, however, one feature in the two

articles of the Dublin University Magazine of this and the last month, which is very worthy of notice ; namely, the tone of *alarm* and irritation expressed in the second column of page 642, in reference to the course pursued by the *Times* newspaper ; a course which the writer in the Magazine designates as "a strange and porten- "tous fact." If the writer in the Magazine had been as well acquainted with the principle on which that paper is conducted, *of pointing out before-hand coming events*, and preparing public opinion for the *adoption of measures of inevitable necessity*, as he seems to be with the language of falsehood and scurrility, the course pursued by the *Times* newspaper, in reference to the publications of your Lordship and of the Earl of Shrewsbury, would not have appeared to him *strange*, though it might have appeared to him *portentous*.

" For months," says the writer in the Maga- zine, " the symptoms were clearly visible, which " indicated that the *Times*, the great Conserva- " tive organ, was beginning to drift from her " moorings. A very decided leaning to the " weaknesses of the Oxford theologians very " clearly appeared. All this we would have " borne, in the confident expectation that the " old English good sense, by which it was dis- " tinguished, would ultimately prevail. But we " can no longer disguise our conviction, that

" such is not likely to be the case............We call
" upon the Conservative gentry of the Empire
" to beware how they suffer their judgments to
" be abused by statements which should never
" have disgraced a journal of the character of
" the *Times.*"

I think that your Lordship will agree with
me, that you have little cause to disturb your
peace of mind at the charge of " drivelling "
brought against you by the writer, who with
such admirable *naiveté,* proclaims the fact, that
the *Times* " has become the vehicle for convey-
" ing to the public and placarding as it were
" throughout the Empire, the delusive plausi-
" bilities of " the Earl of Shrewsbury, and what
the writer in the Dublin University Magazine is
pleased to call your Lordship's " drivellings."

For my part, although I beg to be permitted
to retain, and I hope without offence to either
the Noble Earl or your Lordship, the opinion
I have already expressed in this letter of the
appearance before the public of both productions
at the present moment and under existing circumstances, I consider the notice taken of both
by the *Times* newspaper, as a very *important*
and *cheering* though neither a *strange* nor, at
least in the ill-omened sense of the word, *portentous* fact.

In a style far different from that of the writer
in the Dublin University Magazine, are penned

the published observations, dated Tollymore Park, Co. Down, Nov. 20, 1841, of the Earl of Roden on your Lordship's "Measures proposed for "restoring tranquillity to Ireland." I have no doubt of their being answered by some of his own countrymen, in a manner, which will perhaps make him more cautious for the future, how he presses into the service of the Established Church of Great Britain and Ireland *not* in communion with the See of Rome, the names of Bede, Anselm, and Baronius, as authorities for his very confident but, totally unfounded assertions, that "when the Roman Catholic "Missionaries first visited Ireland, they found "that the Christian religion in its purity had "been professed and practised for centuries "— p. 8, or that "the Irish Christians were under "no obligation....................... to Rome; they ex "tended the right hand of fellowship to the "Missionaries, but they neither recognised nor "submitted to the authority or jurisdiction of "the Bishop of Rome"—*ibid.* As to the words I have omitted in this quotation, "they owed "no allegiance," they remind me of the words of Hamlet *travestie :*

Hamlet—He said each Danish villain was a knave.
Horatio—If that were all, he might have staid in his grave.

Is it possible that the Noble Earl should still be in ignorance of Catholic doctrine on this point as set forth in the Declaration of 1826!!! But I will only hope that whoever may undertake the task, an arduous one, I fear, of *initiating* the Noble Earl in Irish Ecclesiastical History, will not forget the courtesy due to the benevolent landlord who truly describes himself in these words of his pamphlet, p. 32: " during " thirty years' residence in Ireland, I have lived " in harmony and friendship with my Roman " Catholic fellow-countrymen, for many of " whom I entertain a sincere regard."

I now turn to your Lordship's pamphlet.

Your Lordship says, p. 24, that *the great proportion* of the " Roman Catholics in Ireland are " *mere instruments* in the hands of *priests,* who " exercise over them an unrestrained and ex- " cessive power, both spiritual and temporal ; " and as these priests themselves form a *separate* " class of the community, over which the " government has *no authority whatever*, it is vain " to hope that tranquillity and concord, free " exercise of public rights, respect for the laws " and security of property, can prevail, till some " legitimate means are found of controlling " a power *so entirely irresponsible,* and the ex- " istence of which either for good or bad pur- " poses, is contrary to all sound principles of " government, and incompatible with the well " being of the Empire." And p. 25.—" The " *first* step to be taken for this purpose, should be

" a measure for the payment of the Irish Roman
" Catholic clergy."—I presume your Lordship
means to add *by the State.*

I have not the slightest doubt, that your
Lordship *intended* in all this paragraph to state
the truth, the whole truth, and nothing but the
truth ; but your Lordship will not, I hope, be
offended at me for observing to you, that good
intentions sometimes woefully miscarry.

Is it true that the " great proportion " of
the Roman Catholics in Ireland are mere instruments in the hands of priests ? *Would it be
true* to say that they are such in the hands of
Mr. O'Connell, who *is not a priest* ? Put the
case, that the priests to whom your Lordship
alludes, proposed one civil or political measure
for the good of Ireland, and that Mr. O'Connell
proposed another ; does your Lordship believe,
that the great proportion of the Roman Catholics
of Ireland would follow those priests instead of
following Mr. O'Connell ? If not, the Roman
Catholics of Ireland are clearly not, in your
Lordship's opinion, mere instruments in the
hands of the priests to whom you allude. *Is
it true* that " *as* these priests form a separate
" class over which the government has no au-
" thorty whatever, it is vain to hope," &c.?
The priests, to whom your Lordship alludes,
do *not* form a separate class now, any more
that the priests alluded to in p. 8 of your Lord-

ship's pamphlet did in former times. It seems
to me that is precisely *because* the Roman
Catholic priests in Ireland, whether taking a
lead in political agitation or abstaining from
taking such lead, do *not* form a separate class,
that your Lordship is angry with them. There
are several persons, if I am not greatly misinformed, in this country, as well as in Ireland,
who wish all the Roman Catholic priests in Ireland to be pensioners of the State, precisely that
they may all form a separate class, with distinct,
not to say opposite interests, from their starved
and oppressed flocks.

Is it true that the government has no authority whatever over these priests? It has, and
is acknowledged by these priests to have, *all
civil and temporal authority* over them. It is not
fitting, and it would be highly detrimental to
the tranquillity of Ireland, that the British government should have any spiritual or ecclesiastical authority over these priests; and it is any
thing but clear to me, that the scheme of " ac-
" credited Vicars Apostolic in constant commu-
" nication with the government," proposed, p.
32, to be " sent as chosen agents to the different
" dioceses in Ireland," is not a scheme which
your Lordship has stolen from Caliban in Shakespeare's Tempest. I shrewdly suspect, that the
Catholic Church of Ireland would be as little
likely to fall in love with your Lordship's Cali-

B

bans, as Miranda was with Shakespeare's. Nor
am I fully persuaded, that in the principal College for the education of the Roman Catholic
priesthood in Ireland, " government would exer-
" cise a *legitimate* controul over its affairs through
" agents appointed for that purpose."

Believe me, my Lord, all " the extreme severity of discipline," which you attribute, p. 22,
and which I certainly do not attribute, to Maynooth College, though perhaps I have had as
much opportunity of becoming acquainted with
the system of that college as your Lordship has
had, would be requisite to qualify any one brought
up at Oxford or Cambridge, for the task of re-
forming the clergy of the Roman Catholic church
in Ireland. The magic wand required for such
a task, is an Olympian palm, which no alumnus
of Alma Mater would attain, till he had groaned
out more than once in the words of Horace under a much more severe discipline than that of
Maynooth College, whatever he might have
done at Oxford or Cambridge :—

" Quisquis Olympiacæ studuit contendere palmæ
" Multa tulit fecitque puer, sudavit et alsit
" Abstinuit venere et vino."

But we shall have to revert to this subject later,
when we come to the consideration of your
Lordship's third remedy. To return therefore
to your first. *Is it true* that the power of

the priesthood in Ireland is "wholly irrespon-
" sible " — at least the power of the *Roman
Catholic* priesthood? I do not believe that, to
say nothing of the responsibility of that priesthood to the Roman Catholic Hierarchy in Ireland in spiritual and ecclesiastical matters, and
to the Government of the United Empire in civil
and temporal matters, there is any priesthood in
the world more responsible to public opinion.
Your Lordship has, I fear, fallen into an error
always too common with writers, who strongly
influenced by preconceived notions, put their
pen to paper to describe institutions or countries
which they have not had time, leisure, or opportunity to examine sufficiently to become well
acquainted with them; and there is much cause
for apprehension, that to some Irishmen you may
consequently appear to have made a mistake
almost as ludicrous as the honest Mahommedan,
who wrote on a Saturday evening from London,
where he had arrived on the preceding Monday
morning, that he felt himself competent to give
his friend at Constantinople an accurate account
of the Religious character of the People of England. " They are evidently," says the attentive
and sagacious traveller, "a religious people of Ma-
" hommedan descent, and though they are much
" fallen off from the original purity of Islamism,
" still they preserve some of the customs of their

" parent faith. I observe, for instance, early in
" the morning, black priests, like our Muezzims,
" calling the people to prayers with a loud voice
" from the house tops, and waving in their hands
" a sacred symbol." Your Lordship will understand that these Muezzims were chimney-
sweepers—yet continues the devout and true
believer in Allah and Mahomet his prophet:
" I have never yet been able to enter one of
" their mosques, which are rather numerous, but
" always locked up." Your Lordship must observe he had been six days in London. " I had
" understood," he continues, " before I came
" here, that these people believed in a plurality
" of Gods; but I have clearly satisfied myself
" since my arrival, that this is a great mistake,
" and that they worship, and like us constantly
" invoke only one God, whose name is not in-
" deed Allah, but God Dammee."

Your Lordship has it seems to me met with, or
heard and read of that limited portion of the
Irish Catholic clergy, which made such a sorry
figure against my venerable friend the Right
Rev. Dr. O'Finan, Bishop of Killala, in the
Sligo trial of March 1837, O'Finan *versus* Cavendish.

But these exceptional cases are I trust no more
a fair general specimen of the Irish Roman Catholic Clergy, than Sir Harcourt Lees is of the

clergy of your Lordship's Church, in Ireland, or than the present Lord Bishop of Exeter is of that Clergy in England.

Your Lordship has, as it appears to me, committed a still greater error, in considering the refractoriness of a comparatively small number of the Roman Catholic clergy in Ireland since 1834, to the no less wise and patriotic than Christian and Paternal Exhortation of *all* the Roman Catholic Bishops in Ireland in that year, to be the general feeling of the clergy of that religion in that country, instead of the spirit which undoubtedly animates the Most Rev. Archbishop Murray and the great majority of the Roman Catholic clergy in Ireland, than you have committed in imagining that the exemplary conduct of that clergy two hundred or even one hundred years ago, ought to be attributed to Spanish parish priests in Ireland; an idea which has already been so humorously noticed in one of his public speeches by the present Lord Mayor of Dublin, that I may safely be dispensed from making any further remark upon it, as I had intended to do when I addressed your Lordship last October. The deterioration in public estimation, which the acknowledged head and chosen representative of an unruly party, though neither the acknowledged head nor representative of the Roman Catholic Hierarchy in Ireland, has, in

spite of his unquestionable great talents and former services, brought upon himself both in Ireland and at Rome,(*b*) by his conduct at the Sligo

---

(*b*) I have observed in a note, p. 4, that the only *criticism* with
which I have been made acquainted, on my two letters of last
October, has been from the pen of an hon. and learned barrister,
whom some of the readers of that note may perhaps be inclined
to consider as too much transported by aristocratic indignation,
at the idea of a Peer of Parliament treating with levity, or even
condescending to notice, the language of a chartist orator in
England, who, in the fervor of his eloquence, styled the Peers
Spiritual and Temporal of Great Britain and Ireland " a pig-
headed race; " or of an orator on the other side of the Bristol
Channel, who denounced them as a public nuisance. But I must
also admit that I have been favored with another communication
from another learned gentleman, who did me the honor of calling
upon me, and, as I happened to be out of the house, left upon my
table a copy of my two letters, with the following ingenious
discovery in a note, as follows:—

Mr. ————— had the honor of waiting upon Lord Clifford,
in reference to a passage in his Lordship's pamphlet, page 15,
which is calculated to involve *most seriously* the late Cardinal
Weld, unless explained. Mr. ————— leaves the pamphlet
with the passage marked, and will call again at 2 o'clock, or
very shortly after.—Nov. 6, 1841. See page 102 in the collection of letters now left.

With greater curiosity than alarm, I must confess, I referred
as directed to p. 15, and there found the following lines marked
in the margin:—

" Had Gregory XVI. suspected in the most remote degree
that the sentiments of Archbishop M'Hale would have been so
diametrically in opposition to the sentiments of Hierophilos, Dr·

**trial and on the National Education question, (c)
has rendered that party of which he has injudi-**

M'Hale would never have been coadjutor bishop, or afterwards
bishop of Killala, still less would he ever have been Roman
Catholic Archbishop of Tuam."

Upon reflection I think that I should have done better to have
expressed myself on this point as follows :—

I think that if Gregory XVI. had suspected, &c. . . . . . *so
widely different from* the sentiments, &c. Such a mode of
expressing myself might probably not only have precluded any
suspicion that I wished to be considered as *authorised* to declare
what are the sentiments of His present Holiness respecting Archbishop M'Hale, which *I certainly am not ;* but might have
excited a less adverse feeling against myself among the adherents
of that Most Rev. Prelate.

However that may be, what there is in this passage calculated
to involve " most seriously," or in any possible way or degree,
Cardinal Weld, I am certainly at a loss to discover ; and as p.
102 of the (printed) collection of letters, left on my table with
this extraordinary note, and returned by me the same evening to
the learned author, threw no light upon the mystery, not having
any reference to Pope Gregory XVI., Cardinal Weld, or Abp.
M'Hale, I begged to decline further communication.

On reflection, however, it occurred to me that a passage in the
address, see Appendix No. II. to this letter, prefixed to the 2nd
No. of the British Catholic Colonial Intelligencer, dated June 29,
1834, which was certainly written under the eye of Cardinal
Weld, and forwarded with the approbation of His Eminence to
the editors in London, may possibly have been considered as

(c) See Appendix I. to this letter.

ciously, as it appears to me, aspired to be the chief, already the weaker party, and probably one which may be safely left to die a natural death, provided justice be done to the undoubted merits of the *great body* of the Roman Catholic clergy in Ireland. I find fault with your Lordship, because you not only do not do *that* body justice, but in your attempt to remedy an evil which indeed does exist, but not near to the extent which your Lordship supposes, are taking, I am sure without intending to do so, the very course which the M'Hale party would wish you to take, in order to increase, if it were possible, the animosity of that party against England; an animosity, for which I am willing to make every possible excuse, and over the effects of which I am willing to throw the mantle of oblivion wherever it does not attempt to compromise the character of Pope Gregory XVI., whose sentiments towards Enggland, are, as your Lordship ought to know, widely different from those of his official representative in Tuam; and of the unmanageable

---

proof that Cardinal Weld approved of the conduct of Archbishop M'Hale at a period long subsequent to the date of that address. It may be sufficient to observe, that before the case of the Sligo trial was brought before Propaganda, Cardinal Weld had been called to receive the rewards of his labour and virtues in another world.

clerical disciples of that over-ardent politician in his former See of Killala. I am as much averse to any alteration in the present state of the Roman Catholic clergy in Ireland, calculated to infringe upon those limits pointed out to it by the Roman Catholic Hierarchy in Ireland in 1834, as the just and proper limits within which that clergy may, honourably to itself and advantageously, in my humble opinion at least, to public tranquillity in Ireland, exert its influence in assisting the Roman Catholic laity in Ireland to obtain or recover the free and full exercise of the undoubted birthrights of the liege inhabitants of that Country, whether Clergy or Laity, Protestant or Catholic, as I am to giving any countenance to that system of audacious calumny, which was so signally exposed by the Sligo trial of 1836, and by the public declaration inserted by the Hon. Mr. Cavendish in the *Telegraph* newspaper of 24th April, 1839, signed with his name. (*d*) But if your Lordship supposes, that either Archbishop Murray or Bishop O'Finan, however much attached to social order, would be disposed to advocate the payment of the Roman Catholic clergy in Ireland by the State, as a measure to be justified, either by necessity or by expediency, in remedy at present of the

---

(*d*) See Appendix No. III.

evils produced either by the mismanagement of the government in that country, or by a very natural aversion on the part of the People towards the authors or abettors of such mismanagement, or by a noncompliance, on the part of a small portion of the Roman Catholic clergy in Ireland, with the *unanimous* recommendations of the Roman Catholic Hierarchy in that country to their flocks in 1834, all I can say to your Lordship is, that you seem to me to know little of the sentiments of Archbishop Murray and Bishop O'Finan, or of what is calculated to promote tranquillity in Ireland under existing circumstances. I can hardly conceive any measure, including even the Repeal of the Roman Catholic Relief Act of 1829, which would more directly tend to shake to their foundation whatever remains of public tranquillity, the mistakes which have been made since 1829 in carrying the principles of the great measure of justice to the United Empire passed in that year, have left Ireland, than any measure, proposed by a Parliament of the United Kingdoms, for the payment, in the present temper of the public mind in Ireland, of the Roman Catholic clergy in that country by the State. If any such measure is to be proposed in any Legislature, let us wait till the Repeal of the Union has been effected; and I seriously believe, that it would be far less ruinous to the interests of Great Britain then, than it would be now, and perhaps even less difficult to be carried then, than it would be now.

Having said thus much upon the first of your Lordship's remedies, I shall leave for a future letter the consideration of your second ; and beg leave to terminate this, by submitting to the consideration of your Lordship, whether a more efficacious system than can be deduced, either from the pamphlet of the Noble Earl to which your Lordship has alluded in terms of admiration in p. 35 of the " State of Ireland Considered," or from the " measures proposed " by your Lordship " for restoring tranquillity to that Country," may not be deduced from the following words addressed to the House of Lords by an Illustrious Duke, whose name is justly dear to Great Britain and Ireland. It is true that Great Britain alone is mentioned, but Ireland since the Union, and *by virtue of the Union,* is necessarily included in the observation, which I have always admired as full of political wisdom.

" The religious tenets of a people will always
" savour of their political principles, and to them
" they will be ever more or less accommodated.
" Great Britain, insulated from the rest of Europe
" by that element which naturally inspires every
" islander with high notions of self-importance,
" has uniformly and systematically cultivated a
" *peculiar species* of civil and religious liberty,

" unknown almost to any other nation in the
" world." (e)

Every attempt to legislate for Ireland upon
continental models, whether the model be taken
from Russia, Prussia, Spain, or Italy, will most
probably disappoint the expectations of the
legislator ; because it will be found in practice
opposed to *national* feelings, not only in Ireland,
but *in England*. It will most probably not bear
the test of public scrutiny ; and the preliminary
step, with a view to the success of your Lordship's first remedy, must be, unless I am greatly
in error, to destroy the liberty of the press in
Great Britain as well as in Ireland. Whenever,
whether as a consequence of the Repeal of the
Union, or as a consequence of any other great
and violent alteration of the existing state of
things, Great Britain and Ireland shall have become subject to Russia or France, the payment
of the Roman Catholic clergy in Ireland by the
State may perhaps be attempted with success ;
but you will never be able to effect it as long as
Ireland forms part of an united and independent
Empire.

(e) Speech of H. R. H. the Duke of Sussex, on the Earl of
Donoughmore's motion for a Committee on the Roman Catholic
claims, April 21, 1812. Copied into Hansard's Parliamentary
Debates from the original edition published by James Asperne,
Cornhill.

You must be content, so long as the legislative union of 1800 subsists, to " take," in the words of the late Mr. Burke, " the state in the condi-" tion in which it is found, and to improve *it* in " that condition to the best advantage." It seems to me, that the unanimous declarations of the Roman Catholic hierarchy in Ireland in 1826, relative to education, and in 1832, relative to clerical co-operation in political movements, copies of which are subjoined to this letter, constitute for Great Britain a "condition " in Ireland, which we have only to improve upon by wisely seconding those declarations, in order to promote to a very great degree, permanent tranquillity for Ireland ; but if, dissatisfied with that condition, or jealous of the agency which has mainly effected it, any one should unfortunately persuade those who have the power, either on this side of the Alps or the other, to grasp at the shadow of security for public tranquillity, which may be reflected from the waters of the Neva, or of the Vistula, or perhaps even of the Tiber, we shall run a great risk of seeing ourselves laughed at by America, as the dog in the fable. I ventured to observe to your Lordship, in my letter of last October, that a more accurate notion of the real value of Mr. O'Connell to Ireland, and to Great Britain even, though his feelings towards the last-mentioned country are, as well as his action upon her interests and institutions, na-

turally enough essentially different from his feelings and mode of action towards Ireland, might
possibly be formed from a perusal of the pages
of Mr. Gustave de Beaumont, than from those of
the Earl of Shrewsbury. I will subjoin to this
letter, from pp. 84 to 99 of the first of these
works, opinions on the peculiar character of the
Catholic clergy in Ireland, to all of which, perhaps, I am not prepared to give an entire assent;
but to which I should feel much less difficulty
in subscribing *en masse*, than I should feel in subscribing either to the accuracy of your Lordship's
description of the actual state of the Roman
Catholic clergy in Ireland, or, even supposing
that description to be accurate, in subscribing in
any degree, or under any limitation whatsoever,
to the expediency of your Lordship's remedy
for that state, by the substitution at present of
another state, which I fear would be much worse
for public tranquillity as well as for the interests
of Christianity. In the extract from Mr. Gustave de Beaumont's work subjoined to this letter,
your Lordship will find the present numbers of
the Catholic clergy in Ireland stated at " four
" archbishops, twenty-one bishops, and two thou-
" sand and seventy-four parish priests." Let
us, taking the *ancient* rule observed till very
lately in the appropriation of parochial dues
among the Catholic clergy in Ireland, namely,
one-third to the parish priest, and two-thirds to

the bishop; for the *modern* repartition, which *inverts* the proportion, would be evidently too expensive a precedent; assign to each parish priest any sum, say £ 100. per annum.

		£.	£.	
Priests	. . 2074 × 100 =	207,400	
Bishops	. . 21 × 300 =	6,300	Total £ 215,700.
Archbishops	4 × 500 =	2,000	

How says your Lordship? Will the People of Great Britain be satisfied to pay to the Catholic clergy of Ireland, the proportional share of £ 215,700. per annum, which *they* must pay *as long as the Union subsists?* This is a financial not a religious question. To begin with the manufacturing interests. The cotton manufacturer, in defiance of Urban VIII., Benedict XIV. and Gregory XVI., has paid to the American slave-holder, for slave-grown cotton, nine-pence a pound weight, instead of encouraging the growth of cotton by free labour in India, which could have produced it at two-pence half-penny, that is to say, has given, on every pound of raw material, sixpence-half-penny premium to the American slave-holder, instead of employing that sixpence-half-penny in wages to the manufacturing labourer of Great Britain ; and is now reaping the bitter fruits of his mistake, and is told to seek his remedy in measures, which the British agriculturist declares will prove to be no real relief to the manufacturer, but will be the inevitable ruin of the landowner. Surely this is an awkward and unpropitious time to propose to the United Parliament of Great Britain and Ireland the payment of the Catholic clergy in Ireland by the State.

I have the honor to be respectfully,
My Lord,
Your obedient humble Servant,
CLIFFORD.

APPENDIX.

No. I.

RESCRIPT

OF HIS HOLINESS POPE GREGORY XVI. TO THE FOUR ARCH-
BISHOPS OF IRELAND, IN REPLY TO THE APPEAL TO THE
HOLY SEE ON THE SUBJECT OF THE NATIONAL SYSTEM
OF EDUCATION IN IRELAND.

Illustrissime ac Reverendissime Domine,

Quantam negotii gravitatem afferret excitata in Hibernia controversia de recenti Nationalis, ut vocant, erudiendæ juventutis systemate, exploratum adeo Amplitudini Tuæ est, ut mirum tibi esse non debuerit, Sacræ Congregationis de Propaganda Fide responsum de ea re tamdiu fuisse dilatum.

Plenam enim totius rei Amplitudo Tua habet notitiam, penitusque cognita Tibi sunt gravia omnia rationum momenta, quæ controversiæ illius excitandæ occasionem attulerunt, quæque diuturnam prorsus rei deliberationem, postularunt.

Nam Sacram Congregationem magnopere solicitam habere debuerunt, cum diu multumque pro sui instituti munere quæstionem propositam consideraret, Catholicæ religionis tutela, puerilis ætatis instituendæ commoditas, grati animi officium erga Britannici Imperii senatum, qui magnam pecuniæ summam popularibus Hiberniæ scholis decrevit, concordiæ inter Episcopos Catholicos retinendæ necessitas, quietis publicæ fovendæ debitum, metus denique ne ad heterodoxos forte magistros, pecunia tota et auctoritas devolvatur.

Omnibus ergo rei periculis, et utilitatibus accurate perpensis, auditis partium disceptantium rationibus, habitaque præsertim felici notitia, quod per decennium, ex quo id systema studiorum susceptum fuit, Religio Catholica nihil detrimenti passa videatur, Sacra Congregatio, Sanctissimo Domino Nostro Gregorio Papa XVI., probante, censuit, nullum esse definite judicium hac super re proferendum, atque id genus eruditionis in Episcoporum singulorum prudenti arbitrio, et religiosa conscientia esse

My Lord,

Your Grace is so fully aware of the grave importance of the question involved in the controversy which has been raised in Ireland, on the subject of the new system of National Education, as it is called, that you should not be surprised that the answer of the Sacred Congregation of the Propaganda thereon has been so long delayed.

For your Grace is fully in possession of the whole matter, and intimately acquainted with all the weighty reasons that have given rise to this controversy, and which demanded that the subject should be examined with the utmost deliberation.

Because the protection of the Catholic Religion—the facility afforded for the instruction of youth—the gratitude due to the British parliament for having granted a large sum of money for the support of schools for the people of Ireland—the necessity of preserving concord among Catholic Bishops—the duty of fostering the public tranquillity —the apprehension, in fine, lest the entire funds, together with the authority, should be transferred to masters not being Catholics,—could not but have filled the Sacred Congregation with the greatest solicitude, during the long and earnest consideration which, in accordance with the duties of its office, it gave to the question submitted to it.

Having, therefore, accurately weighed all the dangers, and all the advantages of the system—having heard the reasoning of the contending parties—and having, above all, received the gratifying intelligence that, for ten years since the introduction of this system of education, the Catholic religion does not appear to have sustained any injury—the Sacred Congregation has, with the approbation of our Most Holy Father, Pope Gregory the XVI., resolved that no judgment should be definitively pronounced in this matter;

c 2

relinquendum, quandoquidem ejus successum á vigili Pastorum cura, á cautelis variis adhibendis, a futura demum per temporis tractum experientia pendere necesse est. Ne tamen sine idoneis consiliis et providentiis tanta res dimittatur, Sacra Congregatio sequentia interim monenda esse judicavit.

Scilicet 1o. Libros omnes, qui noxium aliquid sive adversus Sacrorum Bibliorum canonem, aut puritatem, sive contra Catholicæ Ecclesiæ doctrinam, vel mores continent, á scholis removeri debere. Hoc autem eó facilius effici potest, quia nulla memorati systematis lex obstat.

2o. Dandam esse pro viribus operam, ut Præceptor Normalis pedagogorum Catholicorum in classe religiosa, morali, et historica, vel Catholicus, vel nullus sit. Nam Catholicum ab Acatholico religionis tradendæ methodum, vel religiosam historiam doceri indecorum est.

3o. Tutius multo esse ut literarum tantummodo humanarum magisterium fiat in scholis promiscuis, quam ut, fundamentales, ut aiunt, et communes religionis Christianæ articuli restricte tradantur, reservata singulis sectis peculiari seorsum eruditione. Ita enim cum pueris agere periculosum valde videtur.

4o. Generatim Episcopos et Parochos advigilare oportere, ne ex hoc systemate Nationalis Institutionis, pueris Catholicis quamlibet ob causam, labes obveniat; eorumdem etiam esse, enixe curare, ut a Supremis Moderatoribus, meliorem in dies rerum ordinem, et conditiones æquiores impetrent. Illud quoque perutile fore censet Sacra Congregatio, si loca ipsa scholarum, in Episcoporum, vel Parochorum potestate,

and that this kind of education should be left to the prudent discretion and religious conscience of each individual bishop, whereas its success must depend on the vigilant care of the pastors, on the various cautions to be adopted, and the future experience which time will supply. That, however, so momentous a question should not be dismissed without suitable counsel and precautions, the Sacred Congregation has decided on giving the following admonitions :—

1st. That all books which contain any noxious matter either against the canon or the purity of the Sacred Scriptures, or against the doctrine of the Catholic Church, or morality, ought to be removed from the schools; and this can be the more easily effected, because there is no law of the said system opposed to it.

2nd. That every effort is to be made, that none but a Catholic preceptor shall give religious, moral, or historical lectures to the Catholic Schoolmasters in the Model School; for it is not fitting that a Catholic should be taught the method of giving instruction in religion or religious history by one who is not a Catholic.

3d. That it is much safer that literary instruction only should be given in mixed schools, than that the fundamental articles, as they are called, and the articles in which all Christians agree, should alone be taught there in common, reserving for separate instruction the tenets peculiar to each sect; for this manner of acting, in regard to children, appears very dangerous.

4th. That generally the Bishops and Parish Priests should carefully watch that no taint be contracted by the Catholic children from this system of national instruction, through any cause whatever; and that it is also their duty strenuously to endeavour to obtain from the government, by degrees, a better order of things, and more equitable conditions. The Sacred Congregation is also of opinion, that

ac proprio jure mauerent. Existimat simul permagnæ futurum esse utilitatis, Episcopos de tam gravi negotio in Provincialibus synodis invicem sæpe conferre. Si autem quid adversum accidet, Sedes Apostolica certior facienda sedulo est, ut ipsa simul provideat.

Denique optat Sacra Congregatio, ut deinceps Episcopi, aliique viri Ecclesiastici abstineant a contendendo super hac controversia in publicis ephemeridibus, vel ejusmodi aliis libellis, ne religionis honor, mutua fama, et Christiana charitas, cum populi offensione lædatur.

Hæc Amplitudini Tuæ, a me Sacræ Congregationis nomine, erant significanda, ut per Te, RR. PP. DD. Episcopis Metropolitanæ Provinciæ Tuæ Suffraganeis communicentur. Quæ vero superius significavi, talia esse Amplitudo Tua quoque facile intelliget, ut iisdem diligentur servatis, in ista re tantæ gravitatis, interea satis religioni, satis tranquillitati, et juvenilis ætatis bono consultum esse concludendum sit.

Precor Deum interea, ut Amplitudinem Tuam, diu sospitem ac felicem servet.
Amplitudinis Tuæ.
Romæ, ex ædibus Sacræ Congregationis de Propaganda Fide
Die 16 Januarii, 1841.
Ad officia Paratissimus

J. Ph. Card. Fransonius, Praef.
J. Arch. Edessen, e Secr.

it would be very useful that the School-houses should be vested exclusively in the Bishops or the Parish Priests. It is further of opinion, that it would be of very great advantage that the Bishops should frequently confer together on this very important subject, in their provincial synods; but that, should any thing unfavourable occur, the Apostolic See should be carefully made acquainted with it, that it may at once provide for the exigency.

In fine, the Sacred Congregation desires, that henceforward the Bishops and other Ecclesiastics should refrain from contending on this controversy in the newspapers, or other such publications, lest the honour of religion, their own characters, or Christian charity, should be injured, to the disedification of the people.

These are what I had to make known to your Grace, in the name of the Sacred Congregation, that they may be communicated by you to the right reverend the Suffragan Bishops of your metropolitan province. Now the matters which I have above communicated to you, your Grace will easily understand to be of such a nature, that if they are carefully attended to, it is to be concluded that, in this most important affair, the interests of religion, of peace, and of the youth, are for the present sufficiently provided for.

In the mean time, I pray God to give your Grace a long and happy life.

Given at Rome, at the Propaganda, the 16th January, 1841.

(Signed)

J. Ph. Fransoni, Prefect.
J., Archbishop of Edessa, Sec^r

TO THE EDITOR OF THE DUBLIN EVENING POST.

SIR,

Permit me to lay before the public a correct view of the document lately received from Rome concerning the National System of Education. It is calculated to preserve the public mind from the impressions of the over-zealous and the ignorant writers on the subject.

CANDIDUS.

It is said, that Rome has not *approved* the system, and that the document in question rather implies disapprobation. We reply :—

1. The System had been going on for ten years, working conformably to the ordinary laws of church government—that is, each Bishop (judge in the first instance) acting according to his judgment in his diocese.

2. After that time, some of the Prelates (from motives which we perfectly respect) brought the matter before the Holy See, and the object of their appeal was necessarily two-fold :—

1o. To supersede the ordinary jurisdiction till now exercised in this cause, by the sentence of the superior tribunal—a sentence binding upon all.

2o. To have this sentence *condemnatory* of the system of education called National—at least, unless essential changes were wrought in it. This appears from the nature of the evidence sent in—viz., that there was danger of perversion—that the books contained errors contrary to faith, &c.—evidence which, if found valid, could elicit from Rome nothing short of condemnation.

3. The Prelates who admitted the system, appeared as Respondents to the appeal; but their application to the Holy See was purely defensive.

1o. They never called upon it to decide; but were

satisfied that matters should be allowed to go on as they had done before.

2o. They never asked for any *approbation* of the system.

4. The cause, therefore, before the Court of Rome was, not "*utrum damnandum aut approbandum*," *whether condemnation or approbation should be pronounced;* but simply, *whether condemnation should be pronounced, or matters left as they were.*

5. The sentence was the latter alternative. Therefore—

1o. The call for an authoritative interference, supersedatory of the ordinary authority, was rejected.

2o. The call for a condemnation was refused.

6. This constitutes all that the decision could be expected to give. But the rejection of an appeal gives the cause, as matter of course, to the Respondent.

7. It is said, this is no *approbation.* True; but *no one asked the Holy See for an approbation.* There was no case before it, on which even to think of granting it.

8. It may be asked, *would* Rome have approved of the system, had formal approbation been asked? We say, probably not. Because—

1o. Every one conversant with the practice of the Church knows that it will condemn error, but does not give formal approbation to what is right. It leaves it to take its course. This is the practice of every tribunal. Acquittal,—"*nec ego te condemnabo*,"—the refusal to condemn, is the only declaration of innocence it will pronounce. This is the case in Rome, especially regarding books: it condemns bad ones, but *never* APPROVES the best.

2o. The respondent Prelates themselves do not consider the National System is a perfect thing to be submitted to Rome for *approbation*. It is a boon not so complete by any means as they would wish: for what Catholic would not be glad to see his own religion taught to all, and everywhere? But it is a boon incalculably better than any ever before offered, and, moreover, offered in good faith; and the system may be kept sufficiently under ecclesiastical inspection, to prevent the evils that might otherwise arise from the imperfection of the system. It is, therefore, not to be expected that approbation would be formally asked for or pronounced. Similar instances have occurred: *e. g.* the taking of the oath of allegiance to the House of Hanover after the expulsion of the Stuarts, whom the Holy See still recognised as sovereigns: this oath was never approved of, but was not therefore condemned, nor even disapproved of; as it can be shown that the Holy See allowed, and perhaps wished, Catholics to take it, without its pronouncing a sanction.——Rome would not *approve* the present parliamentary oath for Catholics, yet its not condemning it, is all that is asked or desired. It is not such an oath as we should ourselves have framed, or could have wished——still, we are glad to have it instead of the oath of supremacy, &c.

9. But there are clauses and expressions in the document in question, which must satisfy us of the wishes and feelings of the Holy See.

1o. The mention of the grant for education, as a subject of gratitude. This could not be so considered, if the Holy See saw even reason to suspect that the motive or the tendency of the grant was to endanger the faith of the children. Would similar gratitude have been expressed towards the Kildare-street grant?

2o. The appeal to ten years' experience of success, is

a clear rejection of the ground brought forward to obtain condemnation, viz.——that there was danger of perversion.

3o. The very fact of adding admonitions and cautions implies anything but condemnation. Like the clause and conditions in a dispensation, they *confirm* what they are applied to.

4o. The very exhortation to the prelates to try to get *better* terms, &c., supposes the contrary of the present ones being bad.

5o. The objection to the masters being taught *certain* things specified by Protestant teachers, implies that no objection is made to their being taught others.

10. The conclusions we may draw from all these reflections seem to be the following :——

1o. That Rome, after a long and full examination of most voluminous evidence, has seen no reason to fear perversion of the faithful by the National Education system.

2o. That it did not think there was ground for condemning any of the denounced books.

3o. That it has rejected the appeal to it for condemnation of the System.

4o. That if it has not formally sanctioned it, such sanction, 1o. is not conformable to usage ; 2o. it was never asked.

5o. That, however, there is sufficient evidence in the document to satisfy the minds of impartial persons of its leaning to the favourable side.

11. We may observe, in conclusion, that none of the modifications it proposes affect essentially the system. In fact, the greater part, if not all, have long existed.

No. II.

EXTRACT FROM AN ADDRESS OF THE EDITORS OF THE
BRITISH CATHOLIC COLONIAL INTELLIGENCER TO
THEIR FELLOW CHRISTIANS IN BRITISH COLONIES.

From the British Catholic Colonial Intelligencer, No. III.

WE call upon YOU to decide for yourselves, upon a
question of high importance indeed to your mother-country,
but not less important to yourselves. The question is this:
Will you be guided by the principles of the British Catholics,
as set forth in their Declaration of 1826, or by the counsels
of those who are not Britons, who are not Catholics, and
who do not profess the principles which British Catholics
profess, and have proved themselves to profess sincerely,
so as to merit the confidence of their king and country?

You would however, fellow-Christians, greatly mistake
us, were you to suppose that, in recommending to you, as
the principles which ought to guide your conduct as well as
ours, the principles of the Declaration of British Catholics
in 1826, we fear to recommend to you, as equally secure,
the principles of Irish Catholics. We do not wish to
appear ignorant of apprehensions which have been entertained, that a difference of *principle*, on points of no small
consequence to the tranquillity of the colonies of Great
Britain, exists between the Catholics of Great Britain and
the Catholics of Ireland; but we know of none. That a
difference of *circumstances*, especially previous to 1829,
did exist between the Catholic subjects of his Britannic
Majesty in the two islands composing your mother-country,
we are well aware; and that the same principles will

operate differently on men's minds in different circumstances, we are equally ready to admit as an undoubted
truth. Inadequate as we feel ourselves to be to the task
we have undertaken, of attempting to influence public
opinion, we trust that we are not so utterly absurd in our
notions of human nature, as to suppose that we could influence public opinion by arguing in opposition to the common
feelings of mankind, upon abstract principles of right and
wrong.

It is with the Act of 1829, usually termed the Emancipation of Ireland, and with the Act of 1833, which in its
86th and 101st clauses * especially, we look upon as the
emancipation of India, in one hand, that we present ourselves before you, holding in the other hand the Declaration of the British Catholics in 1826, to which we called
your attention in our first number,† and together with that
Declaration, the sentiments of a distinguished member of
the Roman Catholic Hierarchy in Ireland.‡

We say to you—Judge for yourselves whether it be
your interest that Christianity or idolatry should be the
religion prevalent in British India, or in the British Colonies
in any part of the world. We have already made up our
minds, that it is the temporal interest, as well as the interest
for another and a better world, of the king and the people of
Great Britain and Ireland, that the colonies of England
should be Christians as she herself became so, and not
otherwise.§

"Man," observes very justly the truly Christian prelate
from whom we quote (Evidences, &c. vol. I, p. 238), " has
a multiplicity of duties to discharge, and it is from the

---

* B. C. C. Intelligencer, No. I. p. 71.   † Ibid. pp. 6, 7, and 74.

‡ The Evidences and Doctrines of the Catholic Church. By the Right
Rev. John Mac Hale, D.D., Bishop of Maronia, and coadjutor Bishop of
Killala. 1828. Dublin : Milliken and Coyne.

§ B. C. C. Intelligencer, No. II. p. 185.

exactness with which the Christian religion adjusts the respective influence of each, controlling the excesses, into which the exclusive practice of one might lead, by the restraints imposed by another, that the beauty of the Christian religion arises, which thus harmonizes the different obligations of its members. It is by a comprehensive and dispassionate view of this kind, that we shall be able to appreciate the full benefits of Christianity. From a long and familiar acquaintance with its advantages, we may become indifferent to many, which would be more strikingly felt, by the melancholy experience of their privation. To impress this observation more strongly on the reader, it may be necessary again to point his attention to the lamentable condition of the pagan world, in order that he may have a clearer view of the happiness for which he is indebted to the Christian religion.

" While the Almighty was dethroned by the impiety of the Pagans, and his place usurped by gods, who were more frequently honoured for their vices than their virtues, the stream of public morals was polluted in its very source. To look for domestic virtue among those who hung up the most licentious images as objects of adoration,* would be to look for conduct at once at variance with the nature of their belief, and the corrupt desires of their heart. Hence, the face of society presented a moral waste, where every virtue withered, under the influence of a wide-spread corruption. If the light of science was kept alive, amidst the schools of philosophy, it assisted but little in exploring the way to virtue. It rather gave a fuller view of the darkness, which it could not dissipate; and might well be compared to those

---

* Après la defaite de Xerxes et de ses formidables armées, on mit dans le Temple un tableau où étoient répresentés leurs vœux et leurs processions, avec cette inscription de Simonides : *celles-ci ont prié la Déesse Venus, qui pour l'amour d'elles a sauvé la Grèce.*"—Bossuet, Disc. 255.

fires that are occasionally lighted on a rocky coast, and which, instead of saving the mariner from shipwreck, cast a more frightful glare over the horrors that surround him. Nor were their political institutions of a more exalted character. With the decay of virtue, every generous motive that inspires true elevation of character, disappeared, and mankind was left to languish under the most oppressive tyranny. Rulers exercised their dominion with distrust and severity, while the obedience of subjects was sullen and constrained. Hence, no indulgence on the one hand, and no respect on the other. Authority lost its reverence with the people, who regarded power rather as an engine of oppression, than as a shield of their protection. Hence the rapid and successive revolutions with which the world was afflicted; now groaning under the weight of despotism, and again, shaken by all the licentiousness of anarchy and disorder. With the exceptions of Greece and Rome, the flame of freedom was extinct in all the nations of the earth; and even in these comparatively favoured countries, its occasional appearance was so irregular and unsteady as to have been productive of but little public benefit. While a few factious leaders abused the name of liberty, by exercising under its injured name the most sanguinary proscriptions, the mass of the people never breathed a respite from servitude. The slaves of either country were the most numerous, as well as the most formidable body of the state.* So late as the reign of Augustus, the policy of that monarch forbad them to wear a distinct habit; lest, from the contagion of their discontent, and the consciousness of their numbers, they should become dangerous to the peace of the empire.† The condition of these miserable beings was

---

* See the curious and learned treatise of the Canon Pignorius, de Servis et corum apud veteres Ministeriis, p. 509, *et seq.* ed. 1674.

† See Senec. de Clemen., l. i., c. 24.

almost beyond endurance.   Invested with the absolute disposal of their lives, their masters treated them with the
most relentless rigour.   The occurrence of every war, and
in those days wars were frequent, exposed the inhabitants
of the conquered country to all the horrors of unmitigated
slavery.   *   *   *   *

"But, scarce was the divine Gospel which Christ came
on earth to preach to the poor, announced, when the face of
the universe was entirely changed.   The rights of humanity
were recognised, and the waters of baptism, which regene-
rated from eternal death, saved many an infant from premature destruction.   Thus, the most spiritual rites became
the instruments of temporal advantages, and the abstract
dogmas of Christianity were productive of the most important practical effects.   However severe the enactments of
legislators, they were insufficient to check the barbarous
practice of exposing infants, so frequent amidst the licentiousness of the Pagan world.   The sacrament of baptism,
and the simple belief of the effects of which it is productive,
has easily accomplished what human laws could not
achieve.   By the infusion of the merciful spirit of the
Gospel, the rigours of despotism were mitigated.   In the
language of the prophets, ' the vallies were raised, and the
mountains were made level.' *   The poor man lifted his
head from his prostrate condition, and the rich recognized
in every being who wore the same form, not only an individual of the same species, but a brother in Jesus Christ,
bought by the same redemption and entitled to the same
inheritance.   In short, the spirit of charity walked abroad,
with all the blessings announced by the prophets in its
train, bringing light to those that sat in darkness, and
solace to the broken-hearted.   At its hallowed touch the

* Isaiah, c. xl. v. 4.

fetters of the captive fell off, and, like the roe on the mountain, he bounded, exulting in his freedom ; * and while the Catholic Church, like a temple seated on an eminence, realized the prophetic vision of Ezechiel, holding forth the torch of its faith, and opening wide its portals to the nations of the earth ; from the threshold of the same temple, to pursue the prophetic image, went forth a torrent of sweetness, refreshing the world as it rolled, and bringing strength, and health, and benediction, to every living thing that was touched by its waters."†

These are the doctrines, fellow-Christians, which we wish you to adopt ; or rather, which we wish you, having, as we doubt not, already adopted them yourselves, not to feel indifferent about causing them to be propagated in the colonies of your mother-conntry. It depends, in our opinion, greatly, if not principally upon YOU, whether " the South and East of India " shall prove the justness of the anticipations of the author of the " Prospects of Britain," which we noticed in our last number, ‡ namely, that they " seem reserved for the influence of Britain, the mistress of the sea, if the goodness of God should preserve her from the dangers which immediately threaten her, and make her the honoured instrument of furthering His own designs.

Great Britain cannot do this good work without cordially inviting and cordially receiving the co-operation of Ireland, long since called the " Island of Saints,"—long before such

---

* Five thousand slaves were manumised by the illustrious martyr Ovinius Gallicanus : eight thousand were restored to liberty by Melania the younger. —*Vide Terentiam in Actis SS. Joh. et Pauli. Surius ad diem* 26 *Junii, et Palladium. ed.* 1680.

† And he brought me again to the gate of the house, and behold waters issued out from the threshold of the house . . . . . and every living thing that creepeth whithersoever the torrent shall come, shall live.—*Ezech.* c. xlvii.

‡ *B. C. C. Intelligencer*, No. II. p. 110.

a term as "ruinous Popery" was ever heard from the
lips, or ever written by the pen of a Christian. It is by
Irish missionaries that Great Britain must propagate the
principles of British Catholics, or she cannot propagate
them sufficiently to meet the necessity for their immediate
extension. But it must depend greatly upon YOU, fellow-
Christians, whether your mother-country will be satisfied
that the principles of Irish Catholics are essentially the
same as those of English Catholics, and whether they
afford, under similar circumstances, equal security. The
question which your conduct has to resolve is, whether
there is the same certainty that the interests of Great
Britain in her colonies will be strengthened by the diffusion
of Christianity through Irish missionaries, which we maintain there would be, if that diffusion were effected by English missionaries, true to the principles of the declaration of
1826. Our reply is in anticipation of its confirmation by
your conduct, unaffectedly and most sincerely—in these
words: *quite as much*, to the best of our judgment and
belief, *under similar circumstances*. We believe that if
the concessions, dictated by sound policy and required by
strict justice, which were made to Ireland in 1829 and to
India in 1833, be honestly adhered to and impartially
acted upon, the Irish missioner in India not only will, but
must feel all the attachment towards Great Britain which
an English missioner *could* feel; and we believe that he
will have this advantage over the English missioner in
many cases, that while the idolater whom he initiates into
the blessings of Christianity, *must be* totally a stranger to
any national feeling or recollection which could make the
voice of truth less acceptable from Irish than from English
lips, the Christian colonists, to whom the missioner will
naturally look for co-operation and support, will certainly
feel not less disposed to second the charitable exertions of

an Irish than of an English missioner, since the majority, we believe the great majority, of the Christian population in British India, is of Irish blood. To them especially we present the following sentiments of the Irish prelate we have just quoted—(Evidences, vol. ii. p. 82):—

" There must be, in every state, a supreme and absolute authority. In a free country, the monarchy may be called limited, on account of the restraints, which are imposed on it by the constitution; but, although monarchy may be limited, there is still in the state an absolute authority, which it is unlawful to resist; and this authority resides in the government, including the executive and the legislature. Constitutional checks, may, therefore, temper the power and modify the form of Government; but they never can annul the obligations of obedience. Nor does this language differ widely from the principles that are laid down by the most eminent Protestant jurists. Grotius, though he leaned to liberty, insists on the sacred obligations that bind the subject to the State. Blackstone supposes that there is as much of absolute power in the British Constitution, composed as it is of King, Lords, and Commons, as was ever exercised by any government. Nay, what are his ideas of the absolute force of English laws, we may learn from his frequent allusion to the omnipotence of Parliament. Paley himself, who, as has been before observed, softens down the most rigid principles of the Gospel by a refined and arbitrary interpretation, requires conditions to justify revolution, which place it beyond the operation of the ordinary principles of human conduct.* Revolutions are events that are seldom influenced by the nice calculations of civilians. They are like the earthquake or the hurricane, beyond the

---

* " Nay, he would not justify the independence of America, unless it were to enlarge the happiness of the parent state."—*Prin. of Moral Philos.* b. vi. c. 3, p. 329.

reach of the ordinary and ascertained laws of society; nor
is it possible for human foresight always to prevent their
recurrence. In the philosophical language of Burke: ' Society is not a partnership in things subservient only to the
gross animal existence of a temporary and perishable nature.
It is a partnership in all science; a partnership in all art;
a partnership in every virtue, and in all perfection. As
the ends of such a partnership cannot be obtained in many
generations, it becomes a partnership not only between those
who are living, but those who are dead and those who are
to be born. Each contract of each particular state, is but a
clause in the great *primeval contract of eternal society*,
connecting the visible and invisible world, according to a
fixed compact, sanctioned by the inviolable oath, which
holds all physical and all moral natures, each in their appointed place. This law is not subject to the will of those
who, by an obligation above them, and infinitely superior,
are bound to submit their will to that law. The municipal
corporations of that universal kingdom are not morally at
liberty, at their pleasure, and on their speculations of a contingent improvement, wholly to separate and tear asunder
the bands of their subordinate community, and dissolve it
into an unsocial, uncivil, unconnected, chaos of elementary
principles. It is the first and supreme necessity alone, a
necessity that is not *chosen but chooses ;* a necessity
paramount to deliberation, that admits no discussion and
demands no evidence, which alone can justify a resort to
anarchy. This necessity is no exception to the rule; because this necessity itself is a part of that moral and
physical disposition of things, to which man must be obedient
by consent or force. But if that which is only submission
to necessity should be made the object of choice, the law is
broken, nature is obeyed, and the rebellious are outlawed,
cast forth and exiled from this world of reason, and order,

and peace, and virtue, and fruitful penitence, into the antagonist world of madness, discord, vice, confusion, and unavailing despair.'* Notwithstanding all the influence of religion to preserve the peace of society, still it will be convulsed by the shock of revolution. Instead of fomenting the lava that is still at the bottom of the crater, the Church labours to repair the damages, which the face of society has already sustained from the eruption. But, though adverse to revolution, she is not hostile to the assertion of constitutional rights; nor do we forget that the Apostle, who so strongly recommends obedience, urged his claims as a Roman citizen, and appealed from the judgment of a vexatious and iniquitous faction to the tribunal of Cæsar.† Thus the doctrine of the Catholic Church is favourable to every form of established authority; it advocates peace, it represses licentiousness and disorder. Governments may entirely yield to the fury of popular violence, or be slowly modified by the influence of deliberative wisdom; while the guardian spirit of religion, which lives in the Catholic Church, still watches over the interests of society, transmigrating through every change, and surviving every revolution."

When, therefore, fellow-Christians, we say with the author of the "Prospects of Britain" in India, that "it is the policy of England, as well as her duty, to give every encouragement to the natives professing Christianity,"‡ and that "the Christian natives of India are our only sure friends;" we confess that we feel as little apprehension of the result of the propagation of Christianity by the disciples of a Mac Hale, or by his countrymen professing the same principles as those we have just quoted from his writings in

---

* Reflections on the French Revolution, p. 144
† Acts xxv. 11.
‡ B. C. C. Intelligencer, No. II. p. 112.

1828, as we do from its propagation by British Catholics holding the principles of the declaration of 1826.

But is it natural that the British Government should feel the same assurance which we feel? Our answer again is, that we should be unjust both to the British Government and to the Catholic Hierarchy of Ireland, if we did not reply that *it is natural.* The same ground for assurance exists in the case of the Irish Catholic missioner, sent by the Irish Catholic Bishop from Ireland to the English or Irish Catholic Bishop in India, as exists in the case of the English Catholic missioner sent by the Catholic Bishop in England to the same Prelate. The religion of both is absolutely, completely, necessarily, the same. The circumstances under which both enter the mission are the same. In the opinion of the author of the "Prospects of Britain," that religion indeed is "ruinous Popery," * but in the opinion of others, *not less* entitled to have their sentiments taken into consideration, by the British Government, the triumphs of Popery over Idolatry, if by Popery be meant, as it would be affectation in us to appear not to know is meant, Catholicity, will probably be considered as likely to be very bloodless, and to be attended with far other results than misery and ruin.

" I should not discharge the duty of one connected with the Government of Ireland," said the Right Honourable the present President of the Board of Control, when Secretary for Ireland in 1819, "if I did not bear testimony to the exertions of that respectable class of men, the Catholic Clergy of Ireland. I have no hesitation in saying, that the present tranquillity is owing to the exertions of those men who go about from house to house at the peril of their lives, to prevent the dissemination of the principles of the reformers.

---

* *B. C. C. Intelligencer*, No. II. p. 113.

Such exertions are not confined to the lower orders, but extended to the Roman Catholic Prelacy. I confess that the check which the wild doctrines of reformers have met in Ireland, may be attributed to the zealous, Christian-like, and patriotic exertions of that respectable class of men."*

We entreat you, fellow-Christians, to compare these sentiments with those of another right honourable member of His Majesty's Privy Council, of whom we have expressed our grateful admiration in our first number,† when acting as Chief Justice, in 1806, of the Supreme Court of Judicature, and first member of His Majesty's Council in the island of Ceylon; and to judge for yourselves, whether it does not depend upon you, that his Majesty's Government, and the British nation, should feel no greater alarm if the Christian subjects of the King of Great Britain and Ireland have their spiritual wants supplied by Catholic priests from Ireland, than Sir Alexander Johnston felt at the inhabitants of Ceylon having their spiritual wants supplied by the excellent priests whose names appear in our first number,‡ and of whose meritorious exertions and candid and respecful behaviour towards the Government of H. B. Majesty in that island, we present you additional evidence in this number, and by their colleagues,§ none of whom were British or Irish priests.

It is quite natural and reasonable, that you should, like the Roman Catholics of Calcutta,‖ feel a decided preference for English or Irish priests. The steps which have been taken during the last nine months by the ecclesiastical authorities of your and our church, prove to demonstration that your wishes have not been disregarded; and the perfect willingness evinced by his Majesty's Government that

---

* Speech in the House of Commons, Dec. 23, 1819.
     † No. I. p, 24.   ‡ Ibid. p. 17.
     § Ibid. p. 26.   ‖ Ibid. p. 78.

those steps should be taken without hindrance on its part, affords the best pledge that there exists an honest intention to act up to the liberal and enlightened policy which passed the acts of 1829 and of 1833.

It is because we feel that it is utterly inconsistent with that liberal and enlightened policy, to feel any apprehension, that priests judged fit for the sacred ministry in the colonies by the Roman Catholic bishops in Ireland, and acting under the superintendence of Roman Catholic prelates, of whose loyalty the British Government has assured itself in India, will betray their allegiance, or act inconsistently with it, when every human and divine motive would, on the contrary, concur, to impress on their minds its obligations and advantages, that we also feel ourselves authorised to assure you, that nothing whatsoever but conduct on your part, opposite to that which the general evidence on the state of our colonies shows our Catholic colonists to have pursued hitherto, could make it probable, that the Government of your mother-country would not feel the same security for the tranquillity of its colonies, whether your priests were British or Irish clergymen.

No. III.

DECLARATIONS OF HON. MR. CAVENDISH.

LETTER of the Hon. Frederick Cavendish, Proprietor of the *Telegraph* or *Connaught Ranger*, inserted in that newspaper, Wednesday, April 24th, 1839, sent to the Right Rev. Francis Joseph O'Finan, O. P., Bishop of Killala, then at Lucca in Italy ; and delivered in to the Secretary of the Sacred Congregation de Propaganda Fide in Rome, Mgr. Cadolini, Archbishop of Edessa, in consequence of a written request to that effect addressed to Lord Clifford, then in Rome, May 9th, 1839.

O'FINAN *v.* CAVENDISH.

Telegraph Office, Castlebar,
20th April, 1839.

Some months back I had a communication made to the Right Rev. Dr. O'Finan at Rome, having reference to the mitigation of the severe punishment I am suffering, for the publication of a libel signed " ALADENSIS," addressed to his lordship, and written by the Rev. Patrick Flannelly, P. P. of Easkey, in the diocese of Killala, and published in the *Telegraph* of June 15, 1836. That letter of a Catholic clergyman, so signed, and privately authenticated to me, contained certain allegations offensive to Dr. O'Finan, and it was, I regret to say, inconsiderately inserted. It was published without comment or observation, and published in utter reliance on a Catholic clergyman's written assurance of its truth.   The subject matter of that letter was such as I did not feel either qualified or inclined to discuss, and my extreme confidence in the author led me into error.   That publication having been highly offensive to Dr. O'Finan, his lordship was advised to bring an action for libel, and I am bound to say that his lordship brought that action in a way which admitted to me, as defendant, the plea of justification in its fullest extent.   In reliance on the assurance, and in compliance with the request, of the writer of the libel, Pleas of Justification were put in.   The verdict of a jury of his countrymen most fully established the falsity of the pleas, as regarded the public and private, the moral and episcopal character of that prelate.   Having been thus induced by the author of the libel to allow pleas of justification in my name, on the express assurance that all the expenses of that suit would be defrayed by him—and having been informed that an idea is now prevalent, and has reached Dr. O'Finan, that I have received £300 as part indemnification for it, I have now distinctly to state, that I have never received, nor has any one on my behalf received, one farthing, directly or indirectly, to aid me in defraying the heavy expenses, losses, and sufferings, that suit and verdict have subjected me to.   For nine years I had directed my time and my pecuniary resources to the advocacy of the Irish people's rights; in a moment of ill-advised confidence, I published a libel, from the pen of one of that people's clergy, and in consequence, I have been for eighteen months a prisoner, within my own house, certainly, but still not less a prisoner.   My property, my health, and the prospects of my family, have all suffered—suffered materially.   Having good reason to believe that my application to the Right Rev. Dr. O'Finan was met in the spirit of peace and christian forbearance, I think it due to myself, to the public, and above all to the sacred character of the right rev. prelate, to render him the most ample and sincere apology for the publication in question. Motives for libel I could have none, having never entertained towards his lordship any other feelings than those of admiration of his talents, and veneration for his sacred position. The verdict of the jury proclaimed the falsehood and gross misrepresentations of that libel, and which was in accordance with the opinion of the learned judge who presided ; and I freely admit it a libel, which had not a shadow of truth to rest upon. I now fully avow the justice of that verdict, as well as the justice ' of the feeling that awarded to Dr. O'Finan, such ample damages, and I must ever deplore the publication and attempted justification of such unfounded calumnies against so pious and so exemplary a prelate.

FREDERICK CAVENDISH.

From the Telegraph of Wednesday, December 8th, **1841.**

To the Hon. Frederick Cavendish.

Gresham's Hotel, Dublin,
Dec. 3, 1841.

Hon. Sir,

During my late visit to Rome in the course of last summer, I ascertained with more regret than surprise, that his Holiness Gregory XVI. still laboured under the same delusion which had been impudently imposed upon him in November 1838, in order to obtain from him, not the *deposition,* which was falsely asserted in the Dublin papers to *have been* obtained even before the suspension had been obtained, not the *resignation* which could only be by the *voluntary* act of the resigning party ; but the suspension or *discharge from the obligation* of doing duty in the diocese of Killala of my venerable friend the Right Rev. Dr. O'Finan, *actual* but not *acting* Bishop of Killala.

The delusion in question is this :—Gregory XVI. was persuaded in November 1838, that his venerable representative in the see of Killala, had brought a *criminal* action before a *Protestant lay* tribunal at Sligo, against one of his parish priests in the diocese of Killala, of the name of Flannelly ; who, thus dragged by his own bishop before a Protestant lay tribunal, was compelled, in defence of his own character, thus criminally, or for a criminal matter attacked, to apply for protection to the Metropolitan the Most Rev. Dr. M'Hale, and to other Bishops of the Archdiocese of Tuam ; who, thereupon, felt it their duty to appear in court, in support of the innocence of said parish priest. Accordingly it is expressly stated in the proceedings (printed though not published) which led to the suspension of my venerable friend, though he himself has been assured within these last six months from unquestionable authority, that the question of his suspension was "*never even proposed*" to the Sacred Congregation of Propaganda during the course of those proceedings, and that " he himself was universally honored and respected." It is, I say, more expressly stated, pp. 48 to 51 of those printed proceedings, that "*the priest Flannelly cited,*" " sacerdos Flannelly quod citaverit," and that Archbishop M'Hale and Bishop Burke were called into court by the priest Flannelly, " vocati sunt a sacerdote Flannelly."

It is needless to observe *to you,* Sir, that the wretched man, who being charged with the translation of the English documents, including the reports of the Sligo trial in the *Telegraph* newspaper, into the Italian or Latin language, for the information of the cardinals deputed by Gregory XVI. to examine into the rights of the case of my venerable friend, knew that he was impudently imposing upon those cardinals a most mischievous calumny, the object and intent of which was to persuade those cardinals, (my lamented father-in-law, Cardinal Weld, being already dead) that my venerable friend, Bishop O'Finan, deserved the displeasure of Gregory XVI. for bringing a criminal accusation against one of the priests of his diocese before a Protestant lay tribunal, instead of bringing it before Archbishop M'Hale; but the object of my addressing this letter *to you*, Sir, is to obtain *from you* a declaration in your own handwriting, upon this point.

Was the trial at Sligo a criminal action brought by Bishop O'Finan against Rev. Mr. Flannelly, or was it a civil action brought by Bishop O'Finan against yourself, a Protestant, and the responsible editor of a public newspaper?

You will oblige me by inserting this lettter in the *Telegraph* newspaper; and inserting in the same paper your answer to it.

I have the honor to be,
Honorable Sir,
Your obedient humble servant,

CLIFFORD.

4th *December*, 1841.

My Lord,

I have received your letter, and shall meet your wishes by publishing it and my reply in the next *Telegraph*. You enquire—"Was the trial at Sligo a criminal action brought by Bishop O'Finan against the Rev. Mr. Flannelly, or was it a civil action brought by Bishop O'Finan against yourself, a Protestant, and the responsible editor of a public newspaper?"

In reply, I have to state that Bishop O'Finan did not take proceedings either by criminal or civil process against Mr. Flannelly. The trial at Sligo was a civil action at the suit of Bishop O'Finan, against myself as Proprietor of the *Telegraph*, claiming compensation in damages for the injury of his character as Bishop of Killala, by the publication in the *Telegraph* of a libel contained in a letter, under the signature "ALADENSIS," handed to me by the Rev. Patrick Flannelly, P. P. of Easkey, who pressed the publication. Bishop O'Finan obtained a verdict for £ 500 damages, and costs. His lordship kindly remitted the damages, and I paid his attorney the costs, which were taxed to £ 328.

I have the honor to subscribe myself,
Your Lordship's very obedient servant,
F. CAVENDISH.

Right Hon. Lord Clifford.

No. IV.

IRELAND; SOCIAL, POLITICAL, AND RELIGIOUS.
By GUSTAVE DE BEAUMONT.
Cap. vii. Sec. III.

But of all the social elements existing in Ireland, and which, favourable to liberty, contain also the germs of democracy, there is perhaps none more fruitful, at least in the present day, than the Catholic clergy. If O'Connell is the summit of the association, the Catholic clergy may be called its base. But O'Connell is a man whose power must end with his life, if indeed the decline of his influence does not commence before his death. The clergy is a body that never dies.

The Catholic clergy is the most national body in Ireland; it belongs to the very heart of the country. We have elsewhere seen, that Ireland having been attacked at the same time in its religion and its liberties, his creed and his country were mingled in the heart of every Irishman, and became to him one and the same thing. Having been forced to struggle for his religion against the Englishman, and for his country against the Protestant, he is accustomed to see partisans of his faith only amongst the defenders of his independence, and to find devotion to independence only amongst the friends of his religion.

In the midst of the agitations of which his country and his soul have been the theatre, the Irishman who has seen so much ruin consummated within him and around him, believes that there is nothing permanent or certain in the world but his religion,—that religion which is coeval with old Ireland,—a religion superior to men, ages, and revolutions,—a religion which has survived the most terrible tempests and the most dreadful tyrannies, against which Henry VIII. was powerless, which braved Elizabeth, over which the bloody hand of Cromwell passed without destroying it, and which even a hundred and fifty years of continued persecution have failed to overthrow. To an Irishman there is nothing supremely true but his creed.

In defending his religion, the Irishman has been a hundred times invaded, conquered, driven from his native soil; he kept his faith, and lost his country. But, after the confusion made between these two things in his mind, his rescued religion became his all, and its influence on his heart was further extended by its taking there the place of independence. The altar at which he prayed was his country.

Traverse Ireland, observe its inhabitants, study their manners, passions, and habits, and you will find that even in the present day, when Ireland is politically free, its inhabitants are full of the prejudices and recollections of their ancient servitude. Look at their external appearance; they walk with their heads bowed down to the earth, their attitude is humble, their language timid; * they receive as a favour what they ought to demand as a right; and they

* I should rather say, evasive. The lion and the bull, says Pindar, defend themselves against an aggressor head foremost; but the fox and the hare, though animals of a very different nature one from the other, are both of them constantly suspicious, and trust rather to their skill in baffling the pursuit of their enemies, than to their physical strength in resisting them. The Irish Catholic has been so long hunted down in Ireland by the Sassenagh, that until he is *sure* no treachery is intended by the foreigner who speaks to him, he, almost in spite of himself, *appears* rather than *is* timid.— His *real* character is the same in his church and in his cabin: it has the courage as well as the resignation of the martyr.—C.

do not believe in the equality which the law ensures to them, and of which it gives them proofs. But go from the streets into the chapels. Here the humbled countenances are raised, the most lowly heads are lifted, and the most noble looks directed to heaven; man reappears in all his dignity. The Irish people exists in its church; there alone it is free; there alone it is sure of its rights; there it occupies the only ground that has never given way beneath its feet.

When the altar is thus national, why should not the priest be so likewise? Hence arises the great power of the Catholic clergy in Ireland. When it attempted to overthrow Catholicism, the English government could not destroy the creed without extirpating the clergy. We have already seen how it tried to ruin that body. Still, in spite of the penal laws, which besides sometimes slumbered, there have been always priests in Ireland. The Catholic worship, it is true, had for a long time only a mysterious and clandestine existence; it was supposed to have no legal existence, and the same fiction was extended to its clergy. Even when the Catholic worship was tolerated, it was not authorised; it was only indirectly recognised when the parliament, in 1798, voted funds to endow a college at Maynooth for the education of Catholic priests. But now the Catholic faith exists publicly in Ireland; it has built its churches, it has organised its clergy, and it celebrates its ceremonies in open day; it counts four archbishops, twenty-one bishops, two thousand one hundred places of worship, and two thousand and seventy-four parish priests or coadjutors. The law does not thus constitute it, but the law allows it to form itself; the constitution affords it express toleration; and now the Catholic clergy, the depository of the chief national power of Ireland, exercises that

E

power under the shield of the constitution. To comprehend this power, it is not sufficient to understand what their religion is to the Irish people, but also what their priest is to them.

Survey those immense lower classes in Ireland who bear at once all the charges and all the miseries of society, oppressed by the landlord, exhausted by taxation, plundered by the Protestant minister, their ruin consummated by the agents of law. Who or what is their only support in such suffering ?—The priest. Who is it that gives them advice in their enterprises, help in their reverses, relief in their distress?—The priest. Who is it that bestows on them, what is perhaps still more precious, that consoling sympathy, that sustaining voice of sympathy, that tear of humanity so dear to the unfortunate ? There is but one man in Ireland that mourns with the poor man who has so much to mourn, and that man is the priest. Vainly have political liberties been obtained and rights consecrated, the people still suffers. There are old social wounds to which the remedy provided by law affords only slow and tedious cure. From these deep and hideous wounds the Catholic priests alone do not turn their eyes ; they are the only persons that attempt their relief. In Ireland, the priest is the only person in perpetual relation with the people who is honoured by them.

Those in Ireland who do not oppress the people are accustomed to despise them. I found that the Catholic clergy were the only persons in Ireland who loved the lower classes, and spoke of them in terms of esteem and affection. This fact alone would explain the power of the priests in Ireland.

The mission of the Catholic clergy in Ireland is the most magnificent that can be imagined. It is an accident, for to produce it there was required an aggregation of miseries which fortunately are peculiar to that country. But the Irish clergy have not neglected their opportunities ; an admirable career was opened to the priests ; they comprehended its grandeur, and entered upon it with sublime devotion : there is no longer any doubt on the continent respecting the life led in Ireland by the Catholic priest, who, in the terrible war waged by the rich against the poor, is the sole refuge of the latter, and who displays, in combating the misfortunes of his fellow man, a zeal, an ardour, and a constancy which the most violent and selfish ambition rarely exhibits in the construction of its own fortune. It appears, besides, that everything in Ireland conspires to exhibit the virtues of the clergy in broad relief.

What must be the feelings of the people when it compares its church, humble and poor like itself, and like itself persecuted, with the haughty and splendid Anglican church, supported by the state, whose power it shares ; when a severe law compels them to pay that church an enormous tribute, for which it receives not a farthing's value, whilst the little that it bestows upon its own clergy is fully paid back, with an addition of care and devotedness which cannot be remunerated ; when, before the peasant's eyes, a Protestant minister, a stranger whom he knows not, occupies a benefice where he only takes care of his family, his pleasures, and his interests ; whilst the Catholic priest, who has no family, no fortune, and no estate, who is the child of Ireland, and has sprung from the popular ranks, lives only for the people, and devotes himself entirely to its service ?

What must he think in the midst of his vast and deep miseries, when every day he hears the rich, almost all of them members of the Anglican church, proclaim charitable almsgiving the greatest of all evils, and a source of demoralisation to the people, whilst the Catholic priest from the pulpit denounces those " who have this world's good, and seeing their brethren in need, shut up their bowels of compassion," and cease not to proclaim those words of charity, " Blesssd are the merciful, for they shall obtain mercy! "

I do not here enquire whether the rich Protestant or the Catholic priest is better acquainted with political economy ; but I am well assured that the mass of the people will take the language of the rich for that of an adversary, whilst the words of the priest, like the voice of a friend, will penetrate to the bottom of the heart. Who now can be astonished at the power of the Catholic priesthood in Ireland? This power has, besides, another foundation more solid than all the rest: in the same way as the Irish people has no prop but its clergy, the clergy has no support but the people. It is the people alone that pays the priesthood, and hence the double bond by which they are mutually linked together—by the bond of mutual dependence, the strongest of all possible ties. Let us add, that in this country, where all the superior and privileged classes are unpopular, the Catholic clergy is the only body more enlightened than the people,* whose intelligence and

---

* This opinion of Mr. G. de Beaumont may perhaps appear to some at variance with the following observations of the late Mr. Burke, in his letter of 1782 to a Peer of Ireland on the penal laws against Irish Catholics :—
" The ministers of Protestant churches require a different mode of education,
" more liberal and more fit for the ordinary intercourse of life. That religion
" having little hold on the minds of the people by external ceremonies and
" extraordinary observances, or separate habits of living, the clergy make
" up the deficiency by cultivating their minds with all kinds of ornamental
" learning, which the liberal provision made in England and Ireland for the
" parochial clergy, (to say nothing of the ample church preferments, with
" little or no duties annexed,) and the comparative lightness of parochial
" duties, enables the greater part of them in some considerable degree to
" accomplish. This learning, which I believe to be pretty general, together
" with a higher situation, and more chastened by the opinions of mankind,

power it gladly accepts. And this power is not purely social; it is furthermore essentially political. The free existence of the Catholic church in Ireland is, perhaps, the matter most directly hostile to the principle of government which has prevailed there for centuries. It is not only a church raised by the side of another church; it is not merely a corps of curates, priests, and bishops organised in rivalry to another clergy, raising altar against altar, and preaching sermon against sermon. There is, in the present free developement of the Catholic church in Ireland, the mark of a new principle, victorious over the old Anglican principle, which was once the very soul of the English government; the Protestant ascendancy is vanquished; it

---

" forms a sufficient security for the morals of the established clergy and for
" their sustaining their clerical character with dignity. It is not necessary
" to observe, that all these things are, however, collateral to their functions :
" and that, except in preaching, which may be and is supplied, and often
" best supplied, out of printed books, little else is necessary for a Protestant
" minister than to be able to read the English language; I mean for the
" exercise of his functions, not for the qualification of his admission to it."
But Mr. G. de Beaumont does not *absolutely* say that the Catholic clergy in Ireland is the only body more enlightened than the people of that country, —he says, as I understand him, that it is the only body more enlightened " *whose intelligence and power the people gladly accepts.*" The intelligence of the Protestant clergy in Ireland, is as *useless* to the people of Ireland, partly on account of the unwillingness of that people to avail itself of that intelligence, partly also perhaps on account of the unwillingness of that clergy to exercise it for the advantage of the people, as it is declared by Mr. Burke to be *unnecessary* for the discharge of the functions of that clergy. But of the intelligence of the Roman Catholic clergy of Ireland, as far as I have had an opportunity of comparing it with the intelligence of other clergymen in communion or not in communion with the See of Rome, whether in Great Britain and Ireland or on the continent, I should be inclined to express myself, were I called upon to give any opinion on the subject, in the words of a highly talented French bishop, of a highly charitable French nobleman : " Whether he has much or little intelligence I will not take upon " myself to decide; but this I know for certain, that he employs all the " intelligence he has in doing good, and he does an immense deal."—C.

is a political, far more than a religious principle that has triumphed.

Thus, the Irish priest does not limit himself to aiding the people in its social miseries, he also protects them against the political oppressor ; he is not content to be a man and a priest, but he is furthermore a citizen, and is not less attentive to liberty than to religion.

During a long period, the Catholic clergy, subjected like their flocks to persecution, had no other care but to withdraw themselves from it, and was humbled too much to preserve any power for protection ; it concealed itself from the penal laws, labouring to procure for the people the spiritual succours of religion, and when it had succeeded in this object, its task was accomplished. Thus, when oppression was at the worst, the Catholic clergy kept themselves strictly within the pale of its church, and continued to shelter itself there when Ireland fought its first battles, and gained its first victories. The priests naturally remained strangers to the agitation of 1778, which was a Protestant movement ; and shortly afterwards, when the Irish Association made an appeal to the nation—they were at first deaf to its voice, and only lent it feeble aid, which was withdrawn when the clouds began to gather that presaged the storm of 1798.

When this dreadful tempest was passed, when the Irish ceased to be revolutionary and became constitutional, when ingenious modes of aggression were discovered, by which the fruits of rebellion could be obtained without encountering its perils,—immense perils, which the priest, anxious both for himself and his flock, keeps constantly in view,— the Catholic priesthood in these conjunctures ended by warmly espousing the cause of the people ; and from that day has been its most efficacious defender and the most formidable enemy of power. There has not been since a political crisis in Ireland, in which the Catholic clergy has not played an important part. It was the constant auxiliary of the association, whose acts and decrees it explained to the people. There has not been an election in Ireland without the Catholic priests giving their advice, not to say their commands, to the people. The priests take part in all the affairs of the country; they attend and speak at all public meetings. The priest is often changed into a tribune of the people, and the same voice that recommends, " to render unto Cæsar the things that are Cæsar's," loudly proclaims, that it is the duty of every good Catholic to vote against the Protestant candidate, and that the most humble tenant should brave the severities of his landlord rather than not give his vote according to his conscience. No one is now ignorant, that the success of the liberal elections in Ireland is almost entirely due to the influence which the priest possesses over the hearts of the people, and to his opposing the menances of the rich and powerful by the promises of heaven and the terrors of hell. It was on the proposal of the clergy that the association resolved to give an indemnity to poor tenants, ejected from their farms for an independent vote ; and thus the Catholic clergy of Ireland introduced charity into politics.

There is nothing, assuredly, in the traditions and principles of the Catholic clergy which would lead them to become enemies of established governments; and when difference of religious principle prevents an alliance, they in general abstain from hostility. Look at Prussia and Belgium. But what do we see in Ireland! Not only a Catholic clergy in presence of a government with which alliance was impossible, but a clergy against which that government waged a merciless war for three centuries, whose laws proscribed its worship and exiled its members;

on which fell the most cruel persecutions, the memory of
which is still alive in Ireland : a clergy, irritated not only
by the evils which it endured, but perhaps still more so by
the protection which the state granted to its most mortal
enemy, the Anglican church ; a clergy, in fine, which,
always at war with the state, has never had any friend but
the people, the poor people of Ireland, who, after having
paid the landlord, the Anglican minister, the taxes levied
by the state, the county, and the parish, found still a trifle
for the proper support of its priesthood. Could any one
desire, that when a struggle began, and continued during
half a century, between the government and the people ;—
when, on a law, a tax, or an election, might depend the life,
fortune, or liberty of all citizens ;—when everything national
was ranged on one side, and everything inimical to Ireland
on the other ;—when alternation of success and defeat
invited every combatant into the lists ;—could any one
wish, I say, that the clergy, placed between this detested
government and this affectionate people, should remain
indifferent spectators of the combat ?

No.   Even if the Catholic clergy wished to remain
neutral, it could not ; but it has no need of doing violence
to itself, to embrace the popular cause.   The Irish priest of
the present day is far removed from those doctrines of
passive obedience with which the Catholic church has been
often reproached, and according to which the people, bowed
down under the most oppressive tyranny, has not the right
to raise their head.   We may judge of the spirit that animates the national clergy of Ireland, by the answer which
Dr. Doyle, titular bishop of Kildare, made before the House
of Commons in 1832, for there is no prelate whose name is
more venerated by the clergy and people of Ireland.

Dr. Doyle had published a letter, addressed to all the

Irish Catholics, exhorting them not to pay tithes to the Protestant clergy, and to maintain their resistance by all legal means.

Thus, said the members of parliament, before whom he appeared, you establish the right to resist law as a principle ; and what is to be the foundation of this resistance ? The individual judgment of each private man is to decide expressly, whether law shall be obeyed or not. Can there be more complete anarchy ?

" I think," replied the Catholic bishop, " that when abuses exist in a state, if individuals were forced to submit their judgment to the authority that protects these abuses, no kind of reform would be possible; and not only would the principle of passive obedience be established on the widest base. but a doctrine even worse than the divine right of kings—the divine right of abuses. What progress was ever made in this country that was not the work of men pursuing justice in opposition to law ? For my part, I know of none. The despotism of James II. was strictly legal. Even on the question of tonnage and poundage, the courts of law decided in favour of the crown. The revolution of 1688 was, beyond doubt, a violation of the British constitution, and yet it was the commencement of national prosperity. Consider Catholic emancipation. During fifty years, it was eagerly sought by Catholics, and many Protestants, and what a multitude of crimes has accompanied the opposition it has met; how many collisions, hatreds, and sanguinary fights ? To speak of something still more recent, is not the present organisation of the House of Commons constitutional? No one, doubtless, will deny that it is so. Nevertheless, the king and the government are endeavouring to modify this institution which the law protects, and their plan of reform has been the cause of riots at Bristol and Nottingham. Who will impute these riots, and the consequent bloodshed, to the government? If a right must be renounced because the establishment of that right involves danger, it would be better to submit to despotism at once; you can never succeed in chaining down my intelligence to the letter of the law, so as to prevent me from pursuing the truth and justice pointed out by my conscience. Let us then take the principle of justice for our guide, and resist abuses as best we may; but let us not, because these abuses are mingled with a principle, sacrifice the principle itself. If we did so, it would be better for us to cease to live in society, and we should assuredly be unworthy of the free constitution which Providence has bestowed on these countries."

Such is at present the language of the priest in Ireland. Thus, an element, favourable by its nature to established governments, is derived from a principle pregnant with liberty to the people,—the principle of political resistance which has become so formidable in Ireland, that it is asked what authority can maintain itself against it; but yet it is a principle which its adversaries dare not touch, because it is the only social safeguard of those whose political power is attacked. The Catholic priesthood is almost the only moral authority that the people of Ireland can consult: it alone teaches the people those rules of conduct in private life, which are the surest guarantees of honesty in public life; and even where its political passions are engaged with its interests, when it adopts the cause of the people, it endeavours, while it follows, to direct the popular cause, and often succeeds. The priests have always condemned the principles and acts of the Whiteboys, and Dr. Doyle excommunicated them more than once. If, in the midst of its democratic agitation, the association succeeded in diffusing ideas of order and obedience to law amongst the people, it was because the Catholic priests were its immediate agents. If the rich landlord and the justice whom the people resist by the counsel of the priest are not robbed or murdered, it is to the priest they owe their safety. What a strange situation for an aristocracy, which, in order to preserve life and property, is in some degree obliged to abandon political power! What a singular destiny for a clergy, which, inclined towards authority by its instincts and its doctrines, has become the most formidable opponent of authority!

When the Irish priesthood, whose Catholic doctrine is not hostile to temporal power, goes beyond its first principle, it is naturally, and by an inclination peculiar to itself, the enemy of the aristocracy.

Christianity is democratic in its essence; it is the great source of the equality perpetually flowing and deluging the world. - Christianity does not cease to be democratic except where it is directed from its natural course.

If the christian principle is the most democratic of all religious principles, it must be added, that of all the forms under which the christian principle is manifested to mankind, the Catholic form is also the most democratic. It alone passes the same level over all men and all nations, which it subjects to the empire of one single chief, the supreme arbiter of the human race. How then does it happen that the Catholic religion is sometimes the ally and friend of aristocracy? The reason is, that the body which represents the religion, the clergy, may be so organized as to lose its original character, and to assume another which does not belong to it.

Suppose a Catholic clergy endowed with great privileges; hence will at once result, the instincts, the passions, and the interests of all privileged corporations. Suppose that, coexisting with nobility in the state, it possesses rights and advantages analagous to those of the nobility; that, like the aristocracy, it possesses great political powers, immense estates, great wealth ; a natural sympathy will be established between the two bodies ; a constant tendency will lead them to approximate and form a close alliance, to league for defence, to unite for attack. Then also its instincts, passions, and interests as a privileged body, will remove it as far from the people, that is to say, the great masses, as its principles of Christian and Catholic equality brought it near to them before they were adulterated : and its distance from the people will increase proportionably as the other privileged body, its equal and its ally, holds itself more aloof ; so that if the aristocracy should go to war with the people, the clergy, the primitive and natural friend of the masses, will become their adversary.

But it is easy to see that nothing like this can happen in a country where the Christian and Catholic clergy possess no privilege and occupy no recognised rank in the state ; where, indeed, an aristocracy exists, ⎡but a Protestant aristocracy in the presence of a Catholic people ; an aristocracy which, instead of attracting the national clergy towards it by parity of position, and thus inviting it to an alliance, on the contrary, rejects it with all the violence resulting from an assemblage of hostile passions, opposite principles, and contrary interests ; in a country, finally, where all the principles, all the interests, and all the passions which sever the clergy from the aristocracy unite it to the people.

Thus, in Ireland, the clergy has complete authority over a people which recognises no authority but the clerical,*— a situation very different from the case in which the clergy,

---

* I presume that the writer means "no authority *over its mind*." The people of Ireland have never been able to love the law which governs them politically, and can have had no other idea of it for centuries than of a law of brute force.—C.

united to an absolute monarch, is strictly kept within the limits of its spiritual influence, and from that where united to an aristocracy it has no political strength, but divided and unpopular. Here the Catholic clergy possesses a double authority over the priesthood,* and exercises it alone. It is thus that a religious body, which we sometimes see the supporter of princes or the ally of privileged corporations, is in Ireland one of the most potent elements of liberty and democracy.

---

* It appears to me that the word " priesthood " has been printed by mistake for the word people.—C.

⮕ The Episcopal Resolutions of 1826 and 1834 alluded to in p. 29 of the preceding letter, lines 23 and 24, will appear as an Appendix to the following letter—the fourth.

LETTER IV.

London, December 13th, 1841.

My Lord,

When I did myself the honor of addressing your Lordship last October, I observed to you, p. 8, that your Lordship had proposed three remedies for the present state of Ireland—a state which I was then even willing to concede to you to be most deplorable, and presenting the most awful prospects. My late visit to Ireland, has confirmed me in the view which your Lordship and I take of the present position of public affairs in that part of the United Empire. The object of that visit was to ascertain on the spot, how far it might be practicable to enlist the feelings and co-operation of the Catholic population of Ireland, in favor of the most earnest wishes of the present head of the Catholic Church, Pope Gregory XVI. for the abolition of that most inhuman traffic, which, the Prospectus published by the Committee of the Society for the extinction of the Slave Trade, previous to the meeting held at Exeter Hall, June 1st, 1840, at which the President, H.R.H. Prince Albert, took the chair, declares to have increased twofold since Great Britain began to exert herself at the expence of fifteen millions sterling for its abolition. An awful fact! I had had, before quitting England, the most frank and unqualified assurances from the present Lord Mayor of Dublin, that I should have his full support; and I must do him the justice to say, that he amply redeemed his promise to me. On Tuesday, the 30th of November, the Lord Mayor of Dublin did me the honor of calling upon me at Gresham's Hotel, to inform me, that no public meeting would take place in Dublin during the few days to which my visit was necessarily limited, except a Repeal meeting, " which, of course," observed the Lord Mayor, " you would not wish to attend;" but that if I thought proper to have a requisition presented to him the next morning, Wednesday, for a special public meeting on the subject which had brought me to Dublin, he would instantly issue the necessary orders, would put the great room of the Mansion House at the disposition of the meeting, and would himself take the chair, and give me every support in his power. On the question, however, of the propriety of calling a public meeting on the subject which had occasioned my visit, or upon the expediency of my presenting myself before any public meeting in Dublin at the present moment, and under existing circumstances, the Lord Mayor wished me to be guided by the opinion of others, especially as my letters to your Lordship of last October, had laid before the public an expression of certain sentiments, which I must be perfectly aware, were far from being in unison with a very influential party, even in Dublin. I perfectly agreed with the Lord Mayor in the propriety of these observations, which entirely coincided with reflections I had previously made to myself; and by application to persons with whom I have the honor and satisfaction to myself of being on terms of intimacy, and in whose thorough knowledge of public feeling in Dublin, not to say throughout Ireland, I could safely rely, I fully satisfied myself that very evening, that it was more than doubtful, whether a requisition for a public meeting at the present moment, on any subject except opposition to the government of Lord de Grey, or Repeal of the Union, would have the effect of securing any tolerable attendance ; but that it was still less likely, that any British Catholic Peer who should so soon after the publication of the recent pamphlet of the Earl of Shrewsbury, present himself before a public meeting in Ireland, without disavowing the sentiments expressed in that pamphlet, and declaring himself in rather stronger terms than I am disposed to use towards Her Majesty's present Ministers, against their administration, and without declaring himself favorable to a measure, the only certain and

F

immediate effect of which would be, in my
humble opinion, the loss of the Lord Mayor of
Dublin, and such men as Mr. Wyse and Mr.
Sheil, to the Parliament held at Westminster,
would run a great risk of being very ill-received.
Of course I decided, that the interests of the
cause I have undertaken to advocate to the best
of my abilities, physical and mental, required of
me, that I should not run the risk of prejudicing
that cause, at the outset, by presenting myself
before a public meeting in Dublin. I contented
myself therefore, with sending to each of the
Roman Catholic Prelates in Ireland, with my
respects, on the 3rd inst. a copy of the address,
which, without my knowledge, though certainly
with great gratification to my own feelings, has
been inserted in the *Times* newspaper, of the
9th inst., and with announcing the re-publication
in the form of a pamphlet, now in the press, of
Mr. Powell, 68, Thomas Street, Dublin, of the
speech of Mr. George Thompson, published
originally in the *Glagow Argus* newspaper, of
the 4th of last November, together with the
Briefs, in Latin and English, of Urban VIII.,
Benedict XIV., and Gregory XVI.

But why do I mention these facts to your
Lordship?—I mention them to shew your Lordship my grounds for believing, that there exists
in Ireland at present a state of public feeling,
which absorbs, or at least outweighs, every other

consideration; and that your Lordship and the Earl of Shrewsbury, have both of you touched, though in very different ways, " that string"— to use an expression borrowed from Sterne's Maria—" on which all her sorrows vibrate,"— when you, both of you, proposed measures for the tranquillity of Ireland, from which the people of Ireland in their present feelings must necessarily shrink with *instinctive* horror, rather than with any *rational* conviction of their inexpediency, or even notion of their import; because neither of your Lordships speak ill of the present administration, or advocate the Repeal of the Union. But do I? No! my Lord, I do not; yet there is this difference between your Lordships and myself, that I do not, with your Lordships, feel inclined to tell the people of Ireland and Great Britain, that the tranquillity of Ireland *may* or can be secured by the State-payment of the Catholic Clergy in Ireland, or by the establishment of an " open" (or any) communication between Rome and Great Britain, *similar* to that which exists between Rome and Russia, or between Rome and Prussia; or by a *relaxation* of the discipline of Maynooth College; or by the committal as a Government measure of the direction of that College to the excellent educationists who now have the direction of the College of Propaganda in Rome, and of Clougowes in Ireland; nor do I, with the Earl of

Shrewsbury, blame the public conduct of the Lord Mayor of Dublin, nor do I feel inclined to blame it.

In my last letter I have, I hope, laid some strong grounds before your Lordship and the public for my belief, that the payment by the State of the Roman Catholic Clergy in Ireland, even were it practicable, on account of the financial difficulties, or anti-catholic feelings of the people of England and Scotland, would not promote the tranquillity of Ireland. I have in this letter not only to explain my reasons for believing that open communication with Rome, *similar* to that which exists between Rome and *Russia,* or Rome and *Prussia,* would not benefit public tranquillity ; but also why I believe, that communication between Rome and Great Britain and Ireland as an United Empire, such as exists between Rome and Belgium, is *all* that *is* wanted to secure tranquillity to Ireland. In these words, however, *all that is wanted*, I must not be understood as expressing an opinion, that the *instantaneous*, and as it were magical effect of the repeal of the Act of Elizabeth, which attaches the penalty of premunire to any Act of the British Cabinet, or of any Member of it, which would amount in the eye of the law to any holding of intercourse or communication with the Bishop of Rome, commonly called the Pope, as spiritual or ecclesiastical head of the

Catholic Church, would be perfect public tranquillity or cessation from agitation in Ireland. No! I mean to say, that such repeal *is*, in my opinion, absolutely requisite, and of immediate necessity for the civil and political interests of the United Empire of Great Britain and Ireland and of the Colonies of that Empire; that it *might be* of great advantage to the spiritual interests of the subjects of the Throne of Great Britain and Ireland; and that it most probably would be, if, in furtherance of the objects of that repeal, namely, of the spiritual, civil, and political interests above-mentioned, a communication between the British Government and the See of Rome, similar to that which exists between the Belgian Government and that See, were established. I mean to say, that such repeal and such communication would be all that would be requisite *on the part of Government,* to enable the prudent, sensible, and loyal portion of the Catholic subjects of the Throne of Great Britain and Ireland to acquire over the far inferior portion of those Catholic subjects who entertain sentiments differing from their own, that decided ascendancy in point of influence and of public opinion, which the existence of the law of Elizabeth, and the absence of legal communication between the Government of Great Britain and Ireland and the See of Rome, absolutely and fatally for public tranquillity, mainly prevents

that far greater portion of the Catholic subjects
of Queen Victoria from obtaining. I mean to
say, that the alteration which I propose, and
which, as it seems to me, your Lordship does
not propose, would give a decided superiority of
influence in public opinion to the Most Rev.
Archbishop Murray and to those Catholics in
Ireland who look up to him ; and that the existing state of things gives a decided superiority of
influence in public opinion to the Most Rev.
Archbishop M'Hale and to those Catholics in
Ireland who look up to him.

I believe, that every measure, really essential
or really advantageous to public tranquillity in
Ireland, would naturally and without any *initi-
ative* act or exertion of authority on the part of
the Government, flow from the single act of the
giving due and proper influence to that far
greater portion of the Catholic population of
Ireland, whose sentiments are in unison with
those of Archbishop Murray.

I will go further ; and I will fearlessly assert,
that it is not merely chiefly, but that it is absolutely entirely to the actual operation of the
Act of Queen Elizabeth upon the interests of
Queen Victoria, that the awfully dangerous influence of Archbishop M'Hale upon public tranquillity in Ireland is to be attributed ; that is to
say, that the talents of Archbishop M'Hale,
great as they undoubtedly are, and that the

present disposition of the Sacred Congregation of Propaganda at Rome, including as it does among its present members the Cardinal Secretary of State, to value most highly, perhaps to over-rate, the talents and the zeal of Archbishop M'Hale for the defence and propagation of Catholicity, would be perfectly innocuous to public tranquillity in Ireland, if the Act of Elizabeth were repealed, and communication between the Government of Great Britain and Ireland and the Holy See similar to that which now exists between the Government of Belgium and the Holy See, were now to be established.

Whatever may be the motives which have induced your Lordship to believe (and it is clear to me that you do believe it, since you assert it expressly, p. 31) that his present Holiness Gregory XVI. and several influential Catholics in Rome, wish that a state communication similar to that which exists between the Holy See and *Russia*, or to that which existed between the Holy See and *Prussia* when the controversy respecting the Archbishop of Cologne arose, should exist between the Holy See and the Government of Great Britain and Ireland, I have no motive whatever for believing any such thing; but I have, I think, much stronger motives than your Lordship can have in support of your opinion, for believing the very reverse. In the doubt in which I am, whether it would be expedient in me to state those motives in this

letter, I shall refrain from doing so; but your
Lordship may easily, with the means which you
possess of learning the truth upon this point,
satisfy yourself that I am not in error upon it;
and that I am perfectly correct in saying that
His Holiness, Gregory XVI. would most willingly see the repeal of the Law of Elizabeth
effected by the Legislature of Great Britain and
Ireland upon a motion to that effect brought forward by the present Cabinet of Queen Victoria,
and would most willingly place the Holy See
in communication with the present Cabinet of
Queen Victoria on terms similar to those on
which he has placed the Holy See in communication with the Cabinet of King Leopold;
or if the phrase be more acceptable, place himself in communication with Queen Victoria on
the same terms on which he has placed himself
in communication with King Leopold.

I will only further observe, and *as my own
opinion only*, but a very decided one,—that it is
ABSOLUTELY ESSENTIAL to the success of a re-
newal of communication between the Throne of
Great Britain and Ireland, and the Pope, that
the representative of that Throne should be a
Member of the Established Church of England,
and a Nobleman of acknowledged high reputation in public business; and that no person in
communion with the Holy See should be attached to such representative as forming *any*
part of his official suite.   This opinion may

appear very startling to some members of the Roman Catholic Church, but it is founded upon my own observations ; and I am decidedly of opinion, that the success of any attempt to renew communications at present between the Throne of Great Britain and Ireland and the Holy See, will depend mainly upon the adoption of this course.

It is not without cause that I have placed before the eyes of your Lordship and of the public, the sentiments of Hierophilos upon the advantages which accrue to Ireland from an intimate connection with Great Britain, since Archbishop M'Hale is at present, far more than the present Lord Mayor of Dublin, the life and soul of the Repeal of the Union party in Ireland. Neither is it without reason, that I have placed before the eyes of your Lordship and of the public, the sentiments of the Bishop of Maronia, coadjutor Bishop of Killala, on civil subordination, since Archbishop M'Hale was publicly announced at the Galway dinner by the Roman Catholic Bishop of Galway, as the most distinguished ornament of the Roman Catholic Hierarchy of Ireland, and about to speak to the Clergy there assembled, the sentiments of that Hierarchy. It is most important to public tranquillity in Ireland, that in the event of any proposition for the restoration of any communication between Gregory XVI. and Queen

Victoria (and none now exists), the subjects of Queen Victoria should clearly understand, that in approving the sentiments of Hierophilos and of the Bishop of Maronia, by the promotion of the coadjutor Bishop of Killala to the Archiepiscopal See of Tuam, Gregory XVI. did not approve the very different sentiments pronounced at the Galway dinner by Archbishop M'Hale, announced as the organ of the sentiments of the Roman Catholic Hierarchy in Ireland.

But your Lordship may perhaps ask me—Is it not desirable that Gregory XVI. should disavow, or publicly disapprove, the sentiments expressed by Archbishop M'Hale at the Galway dinner? My answer to such a question would be—I think that under existing circumstances it would be highly inexpedient that Gregory XVI. should notice in any manner those sentiments.—Certainly the Government of Great Britain and Ireland cannot have any possible claim upon His Holiness, of whose very existence it affects to be ignorant, for any such disavowal, or public disapprobation. If relations similar to those which exist between the Holy See and Russia, were ever, unfortunately for public liberty, to exist between England and Rome, England might then have a *shew* of right to call upon Rome to interpose the moral influence of the Holy See in support even of arbitrary power;

but Gregory XVI. might be baffled as he has been in Russia and Poland, in every attempt that he might make to interpose in favor of oppressed humanity in Ireland, or in any other part of the British Empire, against the most despotic tyranny. It would ill become the noble minded author of the Brief of December 3, 1839, against the abettors of Slavery, to *place himself* in such a position. I know Gregory XVI. too well, to be able to suppose for an instant that he would accede to any such proposition. Liable as he undoubtedly is at present, to be imposed upon by misrepresentation in the affairs of the Catholic Church of Ireland, to the detriment of public tranquillity in that country, as in the Killala case, such liability is a far less evil than those which would result from any *voluntary consent* on His part, to such a substitution for such liability as your Lordship, unintentionally I trust, has undoubtedly proposed, p. 31 of your pamphlet.

Of all the "observations" of the Earl of Roden upon your Lordship's "measures, propo-"sed for restoring tranquillity to Ireland," none perhaps are more curious and exhibitive of the impossibility of coming to any true or practically useful conclusion from erroneous premises, than those contained in pages 24 to 28 of those "observations," on the very point on which I am now addressing your Lordship. They remind me very much of the usual dithyrambics which every Italian opera composer places in the mouth of his primo tenore, to be executed in every note of the gamut, with the utmost skill in cadences and rapidity in demi-semi-quavers, for the obtaining of unbounded applause from his astonished if not delighted hearers, against the perfidiousness of his *crudel tirauna*, until the proper time arrives for protesting with equal musical talent that said *prima donna* is the quintessence of angelic perfection, in short his *bel idol mio;* after which the curtain drops and the *ballet* begins, and Taglioni with a twirl or two of her inimitably graceful leg puts the whole chapter of harmonic grievances and their termination of ecstacy at once out of the heads of the pit, boxes, and gallery. Hapless Earl of Roden, who considers " the present agitations but as a gentle " breeze ruffling the surface of society, in com- " parison with the hurricane which Lord Alvan- " ley's measures are calculated to produce! " What a talent your Lordship must have, in the Earl of Roden's opinion, for raising the wind! This is the *recitative.*——Now for the *aria.*

" Whilst " (andante penseroso) " it is my de- " sire to live on all friendly terms with my " Roman Catholic fellow-subjects," (your Lordship sees clearly that the noble Earl would never wish to see the Beresford Riding House in Dublin, take place again of the National School,) " and not to be wanting in acts of kindness, or

" of courtesy, to them as individuals, I trust that
" it may ever be " (vivace) " the determination
" of *Protestant* Englishmen to make no compro-
" mise with the anti-scriptural doctrines, or anti-
" social principles, of the Church and Court of
" Rome."—(Fortissimo.)

Poor Naldi himself, when singing with his
lovely daughter in " Il Fanatico per la musica "—
" Oh che brava figha, Rassomiglia al suo Pa-
dre "—cannot have experienced or inspired
more thrilling raptures to the breasts of his audience, than the Earl of Roden must have inspired
by this *bravura* into the breast of the writer of
the two articles in the Dublin University Magazine for November and December 1841, which
I have noticed in my last letter to your Lordship.

But what if the equally venerable and amiable
Archbishop Murray, for instance, were to take
it into his head to reply to this *bravura?* It is
my desire to live, as I have always lived, on all
friendly terms with my fellow-subjects who are
not Roman Catholics, and not to be wanting, as
I never have been wanting, in acts of kindness
or of courtesy to them on any occasion; and I
trust that it may ever be the determination of
Catholic Irishmen to prove, by the whole tenor
of their lives no less than by their words and
writings, that the Roman Catholic Church has
no anti-scriptural doctrines, no anti-social prin-

ciples, and that consequently no compromise *can* be made with them. My humble opinion is, that Archbishop Murray's part, though it might not be acted with all the stage effect of the Earl of Roden's, would be in better taste, would be more true to the principles of harmony, and would to good and impartial judges appear better Irish melody than the bravura of the Earl of Roden. But the misfortune is, that before any one has time to test by quiet reflection the merits of the respective compositions, in come, not indeed Taglionis or Vestrisses, but most uncouth morris-dancers, playing antics and yelling out howlings like the crew of Comus; itinerant pedlars in controversial wares, with scriptural texts to be used as shillelahs, instead of being used, as those holy writings should always be used, as exhortations to self-abnegation, humility, and love of God and our neighbour; and the real lover of heaven-born music, half in anger, half in sorrow, retires from a scene, which, however amusing to others, can have no charms for him.

This, my Lord, as far as I am able to judge, has been the misfortune of Ireland since 1829, that agitation never diminishing its energy, however varying in its object, has hitherto prevented Catholics and Non-Catholics in Ireland from dwelling on the harmonious tones of the *Unanimous* Declaration of the Roman Catholic Prelates of Ireland in 1826 and 1834. Had the attention been paid to those Declarations which ought, for the sake of Christianity and social order, to have been paid to them, perhaps ere now the Earl of Roden might have said with St. Augustine, in the quotation so happily prefixed to the Declaration of the British Catholic Prelates, and subscribed by all the British Catholic Laity in 1826 ; " I rejoiced while I blushed, at " finding that I had hitherto barked, not against " the Catholic faith, but against the fictions of " carnal cogitations." Perhaps too, your Lordship might have been able to persuade the noble Earl that he was never more in error in his life, than when he wrote these words, p. 6 of his Observations :—

" No state relation into which we could be " brought with the Court of Rome, could give " greater force to this authority " (that of the Roman Catholic Hierarchy in Ireland) " than is " already given; and instead of such a relation " making the exercise of it safer for our liber- " ties, or our peace, it will only tend the more to " endanger both."

I beg of your Lordship, and I would beg also of the noble Earl who has published his " observations " upon your Lordship's " measures," to read over attentively the sketch of Bishop O'Finan's public career, before the clergy of Killala presented that venerable man first upon the list for the approbation of Gregory XVI., as Bishop Elect of Killala, as it is given in the extract from Mr. West's speech, subjoined to this letter: then to read over the declarations of the Hon. Frederick Cavendish; and to consider whether *such* a state relation as *must* have prevented Gregory XVI. from having been so infamously imposed upon as He was in that case, would have given no greater force to Episcopal authority against such men as the priest Flannelly, and his abettors, both in Ireland and at Rome. I beg of both of your Lordships, and I beg of the people of Great Britain and Ireland, to consider whether it was for the advantage of public tranquillity in Ireland, that the verdict of the jury at Sligo should have been nullified, and a triumph given to the priest Flannelly, by the present anomalous intercourse with the Court of Rome.

Perhaps there never has taken place since the introduction of Christianity into Ireland, any judicial proceeding of such immense importance to the interests of christianity and social order in that country as the trial of Monday, March 20, and of Tuesday, March 21, 1837, at the Sligo Assizes, before Judge Perrin, and a Special Jury; none, which if attentively considered, points out at once to the Holy See the immense evil which must result to Catholicity in Ireland, from the prevalence of an opinion, unfortunately too strong at present even, and assiduously inculcated at the time to the Hon. Mr. Cavendish, who was made the dupe of the assurances given to him at the time; and deserves in consequence much more compassion for his sufferings, than harsh reproach for his error. It must always be of great importance to public tranquillity in Great Britain and Ireland, that attempts from *any* quarter to deceive the Head of the Catholic Church, by misrepresentations and *a fortiori* by calumnies, should be discouraged. How much more so, when the object of such an unwarrantable attempt is, to induce that Head to take, upon such misrepresentation from a quarter whence He had a perfect right to expect nothing but candour and truth combined with full knowledge of the fact, any step, which might with some shew of plausibility at least, be represented as an assertion of right on the part of the Holy See, to set aside a verdict of a British or Irish Court of Justice in an action clearly of a *Civil* nature, between two subjects of the British Crown. Nothing could be further from the intention of Gregory XVI., than to assert any such pretension. With respect to Bishop O'Finan *personally*, the result to that venerable man of the prudential measure taken by Gregory XVI., has been, that an honor has been conferred upon him in presence of ninety Bishops of the Christian world, and of all the Cardinals in Rome, which is not upon record, in regard of any Irish Bishop, since the days of St. Patrick. On occasion of the canonization which

G

took place in May, 1839, four of the Prelates assisting at the Pontifical Throne, were Bishops already named Cardinals ; the fifth, the senior Bishop of Italy ; the sixth, the Right Rev. Dr. O'Finan, Bishop of Killala. Whatever may be the future destiny in this life of the " Venerable Brother " (a) of Gregory XVI., and loyal subject of Queen Victoria, his warmest friends can have little more to wish for his happiness, than that he may persevere to the end steadfast in his faith, in his spiritual obedience to the Holy See, and in his unshaken allegiance to his beloved Sovereign, (b) in order that he may be crowned with still greater honor in Heaven, when called to receive the reward of those who have suffered persecution in this world for justice-sake.

It may have happened, and if so, it certainly was not when I was in Rome, that by some incautious expression my venerable friend may have irritated those, who may have considered, that disrespect to themselves, however unintentional on his part, was proof of his entertaining other sentiments towards the Head of his Church than those, which I have in this letter, and on all occasions, attributed to him. On this point, I shall content myself with transcribing from the

---

(a) The Pope in writing to a Bishop always styles him " Venerabilis Frater."

(b) Mia cara ed amata Regina—words of a letter of Bishop O'Finan to Cardinal Franzoni.

second of two memorials presented by the Earl
of Shrewsbury in 1839, to the Cardinal Secretary
of State, (Lambruschini) the following passage.

" When the Earl of Shrewsbury read to Car-
" dinal Lambruschini, on the 23rd of January,
" 1839, his first memorial in favor of Bishop
" O'Finan, the Cardinal Secretary of State made
" to him a few observations ; one of which was—
" that his Eminence was inclined to believe, that
" Bishop O'Finan had brought upon himself the
" measures taken in his regard, by the tone of
" the letters which he had written to the Sacred
" Congregation, and to the Cardinal Prefect.
" As to these letters, the Earl declared that he
" had no knowledge of them. Another obser-
" vation was—that Bishop O'Finan had threat-
" ened to appeal from the decision of the Holy
" See to the Queen of England, of which the
" Earl again declared himself to be perfectly
" ignorant.

" After this audience the Earl had occasion
" to speak on these two points to the Bishop of
" Killala, who assured him, in the most positive
" manner, that he had never intended to write
" anything but what was very respectful to the
" Holy See, in the defence of which he was
" ready to lay down his life ; nor in reference
" to the Sacred Congregation, for which he pro-
" fessed the most profound respect ; nor in re-
" ference to the Cardinal Prefect (Franzoni) to
" the Secretary (Cadolini) ; nor to any member

" of that Congregation. He equally declared,
" that he had never threatened to appeal from
" the Holy See to the Queen of England; that
" he had never had any such intention; and he
" expressed at the same time extreme surprise,
" and deep regret, that a misunderstanding of
" any of his expressions should have given rise to
" such an ill-founded apprehension."

To this Memorial the Earl of Shrewsbury
never received any answer; nor has my venerable friend ever had any expression in any of his
letters pointed out to him for explanation or re-
tractation. The good breeding of Cardinal Lambruschini forbids me however to suppose, that His
Eminence considered the Memorial of the Earl of
Shrewsbury, Premier Earl of England and of Ireland, the father of Princess Borghese and of Princess Doria, beneath his notice. I must therefore
suppose, that it had its due weight with the Sacred
Congregation of Propaganda, of which His Eminence is deservedly a most influential member. I
consider therefore, the result of the Sligo trial,
so far as it affects Bishop O'Finan *personally*, entirely satisfactory, both in Ireland, where the
verdict was confirmed unanimously upon appeal
to the Exchequer Court in Dublin, and at Rome.

But it is far otherwise with the public result
of that trial. It is but too clear to me, that its
result occasioned the attempt to bear down, in the
subsequent attack upon Archbishop Murray, and
upon the system of National Education in Ireland,

the unanimous resolutions of the Roman Catholic Hierarchy of Ireland in 1826; the great sin of those resolutions being, in the eyes of a certain party in Ireland, that they would tend to teach the Catholic poor children in Ireland, to consider themselves indebted to the Government of the United Kingdom of Great Britain and Ireland, for assistance afforded to their parents and pastors in the execution of the wish so admirably since expressed by Queen Victoria, in Her Majesty's ever memorable words to the Lords of the Council of Committee on Education.— " IT IS MY WISH THAT THE YOUTH OF MY KING- " DOM SHOULD BE RELIGIOUSLY BROUGHT UP, " AND THAT THE RIGHTS OF CONSCIENCE SHOULD " BE RESPECTED."

I watched, my Lord, the progress of that second iniquitous attempt to mystify Pope Gregory XVI. with more disgust than alarm, so far as that clear-sighted Pontiff was concerned; but with far different feelings, so far as the tranquillity of Ireland was at stake. That my hopes have not been disappointed, the production of the Right Rev. Dr. Wiseman, (for that well-informed and able as well as truly Christian Prelate has no reason to conceal himself under the name of Candidus,) whose little tract forms the Appendix No. I. to my last letter to your Lordship, fully proves. Your Lordship's " measures," and the reception with which that pamphlet, and the Letter to Ambrose Lisle Phillipps, Esq.—erroneously and I fear not very charitably imputed, by the writer in the Dublin University Magazine, to Bishop Wiseman, instead of to its avowed author, the Earl of Shrewsbury, who is perfectly capable of writing it; and if he has made *himself* enemies by it, has also, I think, done the public some service by publishing to the world his sentiments, of which I have long been aware, go far to persuade me that my fears also have not been without much foundation.

That which in ordinary circumstances might be unnecessary, nay, perhaps improper in me, appears to me now a duty; and I proceed to lay before your Lordship and the public, in corresponding columns, two versions of an evidence given on oath by Archbishop M‘Hale in a public court, in which he appeared *voluntarily* (c) at the request of the Hon. Mr. Cavendish, the editor of a public newspaper, known in 1837, and for some time previous to that year, by the name of " Lord John's Paper." (d) His Grace appeared not in defence of the character of the priest, Flannelly, criminally accused by Bishop O'Finan, but in support of the

(c) I do not mean to say that Archbishop M‘Hale was not served with a subpœna; but that such were the *known* relations subsisting in March, 1837, and for several months previous to that date, between Archbishop M‘Hale and the Hon. Mr. Cavendish, that that Editor was not at liberty to enforce the subpœna without the consent of his Patron.

(d) Archbishop M‘Hale's christian name is John.

truth of the publication, which has since been acknowledged by the deluded publisher to have been a calumnious libel, and here are the two reports published in the Mayo Constitution and Telegraph Newspapers, of the evidence given on oath by Archbishop M'Hale.

Mayo Constitution,
March 21, 1837, p. 3, col. 1.

Telegraph.
March 22, 1837, p. 3, col. 1.

Dr. M'HALE (Catholic Abp. of Tuam) cross-examined by Mr. BLAKE.*

Q. You said Dr. O'Finan was bound to obey that document relative to the removal of Dean Lyons?

A. Certainly.

Q. Is that any more than a strong advice of the Cardinal's —Is it an official document from the Court of Rome?

A. It is from Cardinal Franzoni; but whether in his own name, or with the concurrence of the Sacred Congregation, I don't know.

Q. When you say that he ought to obey that letter, do you mean that it would be decorous in him to do so?

---

* Of the counsel for Bishop O'Finan, Mr. Blake is since dead; Mr. West's death has, I deeply regret to learn, occurred while these pages were at press. Mr. Fitzgibbon is still alive, as is also his attorney, Mr. Kelly, of Mountjoy-square, Dublin.

Mayo Constitution.

A. I think there would be something stronger than decorum in it.

Q. Is it a mandate from the Court of Rome ?

A. It is not in a strict sense; for disobedience to a mandate would subject a bishop to punishment; he would be liable to ecclesiastical censure.

Q. Would a refusal to comply with the contents of the Cardinal's letter be a crime against ecclesiastical discipline?

A. He would be guilty of an act of disobedience.

Q. I ask you to show me a canon of the church to prove that.

A. I think he would be subject to reprimand ; he would be visited with punishment: in the first instance it is not the practice of the Church of Rome to do so.

Q. Would it not be the duty of the Court of Rome to issue a mandate to him if guilty of disobedience ?

A. No, the Court of Rome does not act in that way : it merely says, *hortamur in Domino ;* and if the commands couched in that shape are not

Telegraph.

Q. You spoke of a letter addressed by the Cardinal Prefect to Dr. O'Finan ; pray was that letter an official document concerning the dismissal of Dean Lyons, or merely a recommendation from Cardinal Franzoni ?

A. I think it is such a document as it would be no more than decorum to obey.

Q. Was it in the nature of a mandate?

A. It was such a mandate as the Bishop would be subject to punishment for disobeying.

Q. Are the words of the document mandatory ?

A. The Court of Rome in its communications generally softens rather than commands ; the usual phrase is, " *hortamur in Domino ;*" if that course fails, they then adopt a harder style.

Q. Are you aware of any case in which punishment has been inflicted without the adoption of the graver style ?

A. I do not recollect that it has.

Mayo Constitution.

listened to, more severe measures are resorted to.

Q. But can a person be punished for contumacy unless a
command be issued ?

A. Very seldom.

Q. Have you ever known an
instance of that having occurred ?

A. Never.

Q. Is it the course at Rome
to send an absolute mandate,
and dismiss an individual without having heard him in his
defence ?

A. Rome appears to have
done so in the present instance.

Q. But then would it not
startle you a little if the Court
of Rome condemned a person
without any investigation into
the truth or falsehood of the
charges against him—and can
that be the course of proceeding
at Rome ?

A. Very often. [A great
sensation in the Court.]

Q. Why, Dr. M'Hale, is
there a secret tribunal, such as
the Inquisition, in Rome, that
would condemn a man unheard
in his defence ?

A. It has been done, I conceive, in the present instance.

Telegraph.

Q. Is it the practice of the
Court of Rome to decide upon
the representations of one party
without hearing the accused ?

A. I should say it is not the
practice, but it is sometimes
done.

Q. Then it is the case that
decisions are sometimes made
without hearing the parties ?

A. Sometimes, when the
representations are made by
parties who should know the
facts.

Q. In point of fact then, Dr.
M'Hale, is there a secret tribunal in Rome which under-
takes to decide without hearing
the accused ?

A. It would seem so.

Mayo Constitution.   *Telegraph.*

Q. So then the Court of Rome issues mandates without having heard the party in their defence? that doctrine surprises me not a litte.

A. The fact is so, however. [A murmur of disapprobation pervaded the Court and Jury.]

Your Lordship, on comparing these two versions, will observe, 1st, that the *Mayo Constitution* report appeared before the public the *day before* the report, which appeared in the *Telegraph*, of the evidence given *on oath* before a public Court by a Catholic Archbishop, on a point materially affecting the character of the Roman tribunals.

2nd. That the report in the *Telegraph* closely and invariably adheres to the word "hearing," and, thereby, does not *in words* violate the truth, for proceedings in political, criminal, and ecclesiastical courts in Rome are not carried on by *viva voce* evidence, but *in writing;* whereas the Archbishop, according to the *Mayo* report, states *a calumny* in asserting that parties are " VERY OFTEN " condemned "without investigation."

3rd. That it may have been important to Archbishop M'Hale's influence with the Catholic Clergy of Ireland, that it should be believed among them, that upon being accused by him "who *should know* " the facts, they would, if they appealed against his conduct to Propaganda, appeal in vain ; and that the Court of Rome would *refuse to entertain the question* whether he *knew* the truth yet accused them *falsely.* But Archbishop M'Hale had no interest whatever in going in his evidence beyond what was necessary to establish *that* impression ; and he was anxious that it should not be supposed in Rome that he had declared on oath what the *Mayo Constitution* reports him to have declared, and Counsellor Fitzgibbon (e) affirms him to have "substantially, if not literally " declared. Counsellor West, (see his letter, p. 145 infra,) and, as I am informed, Judge Perrin's notes, produced on the rehearing of the case on appeal to the Exchequer, confirm Counsellor Fitzgibbon's declaration.

It must naturally occur to your Lordship, as at least a probable circumstance, that when the Sacred Congregation of Propaganda became informed, that evidence to the effect of that reported in the *Mayo Constitution,* had been published in Ireland, as the evidence given on oath in a public Court by a Catholic Archbishop, the first question which suggested itself was—can this be a true report ? It so happened, that the report given in the *Mayo Constitution,* was the first which reached Rome, where I was then residing ;

(e) Vide infra p. 148, l. 5 from the bottom of the page.

and a few days afterwards arrived the *Telegraph*. The essential difference between the two reports struck every body who read both of them; and as it was known that the *Telegraph*, edited by the Hon. Mr. Cavendish, had the reputation of being, if not under the immediate direction, at least under the control to a great degree of Archbishop M'Hale, it was naturally enough concluded, that the report of the *Mayo Constitution*, in so far only as it might be corroborated by the *concurring testimony* of the report in the *Telegraph*, could, in justice to Archbishop M'Hale, be taken as a faithful report. Hence it was generally understood, that the concurring version of both newspapers, and not the report alone in the *Mayo Constitution*, should be held to be evidence even of a presumptive nature, on so serious a matter as a declaration made on oath before a public tribunal, relative to the subject which had naturally excited such strong feelings in the Court in which it was reported to have been made. The report of the *Mayo Constitution* alone being thus generally discredited at Rome, and instructions having even, as it was asserted to me among others, been sent from Ireland to Rome to deny the accuracy of that report, application was made on the part of Bishop O'Finan to Counsellor Fitzgibbon, for his opinion as to its correctness. In consequence of this application, Counsellor Fitzgibbon went before a Notary Public in Dublin, who regularly attested the declaration sent over to Rome, and now in my possession, from which is printed as an Appendix to this letter, (*f*) the document which attests the *substantial* correctness of the report in the *Mayo Constitution*. Your Lordship may perhaps consider, that the report in the *Telegraph*, given in the corresponding column, is also substantially correct as to the greater part of the evidence given; but I must observe to you, that the answer to the question—" Then it is the case that decisions " are sometimes made without hearing the ac-" cused ?" — taking into consideration the public opinion as to the connection between Archbishop M'Hale and the *Telegraph ;* or to speak more properly, the influence which that Archbishop was supposed to exert as to the insertions which appeared in its columns, is, and I think it must have appeared to your Lordship to be, by far the most important part of *either* report as affecting to public tranquillity in Ireland. Archbishop M'Hale must necessarily be supposed to *know the facts* alleged in any representation sent by His Grace to Rome against any priest appealing from His Grace's acts to the superior tribunal of Propaganda—in the case, for instance, of a threatened or inflicted suspension from the duties, and consequently, from the *dues* of his parish, for non-compliance with orders. (*g*)

(*f*) Appendix No. I. p. 148.

(*g*) A very remarkable instance exists at present in a parish in the diocese of Killala, which might be brought forward to shew that the case is not an imaginary one, the object being evidently to compel by exacting an uncanonical and illegal demand, the parish

His station in the Church at the same time, must *preclude the supposition* of an Archbishop wilfully misrepresenting the facts, or denying them altogether.   Except in some *civil* cases, trials are not in general conducted in Rome by *viva voce* evidence, and therefore it is *verbally true* to say, that " decisions are *sometimes* made without *hearing* the accused," as the *Telegraph* reports the evidence.   The accusation and defence are, both of them, conducted in writing; and are submitted alternately by the respective parties or their lawyers to the Judges, who are sworn to secrecy.   This is done, as I have been assured, upon the principle, that there would be an unnecessary exposure of either party to a breach of charity, if the averments of either of the parties were made known to the other, otherwise than through the Judges.

But the answer " VERY OFTEN " given, according to the report of the *Mayo Constitution*, to the question—" Would it not startle you a little if the " Court of Rome condemned a person without an " *investigation* into the truth or falsehood of the " charges against him—and can that be the course " of proceeding at Rome ?"—would imply a *direct* and inevitable charge upon oath by a Catholic Archbishop before a public tribunal in Ireland, of gross injustice against the Roman tribunals, which

---

priest to quit the diocese.   It is the case of the heirs of the priest Jordan, lately deceased, versus the Very Rev. Dean Lyons.

I cannot persuade myself was ever intended, if ever uttered, by Archbishop M'Hale. It was quite sufficient that he should impress upon his hearers, unacquainted with the process of Roman tribunals, the *persuasion*, that to be accused *by him*, and to be condemned *unheard, might* be one and the same thing, and few of the parish priests in Ireland would be willing to try the chance.

I leave your Lordship to decide whether any true lover of Ireland, really desirous of her tranquillity and prosperity, and acquainted, even in a slight degree, with the tortuous course by which advantage has been taken in the case of Bishop O'Finan of the present anomalous state of intercourse between the Holy See and Great Britain, by some of that party in Ireland, which is unwilling to be guided by the advice of the Roman Catholic Hierarchy in that country, as expressed in the Resolutions of 1834, can fail to wish that some *open* communication between the Holy See and the Throne of Great Britain, which might operate as a check upon that anomalous intercourse, should be established as speedily as possible for the protection of the peaceable clergymen of Ireland, who, as long as Archbishop M'Hale has the power to persecute them, certainly require protection. But your Lordship must also observe, that it does not follow of course, that such a wish, which may naturally be supposed congenial to the feelings, and consonant with the interests of every loyal subject of Queen Victoria, should also be the wish of those who are not subjects of Queen Victoria. If there be any nation in Europe, or out of Europe, jealous of the power of Great Britain, that nation cannot naturally be supposed to wish that the moral influence of the Holy See should be thrown into the scale in favor of the Throne of Great Britain or of public tranquillity in Ireland, in any contest that may arise between Great Britain and that nation.

By reference to the pages of the *Annual Register* for 1808— *State Papers*, p. 314—your Lordship may see at once, what great importance the late Emperor of France attached to the circumstance of that moral influence being thrown into the scale in his favor against England. Because Pius VII. refused to comply with his wishes on that point, that implacable foe of Great Britain deprived Pius VII. of his temporal possessions, and carried Him off prisoner to France. There still exists a formidable power in Europe and Asia not less hostile to the power of Great Britain in India, than the late Emperor of France. But it is time to return to the Earl of Roden.

There is, as it seems to me, a strange confusion in the head of the Earl of Roden between Ordination and Jurisdiction. " Up to the twelfth century," says the Noble Earl, p. 8, " they (the " Christians of Ireland) elected and consecrated " their own Bishops." Why, they do so still. " These," (Bishops) continues the Noble Earl, " exercised their jurisdiction in their respective

" dioceses without any reference whatever being
" had to Rome." Whatever jurisdiction these
Bishops exercised, they exercised precisely on the
tenure on which the Bishops of Italy, Spain,
France, and Portugal, exercise it at the present
day. Whether they exercised it on *precisely the
same* tenure on which the Catholic Bishops in
Ireland now exercise their jurisdiction, we will
examine presently; for the question is highly important to the tranquillity of Ireland, at least
in my humble opinion. Whether any *reference*
was made to Rome on the exercise of that jurisdiction, is a question *de facto* not *de jure*. I mean
to say, that if no dissatisfaction to their flocks,
which could not be remedied by internal arrangement in Ireland—for example, by appeal from the
Bishop to the Archbishop—arose previous to the
twelfth century in Ireland, then certainly no reference on points of jurisdiction need have been
made to Rome; but before, as after the twelfth
century, an appeal lay to Rome as the necessary
ultimate resort, and appeal implies a recognition
of jurisdiction.

Now let us see how the great secession of a
considerable portion of the States of Europe from
the communion of the See of Rome, to which, IF
the Church of Rome be the true Church (and
this IF is of most serious practical import, whatever the Religious Peace, as it was called, of the
Treaty of Westphalia may have put on paper to

H

the contrary), the Christian inhabitants of those States, whether sovereigns or subjects, had all and each of them pledged themselves by their baptismal obligation to belong, affected Ireland and its Hierarchy.

Previous to that secession in the sixteenth century, the Catholic Hierarchy of Ireland consisted of Bishops in a country of which the Catholic Religion was the established religion of the state, *and* the sovereign was a Catholic sovereign, Subsequent to that secsssion, with the exception of the reign of Queen Mary, such has not been the case. On the establishment under Urban VIII., if I recollect rightly, of the Congregation called De Propaganda Fide, at which the Pope is supposed to preside in person, the rule was laid down, that all Bishops exercising their Episcopal functions in countries where the Catholic religion was *not* the established religion of the land, *or* the Sovereign was not Catholic, should thenceforward be under the jurisdiction of the Pope *acting through the Propaganda;* and at the present day, every Catholic Bishop in Ireland considers himself in this situation, and has received his Bulls entitling him to exercise that jurisdiction, from the Pope through the Propaganda, not through the congregation of Bishops and Regulars. Every bishop, who has received his Bulls through the congregation of Bishops and Regulars, is entitled, in the event of the Pope judging it necessary to suspend the exercise of that jurisdiction, to have the cause of such suspension notified to him at the time, or within one month afterwards; otherwise the suspension is not held to be valid. But such is not the case with regard to Bishops receiving their Bulls through Propaganda; on account of the peculiar difficulty of their position, they are to exercise their functions of jurisdiction, not *quamdiu se bene gesserint*, but *durante beneplacito*. I subjoin, from the autograph in my possession, the suspension of Bishop O'Finan; (*h*) your Lordship will see that there is no cause assigned. Archbishop M'Hale holds his jurisdiction on precisely the same tenure as Bishop O'Finan held his; and Pope Gregory XVI. might, if he pleased, direct Archbishop M'Hale to consider himself suspended from all exercise of Episcopal jurisdiction in Tuam, and appoint Bishop O'Finan administrator of the See of Tuam; just as he has suspended Bishop O'Finan from all exercise of Episcopal jurisdiction in the See of Killala, and appointed Bishop Feeny administrator of that See. Whatever might be the reason, Pope Gregory XVI. would not be obliged to give it—Archbishop M'Hale would have no right to ask it. Does your Lordship,—does the Earl of Roden,—can any statesman,—see in this state of things no *possible* advantage to the tran-

---

(*h*) Appendix No. III. p. 156.

quillity of Ireland, no security for the Holy See
against fraud and intrigue, in a mutual, open,
State-relation between the See of Rome and the
government of this United Empire? such as exists in Belgium but does not exist in Russia or
Prussia.

I think I may now bring this letter to a conclusion. I flatter myself, that if I have thought
proper to commence this correspondence with
your Lordship in a style of levity, which may
have appeared to some " bad taste," and not according with that dignity of " language in which
" one Peer should address another;" if I have
thought proper to carry that style of levity, in
some degree, throughout my correspondence, and
even into this letter, I have also laid before your
Lordship and the public some matter of very
serious reflection. Recollect, my Lord, that
though every Catholic *must* believe, that the
Catholic Church cannot err in matters of faith ;
though many Catholics believe, and I profess
myself candidly to be one of the number, that the
Head of the Catholic Church speaking *ex Cathe-
drâ*, according to the technical term, or by a formal document which always presupposes due
deliberation *on a matter of faith*, may safely be
considered (though this is not an article of faith)
not liable to err ; and that for all *practical* purposes this rule is the safest ; the infallibility of the
Head of the Church of Rome, or of the Catholic

Church, is limited to articles of faith. There are many acts of the Holy See, which do not relate to articles of faith, but which have a most intimate connection with the social happiness of the countries to which they relate; and in all such cases, it is not wise policy in a state, in which there are several millions of Christians in the communion of the Catholic Church, to render the *knowledge of the truth* difficult to the Holy See. The Holy See, by its peculiar office of watching over the interests of religion, which are essentially pacific; Great Britain, by her peculiar office, as the first commercial country in the world, of watching over the interests of commerce, which are essentially pacific, are two powers, both of them possessing immense moral influence on the destinies of other nations. Such were the wise observations of that great cardinal to whom the assembled statesmen at the Congress of Vienna unanimously assigned the palm of political wisdom. He alone assigned it to the Duke of Wellington, within a very few days after the arrival of that extraordinary man at the Congress; and when I observed to His Eminence, that there were many in Great Britain and Ireland who professed at least to have a less favorable opinion of the noble Duke, and ventured to ask him his reason for thinking so—he gave me this remarkable answer: "I have never met with " any man who possessed in so high a degree the " power of calculating resistance." I venture to submit this "observation" to your Lordship as far superior in importance to any which the Earl of Roden has offered you or laid before the public. Calculate the resistance which the financial distress and the Anti-Catholic feeling of Great Britain *must* oppose to the first of your measures, if attempted,—the payment of the Roman Catholic Clergy in Ireland by the State ; and see if it be a wise measure. Calculate the jealousy pointedly adverted to by the Earl of Roden, pp. 24 and 25, entertained by Great Britain (and long may she entertain it) of taking continental models as our guides ; and see if an attempt to establish a state-communication with Rome, similar to that established between Rome and Russia, or between Rome and Prussia, be a wise measure. If I have adverted to Belgium, it is *only* because the State-relation between that Government, though the Sovereign is not in communion with the See of Rome, is, as far as I am aware, very nearly, if not exactly the same, as the state-relation which existed previous to the reign of Henry the VIII. between OUR OWN COUNTRY and Rome ; and because I wished to direct your attention within the limits of the range you have yourself marked out, p. 31, of *Protestant* States.

We want security for peace abroad—still more, if possible, do we want security for peace at home. There are several, I doubt not, well-meaning persons, who look in Ireland for that security to a

Repeal of the Union,—in England, for that security to a Repeal of the protecting duties on Corn ;—I will not take upon myself to decide, whether either or both of those parties deceive themselves in supposing that either of those measures will *contribute* to public tranquillity. I say decidedly that neither can secure it ; and I think that the measure I have proposed to your Lordship in this letter will.

While correcting the proof as sent me by the printer of this letter, I received on the 23rd inst. from Dublin a copy of the *Telegraph* newspaper, sent to me, as I collect from the letter which accompanied it, with the view of proving to me that the manner in which I have alluded in my second letter to your Lordship to *two* of the Roman Catholic Prelates in Ireland, had excited not only alarm, but great disapprobation in that Country. This disapprobation I appear to have incurred, especially by the manner in which I have expressed myself in reference to the Galway dinner at which the Right Rev. Dr. Brown presided, and by the terms in which I had mentioned that Right Rev. Prelate's conduct at that dinner, in p. 14 of that letter—I have been also assured, that it is generally said, that I have done my venerable friend, Bishop O'Finan, no service, by alluding, in my second letter to your Lordship, to the Sligo trial of 1837. Your Lordship will have observed by the note on p. 23 of my third letter to you, of which I brought over with me to

Dublin towards the end of last month the printed proof, that I had already then become aware of the misapprehension, which the manner in which I had expressed myself in p. 15 of my second letter was liable, not to say likely to produce; and I must hope that it is unnecessary to add much here to what I have said in that note. But I am desirous of availing myself of this opportunity of rectifying in few words an expression in p. 14 of that letter, which I regret to learn has occasioned considerable pain to the Right Reverend Dr. Brown. Unquestionably, I *meant* to express in that letter my disapprobation of the credulity of the meeting which Bishop Brown addressed; if that meeting considered that Archbishop M'Hale was speaking to it, the sentiments of the Roman Catholic Hierarchy of Ireland in his observations upon the toast proposed in the following words,—" The people, the true source of legitimate power." (*i*) Even in a civil or political sense, that toast is very ambiguous—in an ecclesiastical sense it is yet more objectionable—still more objectionable were the observations of Archbishop M'Hale (introduced as he was to the attention of the meeting as "the " brightest ornament and lustre of the Catholic clergy of Ireland," and about to lay before the meeting the sentiments of the Catholic Hierarchy of Ireland, see note (*e*), p. 91 of part I. of

---

(*i*) See the words of the Divine Founder of the Christian Religion before Pilate, St. John xix, 11, and in the note, p. 185 of these letters, the words of St. Paul to the Romans, xiii, 1.

these letters), as to vote by ballot being recommended to the people of England or Ireland on political elections by the example of "the election "of the Head of our Holy Church;" I certainly, in the passage in question, meant to declare *my opinion* that Gregory XVI. would not approve of his name or station being thus used to influence the Catholics of Ireland *one way or the other, by* Archbishop M'Hale, on such a subject.

But, unquestionably, I did *not* mean to assert or to insinuate, that Archbishop M'Hale himself, still less Bishop Brown, had asserted what either of them *believed to be untrue;* though it is in my opinion *materially* untrue that Archbishop M'Hale is "the brightest ornament and lustre," or, in his political career, and especially as a newspaper writer, or speaker after dinner, any ornament whatsoever to the Catholic Hierarchy of Ireland, or to the Catholic Church. In a letter which that Archbishop has addressed to the *Freeman's Journal*, he has asserted, in opposition to the assertion of Counsellor West in his admirable speech at the trial at Sligo, O'Finan *v.* Cavendish, Monday, March 20, 1837 (see appendix No. I. to this fourth letter, p. 138), that he was *not in* Ireland when the unanimous resolutions of all the Roman Catholic prelates *in* Ireland respecting Clerical Agitation (appendix IV. to this fourth letter, p. 174) were passed, and that his name was *not* affixed to them; and he attempts to shew, that *because* he was made

Coadjutor Bishop of Killala in 1825, and *because* His Present Holiness was not elevated to the Papacy till 1831, *therefore*, my assertion respecting the diversity of sentiment between Gregory XVI. and himself, since he has become Archbishop of Tuam, is disproved by chronological evidence. But your Lordship and the public will at once see the value of this sophism by a moment's reflection on the undoubted fact, that Cardinal Cappellari, now Pope Gregory XVI. was, under Leo XII., Prefect of the Propaganda, through which (see p. 114 of this letter) Archbishop M'Hale received his bulls as Bishop Coadjutor of Killala, and that Cardinal Cappellari, even before he was Prefect, was a most influential member of the Sacred Congregation.

Cardinal Cappellari admired the sentiments of Hierophilos, and of the author of the " Evidences and Doctrines of the Catholic Church," vol. I., p. 238 ; and vol. II., p. 82, (see Appendix to the second of these letters, p. 21, and to the third, pages 45 and 51); and Gregory XVI. does not and cannot admire the newspaper writings and after-dinner speeches of Archbishop M'Hale, on the sovereignty of the people, and vote by ballot, as recommended in Irish political elections, by the example of the Head of the Catholic Church, any more than the present Lord Mayor of Dublin approved of Mr. Callaghan's proposition of the introduction of vote by ballot in the election of a Lord Mayor. But it certainly cannot be argued, that because the present Lord Mayor opposed vote by ballot in the Corporation of Dublin, he is opposed to vote by ballot in Parliamentary elections. Mr. O'Connell considered the two cases perfectly different and non-analogous, and so *ought* Archbishop M'Hale at the Galway dinner to have considered a Papal conclave, and a Parliamentary election in Ireland, as two cases perfectly different and non-analogous. But it suited the political views of the speaker, addressing that assembly in the character in which the Bishop introduced him to its attention, to represent the two cases as analogous.

Perhaps it may appear unnecessary in your Lordship's eyes, that after what I have already observed to you on the character of the Sligo trial, and on the evidence it affords of the propriety of substituting, in lieu of the present anomalous intercourse between Great Britain and Rome, to which is mainly to be attributed the elevation of Archbishop M'Hale to his present situation, notwithstanding the representation transmitted through Sir Henry Seymour, then Minister Plenipotentiary at Florence, an *open* communication such as exists in Belgium—it may I say, appear unnecessary, that I should make any other remark to your Lordship on the article in the *Freeman's Journal*, of the 20th inst., signed " A Roman Catholic Priest of Killala," than that it is a miserable specimen of special pleading and sophistry. Bishop O'Finan, up to the moment of going into Court in 1837, offered to withdraw the suit, on condition that the subject matter of the libel were acknowledged by the author of the libel, and by the publisher of it, to be false. This both refused to do; and on account of that refusal alone, and because that refusal was *advisedly* persisted in, the advisers of Bishop O'Finan insisted upon his going before a Jury of his Countrymen.

I have the honor to be respectfully,
My Lord,
Your obedient humble servant,
CLIFFORD.

NOTE.—By reference to App. V. to this letter, it will be seen that the *author* refused to make this *acknowledgment*, which would have frustrated the end he proposed to himself in having the matter referred to Rome, where Archbishop M'Hale had promised him his protection.—Of course the *publisher* could not acknowledge the falsehood of that which the priest Flannelly, backed by the Archbishop M'Hale, who was the great patron of his newspaper, assured him was perfectly true.

APPENDIX.

No. I.

From the " Mayo Constitution " Newspaper, Tuesday, March 21st, 1837.

SLIGO ASSIZES.—LIBEL CASE.—MONDAY.

RIGHT REV. FRANCIS JOSEPH O'FINAN, a. THE HON. FREDERICK CAVENDISH.

Before Mr. Justice PERRIN, and the following Special Jury :—John Wood—Richard Wood—Samuel Barret—Henry Irvine—Rutlege Tibbs—Edward Loftus Neynoe—Bryon Fury—Lawrence Vernon—Booth Jones—James Wood—Robert Moore—and Abraham Reed, Esquires.

MR. O'DOWD opened the pleadings.—This was an action on the case brought by the Plaintiff against the Defendant for a libel printed and published of and concerning the Plaintiff, in the form of a letter, in a certain Newspaper called the *Mayo Telegraph*, of which the said Defendant was proprietor. The declaration contained one count—it averred that the Plaintiff was a Roman Catholic Bishop of the Diocese of Killala, that he appointed one John Patrick Lyons to be his Vicar General of said Diocese, that he removed one John Barrett from Crossmolina and appointed him to the parish of Lacken. It then set out that Libel, charging the Plaintiff with injustice, oppression and misbehaviour, in reference to said appointment and removal, and with misconduct generally as Roman Catholic Bishop of Killala. To this the Defendant pleaded, first, the plea of not guilty to the whole declaration, and nine other pleas in justification of certain portions of the libel. To five of these the Plaintiff demurred, and to four, viz., the 4th, 6th, 8th, and 10th, he filed the replication *de injuria*, Defendant rejoined by joinder in Demurer, with a similiter. The damages were laid at £3,000.

Mr. West, K.C., stated the case for the Plaintiff in the following terms:*—Gentlemen of the jury, in the month of August, 1834, the Roman Catholic See of Killala became vacant by the translation of Dr. M'Hale to be Titular Archbishop of Tuam. A new rule had been introduced into the Roman Catholic Church, relative to the appointment of Bishops—a few years ago the appointments were made on the recommendation of the Bishops of that Church, but some few years since the second order of the Romon Catholic Clergy, the parish Priests, made an application that they should be the persons whose recommendations should be taken on the subject, and it was granted to them to return the names of three Clergymen for the appointment; from these three the See of Rome, though not obliged to do so, selects the new Bishop. On the See of Killala becoming vacant, three names were selected for the office of Bishop, these were the Rev. Mr. Flannelly, Costello, and Dr. O'Finan, the present Plaintiff.† Dr. O'Finan was unanimously elected, that election was confirmed by the See of Rome, and he was consecrated at Rome in the month of March, 1835. Gentlemen, it was not without reason that the Clergymen of Killala diocess selected Dr. O'Finan, if

---

* The report here given is abridged from the report given in the *Mayo Constitution*, that is to say, passages of that report are occasionally left out as irrelevant to the object for which this appendix is added—in the passages given not a word is altered.—C.

† Dr. O'Finan was first on the list.—C.

their object was the true interest of religion. I believe it is a natural feeling amongst all men to respect and honour those of their countrymen who, by their talents or merits, acquire eminence amongst strangers. The Plaintiff, Dr. O'Finan, was personally unknown to every one of the Clergymen of the diocese of Killala, who gave him their votes, but he was perfectly known to all as a man distinguished for talents and learning ; and if, gentlemen, in the cruel situation in which he is now placed, he appeals to a Jury of Sligo, he only appeals to men of his own county, for he was born in the county of Sligo, and in the very parish which is his mensal parish, given him for his support as a Bishop. His family is of Sligo, and connected with some of the most respectable in Ireland. I could mentioned many of his connexions—he is a near relation to Mr. Moore O'Farrell ; he is a relation of the Dillons, O'Dowday's, and many other families whom it is only necessary to mention, because you are perfectly acquainted with them. He was not seeking to attain eminence as a needy adventurer, for he has been devoted to study from his early years. In the year 1792, being then twenty years of age, he went to Rome for the purpose of receiving the best education to fit him for the Ministry, in which his life has been spent ; and for three years he studied in the College of St. Clements, where he excelled as a man of talents. In 1795 he went to Madelona,* celebrated as a theological seminary, where he remained for two years. In 1797 he became a member of the Neapolitan College, and read during five years the course necessary for a Minister

---

* I believe this name to be a mistake for some other, but I have not an opportunity at hand of correcting the mistake. It is so in the newspaper.—C.

of the Christian Religion. In 1802 he returned to Rome, and was appointed Syndic, something like Bursar in our Colleges. He filled that responsible situation in the College of St. Clements, where he passed his noviciate, but in some time after he was transferred to Lisbon, for it is a principle in the Dominican order that the members may be sent to any place where their services may be useful. He was appointed professor of Theology in the Irish College in that city, and discharged the duties of his office so as to merit universal approbation. In 1805 he returned to Ireland, being sent to Waterford, where, during seven years, he acted as Professor of Theology in a new episcopal seminary in that city. This brings me to the year 1812, in which a circumstance most creditable to the character of my client occurred. At this time it is well known that surprising events took place in Europe; French principles were spread almost over the entire Continent, and in Portugal, a country long attached to England, they were beginning to take root. It was feared that the College of Corpo Santo, resorted to by students from this country, might become infected by those principles, and the Portuguese being jealous of their introduction, selected Dr. O'Finan to become Professor of that College, for the purpose of showing the Irish students the value of the British Institutions over the French. He remained during several years Professor of that College, and might, if he wished, in the year 1814, have been appointed to the See of Killala, which was then vacant, for he enjoyed the friendship of Cardinal Macchi, at that time the representative of the Pope, who was in exile, so that the Cardinal wielded the powers of the See of Rome.* In 1816, up to which time Dr. O'Finan retained

---

* Here again is, I think, a mistake,—Cardinal, then Mgr., Macchi, was inter-nuncio at Lisbon when I was there in 1811 and 1812 ; but he was not

his professorship, he returned to Rome, and was appointed Prior to his old Church of St. Clements, where he passed his noviciate; and his Order in Rome have reason to remember him with pleasure, as they enjoy the Pope's munificence to him in bestowing upon him two magnificent Churches, one at Tivoli and another at Rome. Dr. O'Finan remained at Rome until the year 1824, so much respected, and I believe deservedly so, that, though then advanced in life, he was selected to be the Preceptor* and Confessor of the Duchess of Lucca, sister to the Emperor of Germany. He spent seven years at her Court, and enjoyed there the society of the most distinguished characters in Europe. Dr. O'Finan is proud of possessing letters from her Royal Highness, from her husband, and from other persons of distinction, both English and Foreigners, bearing testimony of their high opinion of his character, and expressive of their pleasure at enjoying his acquaintance. Gentlemen, this brings me to the year 1831, in which Dr. O'Finan returned to Rome, and was appointed companion to the General of the Dominican Order, an office next in rank to the head of the Order; in fact, unless he were appointed to be head of the order he could attain no greater object of ambition. Here he remained until the year 1835, when he abandoned Rome, and valued friends, and elevated society, to settle himself as Bishop of Killala, and become the object of foul and revolting calumny in the columns of the *Mayo Telegraph*, the respectable property of the Hon. Frederick Cavendish.† Certainly, gentlemen, the love of country must

---

the representative of Pius VII. for the affairs of Ireland, or of the Church in general.

* Another mistake—he was Confessor to the Duchess, a Princess of extraordinary virtue and talent, who had and retains the highest veneration for him, but not Preceptor to her son.

† See page 153, note. The more the conduct of the Hon. Mr. Cavendish, in reference to Bishop O'Finan, who is a relative of that gentleman's wife, is considered, the more it will appear that advantage has been taken of his

I

be a powerful instinct when it could cause such a voluntary
sacrifice as this. Gentlemen, having stated so much with
respect to the course of life of Dr. O'Finan, it is necessary
to mention some matters which may appear in some degree
irrelevant to the matter at issue, but to which I must direct
your attention, in order that you may understand the point
and virulence of this libel. The Plaintiff was consecrated
in Rome in March, 1835, and immediately on his appointment to the Bishoprick he was nominated one of the domestic Prelates of Pope Gregory the XVI. In September
1835, he set out for Ireland, and arrived on the 15th
October, and met with a reception disgraceful to those who
gave it. He accepted the office of Bishop, and came to
Ireland, not at his own solicitation, but at the solicitation
of every parish priest in that diocese, and he found even
before he left Rome that cabals were at work to counter-
act his promotion. He that was recommended to day by
the unanimous voice of the Clergymen * of the diocess
was pronounced unfit to-morrow. It was not, indeed,
stated openly, but it was insinuated that he was too old to
be made a Bishop, and that he must have forgotten the
language, as if all this was not equally known before to the
Clergymen who selected him. On the 16th of October he
arrived in Ballina, that was on Friday ; and on the Tuesday following he was waited on by thirteen of the Clergymen who elected him ; and they demanded that he should
make an alteration in the revenue of the diocese. They
required an alteration in the marriage fees, from which

---

ardent temper and aversion to oppression, to mislead him into steps which he
was sure to regret and disapprove when he came to know the truth. Every
allowance, therefore, should be made for his error. Such was always the
opinion of Bishop O'Finan, as his act mentioned p. 160 proves.

* This is a very important fact, as shewing that the subsequent abuse and
ill-treatment which Bishop O'Finan experienced from some of the Clergy of
Killala, did not arise from any previous dislike to him, or any objection on
their parts to his promotion to the Bishoprick.—C.

he derives his chief support as a Bishop. They did more, they presented a protest against the appointment of the Rev. Mr. Lyons, of whom I shall have something to say shortly. With respect to the fees of marriage, called Bans money, they said Dr. O'Finan should place it on the same scale as in other diocesses. In some diocesses the Bishop receives one-half, and in others one fourth of the marriage money. With respect to those questions, he told them in the first place that he was not yet a week in the diocess, and could not give them an answer at that moment as to the appointment of Mr. Lyons; and in the next place he told them that as Bishop of the diocess he had no power to make any alteration in the marriage fees, because it was perfectly well known that he could not make any alteration to the amount of one farthing in the episcopal revenues, as that is a right most scrupulously and jealously restricted to the See of Rome; so that he could make no change for better or for worse. Gentlemen, though this regulation must have been perfectly well known to these Clergymen, they appealed against Dr. O'Finan's verdict, if it could be called such, to a provincial synod, of which Dr. M'Hale was head, and though he must have been aware that he could not legitimately interfere, he did admit and accept that appeal. Gentlemen, I had the curiosity, knowing that Doctor M'Hale had been Bishop of Killala, to ask what was the rule respecting these fees when he was bishop there, and I learned that he had received them exactly as his predecessor had, and as Dr. O'Finan does, that is, one half, which he required to be paid him even to the last farthing.* Gen-

---

* Another important fact, as shewing that the question of the division of marriage fees between the Bishop and the parish priests could not *of itself* have made Bishop O'Finan objectionable in the eyes of his predecessor. See also p. 158, 6th proposition of Mgr. Cadolini, and observations upon it. p. 159.—C.

tlemen, that is one of the facts necessary to be understood as regards these marriage fees. Now with respect to the Rev. John Barrett. Amongst the clergymen most forward in pressing these demands upon Dr. O'Finan within one week after his arrival in the diocess, were the Rev. Messrs. Flannelly and Costello, competitors for the See of Killala, and the Rev. Mr. Barrett. And now gentlemen with respect to Mr. Barrett I will ask your attention. When Doctor Waldron, whom many of you probably knew, was Bishop of Killala, Dr. M'Hale was his Coadjutor Bishop. Bishops in the Roman Catholic Church have parishes, called mensal parishes, given them for their support, and the Bishops are in effect parish priests of these parishes so far as regards the revenues of them. In each diocess this parish is well known, but in the case of a Coadjutor Bishop he should have a different one, which is to all intents and purposes his mensal parish. It is a rule in the Church of Rome that when a Bishop vacates a See the right of appointing to the mensal parish devolves on the See of Rome itself, and the Bishop is deprived of all power in the matter, it is something like our First Fruits. So clear is this right, and so scrupulously is it guarded by the See of Rome; that it is a matter of excommunication to interfere with it, or to usurp it. The parish of Crossmolina was the one belonging to Dr. M'Hale as Coadjutor Bishop, and when on the death of Dr. Waldron that parish became vacant in consequence of the succession of Dr. M'Hale to the See of Killala, the appointment rested solely with the See of Rome. Yet Dr. M'Hale, either ignorantly, or in opposition to the generally known right of the See of Rome, appointed to this parish the Rev. John Barrett,* an appoint-

---

* The same clergyman whose unhappy end is mentioned in page 159. He was present at the Crawfurd Dinner (see App. No. III.); and his speech on that occasion is reported in the *Telegraph*, concluding with these words:

ment which was *ipso facto* null and void.* Gentlemen, then came the election of my client to the diocess of Killala, an election made by parish priests alone ; and at that election the vote of the Rev. Mr. Barrett, so appointed by Dr. M'Hale, was objected to by some of the clergymen, on the ground of his appointment by Dr. M'Hale being null and void, as he had no power to make the appointment. The question of Mr. Barrett's right to vote under these circumstances was referred to Dr. M'Hale, even to him who had made the appointment objected to, and he, not being perhaps aware of the validity of the objection, decided the point in favor of Mr. Barrett, and he voted at the election. Dr. M'Hale, after this having his attention directed to the subject, and seeing that his error was found out, made application to the Court of Rome to get the appointment for Mr. Barrett to the parish of Crossmolina ; and he was distinctly refused. The Court of Rome acted peremptorily in the matter, because it did not wish to establish such a precedent as it must have established by acceding to the request of Dr. M'Hale. All this occurred before Dr. O'Finan left Rome, and before he ever heard a word on the subject. It was at Rome some friend acquainted Dr. O'Finan of the matter, and of the refusal which Dr. M'Hale had met with ; and he was also told that if he would apply to the Sacred College he would get the right of appointment. He did apply therefore for the right to appoint to the parish of Crossmolina, and I hold in my hand the appointment given to Dr. O'Finan ; it is written in Italian and Latin, and is certified by Monsignor Mai, granting to Dr.

" He could assure them there was not a clergyman in the diocese of Killala who did not participate in his opinions, and who was not ready to co-operate in them."—A slight mistake !

* See p. 160, as to the serious consequences of this unauthorised act.—Another important fact, shewing that Archbishop M'Hale was *not* sure in 1835 of obtaining all he asked for at Rome. See again on this point, p. 144.

O'Finan the appointment which had been expressly refused to Dr. M'Hale. Gentlemen, if ever a case of title was demonstrated with mathematical certainty, and placed beyond the possibility of doubt, here it is. For not only did Dr. M'Hale apply to Rome for liberty to appoint to Crossmolina, and was refused, but here is the rescript from Rome, giving it to Dr. O'Finan, and that is an authority to which even Roman Catholic Bishops bow. Gentlemen, I must qualify that observation, for there are many Bishops willing to bow to the wishes of Rome, but that is a document to which Dr. M'Hale himself must bow. Gentlemen, I have told you that Mr. Barrett came with other clergymen to Dr. O'Finan, within a week after his arrival in the diocess, to make a demand for, or to require an alteration in the fee I have mentioned; and that being a matter confined to parish priests, Dr. O'Finan told Mr. Barrett that he had no right to be there because he was not a parish priest. Mr. Barrett said that he had been appointed by Dr. M'Hale, upon which Dr. O'Finan produced the Rescript from Rome; and that being too strong to admit of open resistance, none was made at the time; but it did not prevent intrigue in the parish. The congregation was worked upon and excited to resist—the friends of Mr. Barrett, if not himself, were busy in stirring up the people to opposition on all occasions. Dean Lyons remonstrated with Mr. Barrett, and even went the length of procuring for him the office of administrator of the parish of Lacken, placing him in the same situation as when Dr. M'Hale appointed him erroneously, I will not say otherwise, to the parish of Crossmolina. The plaintiff waited for three months after his arrival to see if Mr. Barrett would acknowledge that his conduct had been improper, and it was not until the six months within which the appointment should be made had nearly elapsed, that he was compelled by the contumacy of Mr. Barrett to confer the parish upon Mr. Murray. And, gentlemen, here is a fact to which I beg your attention.——Notwithstanding the contumacy of Mr. Barrett, and the clearness of his own right as to the appointment, Dr. O'Finan permitted him to remain in the parish of Crossmolina until after the Christmas festival, giving him the advantage by that means of receiving the voluntary offerings made at that season to clergymen of the Roman Catholic Church. Gentlemen how was Dr. O'Finan requited for this ? When Mr. Murray went to take possession of the parish he was resisted with violence——a tumult and a riot took place ; the brother of Mr. Barrett was the foremost in all this, and Dean Lyons and Mr. Murray were obliged to fly from the town in consequence of the violence of the party in the interest of Mr. Barrett. The Plaintiff, Dr. O'Finan, seeing himself set at defiance in that manner, suspended Mr. Barrett, upon which his partisans closed the chapel doors, and for several months there was not a clergyman to officiate in the parish of Crossmolina, as the one appointed to the parish by Dr. O'Finan was obstructed in the discharge of his duties by the people, who were excited by I know not whom. Gentlemen, you will be easily, I think, able to say which party was to blame on that occasion. It is true that Mr. Barrett appealed to Dr. M'Hale, the Metropolitan, who again assuming a power which did not belong to him, nor to any one but to the Holy See, that of citing a Bishop to appear before him, accepted the appeal, and cited Dr. O'Finan to attend a Provincial Synod, of which he was the head. And gentlemen, I say it is much to be lamented that Dr. M'Hale did not represent to Mr. Barrett his outrageous conduct——that he did not explain his own error in appointing him to the parish——and that he did not restore peace to it by advising the people to receive the parish priest sent to them by their Bishop, Dr. O'Finan. One word from Dr

M'Hale would have effected this; and such a course would have been more creditable to him than that of encouraging a priest who had been suspended by his Bishop, by inviting him to his table at Tuam.*

Gentlemen, my client who sits beside me is, in my opinion, fully competent to teach every one of the Roman Catholic Bishops and Archbishops in Ireland the rules and discipline, and the canon laws of that Church; but that is not surprising when we consider the society in which he has spent the most part of his life. Gentlemen, Dean Lyons has the misfortune of being particularly obnoxious to Dr. M'Hale, it is a dislike of an old standing, going back, I believe, as far as twenty years, and late occurrences have not tended to soften the anger of Dr. M'Hale. On the appointment of Dr. O'Finan, Dr. M'Hale was led to do as is done in the Protestant Church, to make a union between the diocess of Tuam and Killala; and he made an application to Dean Lyons and other Clergymen on the subject. But the Dean replied that though he was not in principle a repealer, yet he was opposed to that union; and so it passed off as a good joke. But as the next best thing to such a union, Dr. M'Hale was desirous to have a nominee of his own appointed.†

---

* Rev. Mr. Barrett was the most active of the *political* partisans in the diocese of Killala of Archbishop M'Hale, who is said to have boasted that he could return his cow-boy to parliament, as member for the county, if he pleased. The Archbishop durst not disoblige him for fear of losing his political services and those of his brother.

† This has now taken place by the appointment of Bishop Feeny, one of the priests of Tuam, not of Killala, as administrator. When the Sacred Congregation decided upon appointing an administrator to the See of Killala, it applied to Archbishop Murray to recommend one; but as Killala is in the archdiocese of Tuam, not of Dublin, Archbishop Murray declined interfering, and Bishop Feeny was consecrated by Archbishop M'Hale, Rev. Mr. Flannelly assisting.—C.

Now, gentlemen, having made you acquainted with what may appear somewhat irrelevant, I will come to the facts more intimately connected with the case. I first turn to the Defendant in the case, and I feel that it is only necessary to state that he is the *Honourable* Frederick Cavendish. What, gentlemen, could have induced him to attack a respectable old gentleman like Dr. O'Finan. I will do the Defendant the justice of saying that his motive was not mere malice.

The Plaintiff came to Ireland in October, and in two months after, * * * this print began to attack him : and every number since issued * * * * teemed with the most revolting libels on the character of Dr. O'Finan. Gentlemen, it is not only the malignity of those libels but their variety, which is remarkable. One calls himself a Kilmore man, another a Tyrawly Catholic, and another gentleman styles himself Aladensis. A fourth writes under the signature of Viridicus, and a fifth delights in the title of Mr. Higginbottom—(laughter). Then there are the admirable articles of Mr. Cavendish himself, boasting of the powerful auxiliary he had in Aladensis, who never wrote but for the purpose of vilifying my client ; at least that was the object of his letters under that signature. Gentlemen, * * * * on reading over the mass of filth and scandal which is the subject of the present action, I have not been able to see anything but what displays the most perverse malignity of heart and mind. On the day the thirteen Clergymen waited upon Dr. O'Finan, it was, as I have stated, the first time he had seen them, and he took the liberty of delivering to them an exhortation, credible to his head and heart. An Election for the county of Mayo was about to take place, and he told his clergymen that it would be more creditable in them to content themselves with recording their votes than take any active interference in the

Election. He told them that while he did not assume any right to control them in the exercise of their franchise, he implored them as Ministers of God's word to do nothing inconsistent with their characters as Ministers of Religion.* Gentlemen of the Jury, I am afraid that advice was more unpalatable to the gentlemen than even the answer about the marriage fees; and I believe that that answer was the chief means of calling forth the persecutions which this old and peaceable gentleman has since experienced from his refractory Clergymen. Only consider the gross injustice done to my client—he came to Ireland after an absence of almost his whole life, and because he delivered his sentiments respecting the share which his Clergymen should take in politics, he has incurred their enmity. But mark this—that advice was in the year 1834, the advice of every Prelate of his Church in Ireland. Here are two short resolutions agreed to by the Roman Catholic Prelates in that year on this very subject; and amongst the signatures which are affixed to them, is that of Dr. M'Hale himself. (Mr. West then read the resolutions—they were to the effect that the Roman Catholic Chapels should not be used for any purposes except those devoted to charity and religion; and that the Roman Catholic Clergymen should not interfere with the civil rights of their flocks, nor make any reference from their altars to political subjects, but confine themselves to the discharge of the duties of their office. They were also recommended not to connect themselves with political clubs, nor become secretaries to them.)† Now,

---

* It was this advice which occasioned the speech of the Hon. Mr. Cavendish at Mr. Sharman Crawfurd's dinner, in which he designated Bishop O'Finan, who was not present, by the term with which he concluded his address. Archbishop M'Hale, who sat on the left hand of the Chair, remained silent.—C

† See Appendix No. II. at the end of the fifth of these Letters.

Gentlemen, these resolutions were highly creditable to these Prelates, if it be permitted to a person of a different faith to say so; but because Dr. O'Finan, coming from Rome the following year, gave a similar advice,* and recommended to his clergymen the same things, he is persecuted and stigmatized as a man unworthy to hold the station of Bishop. In fact, every attempt has been made to drive him from this country and compel him to return to the place in which he was so much esteemed and cherished. Now, gentlemen, to show you that this is the true motive of these libellers, I will read an extract from the very first letter of this ' Aladensis,' the author of the libel in question. There is nothing more horrible in these letters than the use made of the Scriptures in them—for every one of them begins with a text of Scripture. I will read a passage from the very first letter of ' Aladensis '—in which the words used by Dr. O'Finan at his first meeting with his clergy are put in italics. I find it in the *Telegraph* of the 6th of January, 1836.†

Now, gentlemen, I come to the publication in question, to the libellous matter which is the subject of this action, and which is contained in a letter published by the Defendant in his paper of the 15th of June, 1836. Like all the others, this letter begins with a text of Scripture. I do not mean to say that Mr. Cavendish is the author; I understand that it is the work of a parish priest; but, gentlemen, there is something in it which induces me to think that it has not emanated from a parish priest; and I mean no disrespect when

---

* It is remarkable that Bishop O'Finan did not even know on this occasion of the existence of the resolutions of 1830, 1832, or 1834, having been out of Ireland at the time that they were passed, yet his advice was to the same effect.—C.

† I have not been able to procure this file of the *Telegraph* in time for insertion in this place.—C.

I say that I would not expect such a production from the pen of one of these gentlemen.* I shall, gentlemen, read for you this foul tissue of misrepresentation and calumny.

Now, my lord, I will take the liberty of calling your attention to the state of the pleadings in this case. Your Lordship sees that the declaration, containing but one count, sets out the libel, and to this there are the plea of the general issue, and other pleas put in. To five of these demurrers have been filed, and on four of them, which contain matters of more importance, the Plaintiff's counsel have thought proper to join issue. With respect to those which have not been demurred to, our proper course will be to have contingent damages assessed upon them. As to the four pleas upon which issue has been joined, I will make a few passing observations. Gentlemen of the Jury, the Defendant proposes to justify what has been stated in the libel, and claims your decision on the truth or falsehood of the charges.

The next plea is, Dr. O'Finan has neglected the most or-

---

* This passage in counsellor West's speech will, perhaps, be best elucidated by the following words of the letter of Archbishop M'Hale to Cardinal Fransoni, dated April 10, 1837, and forming No. 12 of the case submitted to Propaganda. In it the Archbishop gives *his* account of the Sligo trial, and (p. 49 of the printed case) of the priest Barrett. In p. 50 his Grace says, ubique spargebant ipse (Dean Lyons) et episcopus me libellorum famosorum auctorum fuisse. As far as these words relate to Bishop O'Finan, they are not only not true, but have so much the appearance of having been written for the express purpose of misleading the Cardinal Prefect on a most important part of the case on which His Eminence was to decide, that it is to be hoped Archbishop M'Hale will see the propriety of rectifying in the proper quarter the misapprehension he has occasioned. Bishop O'Finan merely asserted (and that not everywhere) that Archbishop M'Hale protected the author and publisher of the letters of Aladensis, and was cognisant of their contents before publication. On the above words, as far as they relate to Dean Lyons, it is not necessary for *me* to make any remark, since the Dean is in Ireland and fully able to defend himself.—C.

dinary duites of his station, having not preached or exhorted his flock since his arrival in the diocess. Now, gentlemen, this is a most atrocious libel, and you will deal with it as such. Preaching is not the ordinary duty of a Bishop; there are many Bishops in the Roman Catholic, as well as the Protestant Church, who do not preach. Gentlemen, there is not a word of truth in this letter, except that Dr. O'Finan has not preached in Ardnaree; the reason he has not preached is, he is 66 years of age, and of a delicate constitution, and from the unfinished state of the chapel, it not being even glazed when he came from Rome, it would be extremely dangerous for him to preach in it. Added to this the chapel is of immense size, so that his voice, though it might be of benefit to those who heard him, could not be heard by many. It is not an absolutely necessary duty of a Bishop to preach, but Dr. O'Finan would have done it if his health permitted him; however, he celebrated Mass in the chapel regularly, and did all the duties he could. And though he did not preach in the cathedral, I will undertake to say, that since his appointment to the diocess there has been more preaching in that edifice than during any equal period previous to his arrival. There is one more plea, and it is this, " No efforts are made to provide for a competent succession in the ministry by any encouragement given to schools, or young men of talent." With respect to the schools, the facts are these. Some time previous to the arrival of Dr. O'Finan there had been five or six schools got up by Dean Lyons, when he was administrator to Dr. Waldron's mensal parish, but they had been suffered after the departure of Dean Lyons to fall into decay, so that when Dr. O'Finan came to the Diocese there was not one of them in existence. On his arrival he re-established one of them for females, and procured a person to teach them, so that it is now going on well; and there is another boy's school in operation, which he also established. Was that, gentlemen, neglecting the education of the people? With respect to the other charge, not providing for a competent succession to the Ministry, see the malice of the libeller. Those designed for the Ministry are educated in Maynooth, there are ten places for Killala diocess—these were filled up by Dr. O'Finan, and in addition he has four more than this regular number now studying in Maynooth, and another he has sent to Rome to be educated. Dr. O'Finan then has four in Maynooth and one at Rome more than the number he is bound to have. Now, gentlemen, these are the few pleas on which issue has been joined, and on which you are to find a verdict ; but the other atrocious parts of the libel are not attempted to be justified—they are left to the general plea, that Mr. Cavendish did not print or publish the libel. The first crimes that are charged against the Plaintiff is, that he is labouring to bring reproach and obloquy upon the Ministers of Religion, that he practices intense persecutions and unnatural atrocities against his Clergymen, and sheltering the retreat of the ill-chosen object of his choice. Mr. West then read over the libel, commenting upon the most wicked parts of it as he proceeded.* On reading the conclusion of the article which was as follows —" The father of the faithful will shudder at the perversion of order which they will be able to establish against your Lordship, but he will have great difficulty in believing that, in a parish within six miles of the Bishop's residence, it would be necessary for the maintenance of order to permit adults to die without the consolations of religion, and infants to vanish untouched by the waters of regeneration." The learned gentleman observed—Gentlemen, mark the charge made here against my client, and consider for a moment

---

* It was, I think, in this letter that Bishop O'Finan was declared to be " the greatest persecutor of the Christian Church, who had appeared since the days of Nero."—C.

who was the really guilty. The disorder alluded to arose
from the conduct of Mr. Barrett's party, who closed the
chapel doors, and the people of the parish were excited to
the greatest violence by I know not whom; and, because,
owing to this turbulent conduct, no clergyman was suffered
to officiate in the parish, and discharge the duties of religion,
the Plaintiff is charged with that omission. Finally, gentlemen, this libeller concludes in the most pacific manner,
calling himself my client's most obedient humble servant.
Were it not for the peaceful character of my client we
should have heard nothing of this calumniator's attack
upon him. And that he might meet such treatment as this
the Clergymen of the Diocess of Killala unanimously invited
this aged, learned, and respectable gentleman, to desert the
society of men of letters, a country in which he lived in the
enjoyment of the esteem of the highest characters and
friends whom he loved. This, gentlemen, is the manner in
which they realised the hopes they gave Dr. O'Finan of
returning to spend his closing days in peace, and lay down
his head at last in the land of his fathers. Why did they
not tell him, as his libeller told him, the great difficulty he
would have in believing the revolution that had taken place
in the public mind—if he was not acquainted with the
mysteries of agitation—if he was a person horribly un-
skilled in the great work of tithe abolition, and more un-
skilled in electioneering tactics; had his libeller no heart to
consider that my client had been for a long time in a
country where such things were not even talked of. Come,
then, whoever you are that have employed this execrable
and slanderous print as a vehicle to vilify and traduce the
spotless character of this old and venerated gentleman—
come and say now if you have been engaged in an honourable course. How much has been done within these three
days for the interest of religion, how often has it been
within that period said that a Sligo Jury was not the proper

tribunal before which to investigate this matter, but that it should be left to the decision of the See of Rome. Gentlemen, only think of Frederick Cavendish appearing before the See of Rome. I here on behalf of my client say that he is willing to refer on all points of discipline and on ecclesiastical questions to Rome; he asks for no other tribunal while the matters to be decided are confined to those partaking of this character; but when he sees appeals made from the Pope to Frederick Cavendish, and from Rome to Castlebar, my client does not think it against ecclesiastical authority to appeal to a jury of the county of Sligo.—Gentlemen, as a Prelate my client would not suffer it to be said that the interest of religion can suffer by a manifestation of truth—bad passions and conduct may suffer, but not religion, for it is not in the power of man to injure the one by holding it in the light of the other. My client cannot but ask himself how it is that during fifteen months, while calumny was incessantly heaped upon him, no friendly voice interfered to implore mercy from the Honourable Frederick Cavendish for the character of a man who had never offended him; that no command was issued by the competent authority to put a stop to the libels of "Aladensis" and the "Tyrawly Catholic." Gentlemen, my client is willing to submit the entire matter to a jury, and abide by their decision. It is easy to transmit to Rome statements without truth or charity, but it is not so easy for a parish priest to unmask the slanderer to the Holy See. Gentlemen, I know, for I too have been at Rome, that a conviction is entertained there that the decisions of our law are just, and that its judgments, passing between man and man, are founded on truth and uprightness. It is for that reason that we have submitted the case to your decision. * * * * * * * We are in a country where virtue is predominant—and your verdict will decide the peace and welfare of my client. Gentlemen of the jury, I say that you are the arbiters of his fate here, for he sees the day not far distant when he will have shelter from all these attacks—when meekness of disposition and good will towards all men shall fit him for a place where neither the agitator nor the calumniator can come.

Gentlemen of the jury, it is your province to mark your disapproval of the course pursued by the defendant; and I know that whatever the verdict of the jury may be, this old and ill-treated gentleman is satisfied to leave the case to the decision of twelve honourable men, who hold the administration of impartial justice in their hands.

———————

The following letter from Counsellor West is printed from a copy collated by Lord Clifford, with the autograph, and afterwards forwarded to that Hon. Member of Parliament for the City of Dublin, in September, 1841, and returned to Lord Clifford revised and signed by Mr. West in his hand-writing, with permission to Lord Clifford to publish it.

Copy of an autograph letter, addressed to Peter Kelly, Esq., attorney for Bishop O'Finan in the trial at Sligo, March, 1837, by Counsellor West, K.C., first counsel for that Prelate at that trial.

London, June 3, 1837.

My dear Sir,

I have this morning received from you the *Mayo Constitution* newspaper, with a request from you that I should state my opinion of its accuracy in the report of Dr. O'Finan's case at Sligo; my opinion is, that as far as it goes, particularly in the evidence, it is accurate; but as the

K

leading counsel for Dr. O'Finan, and having watched the trial with considerable anxiety and all the attention in my power, I have no hesitation in saying that the whole report there given is a very faint and imperfect representation of the case as it actually appeared—of the calumnies and villainous abuse heaped without provocation and without justice on that pious and excellent man, and of the very discreditable and unwarrantable conduct of those, who, if they had any of *his* benevolence and Christian charity, would have been the foremost to protect an unoffending old gentleman, whose whole life appeared to do so much honour to themselves. The only accurate report of my statement is in the *Evening Mail,* and even that omits a great part of the case. Dr. O'Finan ought long since to have published it himself in a distinct shape, and as a pamphlet: it is equally due to himself, to the religion he professes, and to justice.* The whole attack upon him was in every part of it the most audacious, and the most unwarrantable that I have ever met with in my experience. It was so considered and condemned by the Judge, and I was truly rejoiced to find after the trial, the universal sentiment of gratification which his success produced, not only amongst ALL the respectable Roman Catholics of his own diocess, but those whom I have since met with in every part of the country.†

---

* At this distance of time it is to be hoped, that without resorting to the measure recommended in 1837 by Mr. West, a sufficient insight has been given by these pages into the nature of the persecution raised against Bishop O'Finan, and of the means taken to verify the threat made at Mr. Sharman Crawfurd's dinner, by the editor of the *Telegraph*, in presence of Archbishop M'Hale, who appeared as witness in proof of the truth of the libel, evidently as a *voluntary* witness. See note on p. 102.—C.

† This declaration of Mr. West perfectly corresponds with the letters sent to Bishop O'Finan at Rome from different parts of Ireland, and now in my possession.—C.

If any other feeling than this, or any other opinion as to the result of this trial should be entertained at the Court of Rome,* or elsewhere, then the misrepresentation of the truth must be great indeed, and falsehood will have been more successful in its attacks upon Dr. O'Finan at that distance, than it was before a jury of the most honourable and respectable men of his country, without any motive of partiality for either, and discharging a sacred duty under the most solemn of all obligations. For my own part I shall always consider it a matter of pride and gratification to have known Dr. O'Finan, as I was enabled to do by reason of this case, being fully satisfied that the example of such a man will do more to ensure good will and brotherly feeling amongst all classes in Ireland, than any other means that could be suggested, and this I believe (if I may be so presumptuous as to express such an opinion) with less abandoment of the principles of his Church, as known and practised at Rome itself, than those men can boast of, who, to their shame, forced him to the inevitable necessity of vindicating himself before the world, or setting down with a ruined character, and as a disgraced Minister of the Word of God.

I write to you in the greatest hurry, and send you back your newspaper; but I could not suffer a day to pass without expressing my perfect readiness to assist at any time in making out a true and perfectly accurate statement of the case, which would be much more honorable for Dr.

---

* See Appendix No. III. to my third letter. It was considered at Rome, in consequence of the misrepresentations made as to the real character of the Sligo trial, that Bishop O'Finan ought to be held answerable for whatever discredit the evidence of Archbishop M'Hale had brought upon Propaganda, because Bishop O'Finan, by bringing a criminal action against one of his own priests before a Protestant lay tribunal, had obliged that priest to cite Archbishop M'Hale to give evidence in his defence.

O'Finan, and more damaging to his enemies than that
which you have sent me in the *Mayo Constitution*.

My dear Sir,

Faithfully yours,

(Signed)   J. B. WEST.

To P. J. KELLY, Esq.

DECLARATION OF COUNSELLOR FITZGIBBON.

Dr. O'Finan having applied to me to express in writing
my opinion of the correctness of a report of Dr. M'Hale's
evidence, in the trial of Dr. O'Finan's case against the Hon.
Frederick Cavendish, given in the *Mayo Constitution* of
Tuesday, the 21st of March last; I have read that report,
and I have marked with a circumflex and my initials in the
margin of the newspapers the passage to which my attention
has been more particularly directed. I have a clear recollection of the substance of Dr. M'Hale's evidence touching
the subject matter involved in the passage which I have
marked, and the more so, because the evidence of Dr.
M'Hale stated the existence of a principle of decision in the
proceedings in the Court of Rome, which could not fail to
excite the attention, if not surprise, of any person accustomed to view the administration of justice in these
countries, where no charge, however trivial, can be even
entertained against the poorest individual, without giving
him full notice and ample opportunity to appear and defend
himself. The passage I have marked is, in my opinion, and
according to my recollection, substantially, if not literally,
correct. Dr. M'Hale expressed his opinion, that the letter
of Cardinal Franzoni, although not mandatory in its terms,
was yet to be received, and understood, and obeyed as a
mandate; and that the terms of exhortation in which it

was couched, were adopted, not for the purpose of affording any excuse for disobedience, but to characterize the mildness of the tribunal from which it was issued. He very clearly intimated his opinion to be, that the letter of Cardinal Franzoni was, in substance and effect, a final judgment of the Court of Rome; and stated that the terms—"Hortamur in Domine"—were used as being the customary, mild, and courteous expression of the judgment and command of the Court of Rome. The libel charged Dr. O'Finan with having cushioned the verdict of Rome. The letter of Cardinal Franzoni was the thing designated by the word verdict, and was what the writer intended to charge Dr. O'Finan with having suppressed. To maintain this issue for the defendant it was necessary to prove that there was, in fact, a verdict; *i. e.*, in substance a judgment actually pronounced and transmitted to Dr. O'Finan. If the opinion of Dr. M'Hale were received as correct, the issue was substantially proved for the defendant; and when Dr. M'Hale expressed that opinion, it appeared to me that he had forgotten the fact, that when the letter of Cardinal Franzoni was written, Dean Lyons had not been heard in his defence, nor even apprized of the charges against him; and this being a notorious fact in the case, and one which could not be controverted, it followed, as a necessary conclusion from Dr. M'Hale's opinion as to the character of the letter, that judgment had been pronounced on Dean Lyons, without affording him any opportunity of defending himself; and having thus established, by his opinion applied to the undoubted facts of the case, that in Dean Lyon's instance a man had been condemned by the Roman tribunal unheard and undefended; he was in some degree compelled to admit the existence of this principle in the ecclesiastical jurisprudence of the Romish Court.

The foregoing is as accurate a statement of the facts, and as good a solution of the reasons for Dr. M'Hale's evidence, as my recollection and understanding enable me give. I should add that I was one of Dr. O'Finan's Counsel in the case, and attended the whole trial.

(Signed)   GERALD FITZGIBBON.

August 9th, 1837.

_____

Dublin, 29, Upper Gloucester Street,
Loc ✠ Sigilli.

I, Hugh Stafford, Public Notary by Royal authority duly admitted and sworn, dwelling in the City of Dublin, do hereby certify that the signature—(Gerald Fitzgibbon)—to the foregoing statement, is the genuine signature of Gerald Fitzgibbon, Barrister-at-law, Esq.; and that by his desire I have hereunto annexed a copy of the *Mayo Constitution* newspaper, with a report of that part of the trial O'Finan *v.* Cavendish referred to, and marked as in the above statement.

Given under my hand and notarial seal of office this eleventh day of August, One thousand eight hundred and thirty-seven.   Which I attest,

(Signed)   HUGH STAFFORD,

(Loc ✠ Sigilli.)   Not. Pub. Dublin.

After I had written the statement on this sheet at the request of Dr. O'Finan, it struck me that for the purpose of authentication, it would be useful to get it attested by a notary, which I have therefore done.

(Signed)   GERALD FITZGIBBON.

_____

* In the autograph now in my possession, with the copy of the *Mayo Constitution*, to which it is affixed with a green ribbon and the Notary's seal, the date, instead of being 1837, is written one thousand eight hundred and twenty-six, which is an evident mistake, though overlooked at the time, both by the learned Counsel and the Notary.—C.

No. II.

Extract from printed and manuscript papers forming one hundred and two pages folio, entitled Documents Regarding the Diocese of Killala in Ireland, communicated to His Eminence Cardinal Weld,* by the Bishop of of Killala, Francis Joseph O'Finan, O. P.

Printed Slip from the " Telegraph " newspaper, p. 68, No. 29.

PUBLIC DINNER TO W. S. CRAWFURD, ESQ., M.P.

WALTER BOURKE, Esq., Barrister, Chairman.—On the chairman's right sat the distinguished guest, and on his left the Most Rev. the Catholic Archbishop of Tuam.—The Chairman.—I have now, gentlemen, to propose the health of the Catholic Archbishop of Tuam. [The whole company here rose, and the cheering was loud and long continued.] I have, gentlemen, the learned chairman continued, known him from my infancy, and in common with Irishmen of all classes, I am proud of him. (Cheers.) He is an honour to his country and his creed. (Loud cheers.) In whatever point of view we regard it, his career reflects the highest credit on himself; whether as filling the Professor's chair at Maynooth† (cheers), or when as Bishop of Killala he so

* It may be proper to prevent misconception, that this collection of documents having been read over by me to Cardinal Weld, was subsequently returned in 1836 by request to Ireland, whence it was sent to me in December 1841, with permission to extract the contents of pages 68 and 83 for publication in these letters.

† Chief Remembrancer Blake might not, perhaps, agree on this point with the learned chairman. See Letter V.

much advanced the interest of that diocess,* or in the more
elevated position in which he is now placed, his energies
have been uninterruptedly dedicated in the first place to his
God, in the next to his country. (Immense cheering.)
But if we pass over the prelate and the politician, where is
the living man more distinguished in literature than the
Archbishop of Tuam? It was not, perhaps, known to all
those present as it was known to him (the chairman), that
the letters of " Hierophilos " had been translated into the
French, Italian, and Spanish languages, an honour which
the works of very few living authors could boast. He
would, without further preface, give them the health of the
" Catholic Archbishop of Tuam."

The applause which followed this toast was tremendous.
We regret that our limits will not permit us to-day to give
to our readers the very eloquent address pronounced by
His Grace on returning thanks—we shall insert it at
length in our next.

(Among the toasts of the evening was) The Honourable
F. Cavendish and the " MAYO TELEGRAPH. " Nine times
nine, and loud and repeated cheers. The Honourable Mr.
Cavendish rose, and was received with loud cheers. After
six years devoted to the arduous duties he had undertaken,
he was now rewarded with their approbation. When he
commenced his journal he found the county of Mayo bowed
down by force, and backed and aided by the Roman Catholic Clergy, he had raised her from that state to one of
freedom. He had adopted in his paper the exposure of
those parties who used their power for the oppression of
their fellow-men ; and he had succeeded, if not in procur-

---

* It would seem that the learned chairman and Counsellor West had
been differently informed on this point, so far at least as schools were concerned. See p. 141.

ing redress in all cases, at least in preventing a repetition of the injustice.* (Hear.) * * * He should now advert to another subject. He had been furnished with documents of a most extraordinary character, relating to another body of this county, and he had delayed to publish them only because he believed they were calculated to destroy that cordiality and that kind feeling which ought to subsist between certain parties. But he would warn any man, no matter how high his rank or how exalted his character, or how great his influence, not to suffer himself to be led away by evil advisers, or to endeavour to warp those under his control from the display of political integrity which they have hitherto, and ought to continue to pursue. He would tell him from that place, as he preferred that mode to the alternative of making it the subject of an editorial article in his paper, and it would probably reach his ear, not to persevere in the evil course he had chalked out for himself. And, however honest and praiseworthy and venerable he might be, not to pursue the advice of any man, who, for an object either of a public or private nature, should endeavour to cause any body of men to desist from their support of the rights of the people. (Hear, hear, and cheers.)

On the same page, 68, of the Documents forwarded in 1836 to Cardinal Weld, is the following :—

---

* Upon comparing these words and the words almost immediately preceding "the exposure of those parties," &c., with the declaration of the Honourable Mr. Cavendish above given, pages 57 and 58 (Appendix to the third of these letters, No II.), it must be evident to any impartial person that the Honourable Editor *sincerely* believed on the faith of the assurances given him, that in publishing the letters of "Aladensis," he was "preventing a re-" petition of the injustice of those who used their power for the oppression "of their fellow-men."

" Mr. Cavendish to Dean Lyons, accusing Dr. O'Finan as an enemy of the people.

" No. 30.

" *Castlebar, December* 3, 1835.

" My dear Sir,

" I should regret that any publication in the *Telegraph* should give you annoyance. But if I had published the documents sent me from Ballina, you might then with some reason complain of annoyance. I have suppressed many that I hardly think I was justified on public grounds in suppressing. The conduct of Dr. O'Finan, as it is said, recommended by you, which would go to suppress the display of independence, and again reduce that county to a state of degradation, and place it in the hands of the aristocracy, is what, as an advocate of civil liberty, I can't quietly submit to.

" I remain,
" With perfect sincerity
" Your's very truly,
"FREDERICK CAVENDISH.

" To the Very Rev. Dean Lyons, &c., &c., Ballina."

Documents, p. 83.—No. 45.

" Most Rev. Dr. Kelly to Right Rev. Dr. Waldron.

" *Tuam, January* 20, 1833.

" My dear and ever esteemed Lord,

" Our mutual friend, Mr. Kelly, will have the sincere pleasure of handing you these hurried lines. I have not time to enter into details. We live in times when the exercise of the most pure and unsophisticated principles of Christianity are to be enforced. Patriotism is a virtue which I admire as much as any member of the Christian community. But I would not surrender one particle of the genuine principles of Christianity to obtain the greatest temporal blessings. If the people are in pursuit of rights which I know and feel have been long withheld, let it be done without tarnishing the principles of the Catholic religion, which teaches us that the end is not to be gained by cruel means, or that evil is to be done that good may eventually result. We are summoned to appear in Dublin on the 29th. Your Lordship will send the Right Rev. Dr. M'Hale* to say your own feelings and his on passing events."

If his Lordship should make Tuam his route, I shall feel pleasure in awaiting his arrival, and hence we shall proceed with the determination of doing what may appear most advantageous to our province and to the Irish Church at large. Make my best respects to his Lordship, and believe me, my ever dear Lord,

" Yours most devotedly,

" ✠ OLIVER KELLY."

---

* The reader of this passage is requested to bear in mind that Archbishop M'Hale in his letter " to the Honourable Lord Clifford," published in the *Freeman's Journal* of December 20, 1833, declares that he did not sign the resolutions of the assembled Bishops respecting clerical agitation, and that he was not in Ireland at the time.

No. III.

Letter of His Eminence Cardinal Franzoni, Prefect of the Sacred Congregation called De Propagandâ Fide, to the Right Rev. Francis Joseph O'Finan, Bishop of Killala, notifying to him his suspension from the administration of that See, and the wish of His Holiness Pope Gregory XVI. that he should not quit the Papal States without the previous permission of His Holiness. Copied from the original, signed with the autograph of Cardinal Franzoni.

Dalla Propaganda, 26 *Novembre*, 1838.

Questa Sagra Congregazione Generale con suo Decreto de 19 Corrente sanzionato dalla Santità di Nostro Signore, dietro il puì maturo esame delle varie controversie insorte fra V. S. Illmã e Revmã e il Clero di sua Diocese, ha guidicato essere pel bene, e per la tranquillità della Chiesa di Killala indispensabile, che venga a V. S. Illmã interdotto e sospeso sin da ora ogni esercizio di sua Episcopale Giurisdizione in detta Diocesi, il di cui governo sarà affidato ad un Apostolico Amministratore a tal ùopo appositamente nominato.

Dolente di dover porgere somigliante partecipazione a V. S. Illmã perchè appieno vi si uniformi, il Cardinale Prefetto di Propaganda deve in pari tempo prevenirla, che come naturalmente richiede del pari e il sagro carattere ond' Ella è rivestita, e la riverenza dovuta al Sovrano Pontefice non è spediente che V. S. Illmã partasi dagli Stati Ponteficj senza il previo Beneplacito di Sua Santità.

Ne altr' oggetto avendo il presente foglio, il Cardinale Sottoscritto passa con vera stima a baciarle di cuore le Mani.

Servitore Vero,

J. F. CARD. FRANZONI, Pref.*

Mgr. Francesco O'Finan dell ordine de Predicatori Vescovo de Killala.

---

* This is the document alluded to in the article inserted in the *Telegraph* newspaper, December 30, 1841. See Appendix No. III. Mr. Cavendish's mistake has, in my opinion, arisen from having confounded this document

TRANSLATION

*Of the Letter of H. E. Cardinal Franzoni to Bishop
O'Finan.*

From the Propaganda, 26 November, 1838.

This Sacred General Congregation by its Decree of the
19th of this month, sanctioned by His Holiness our Lord,
after the most mature examination of the various contro-
versies which have taken place between your Lordship and
the Clergy of your Diocese, has judged it to be indipensable
for the good and for the tranquillity of the Church of Killala
that your Lordship should be interdicted and suspended
from the present time from every exercise of your episcopal
jurisdiction in said Diocese, the government of which will be
entrusted to an Apostolical administrator expressly named
for such purpose.

The Cardinal Prefect of Propaganda grieving to be obliged
to transmit to your Lordship such a notification, in order
that you may fully conform to it, must, at the same time,
warn you that it is not expedient that your Lordship should
depart from the Papal States without the previous pleasure of
His Holiness to that effect ; such a course being naturally required of you equally by the Sacred Character with which
you are invested, and by the reverence due to the Sovereign
Pontiff.

And the present letter having no other object, the under-
signed Cardinal proceeds with true esteem heartily to kiss
your hands.

Your true Servant,

J. F. CARD. FRANSONI, Pref.

To Mgr. Francis O'Finan, of the Order
of Preachers *(Dominicans)*, Bishop of Killala.

---

with the following one, in which no mention is made of suspension, and the
renuntiation of the damages awarded in the Sligo trial is mentioned only as
one of the six propositions.

Note.—From the foregoing letter, it must be evident to every unprejudiced person that the suspension of Bishop O'Finan from the exercise of his episcopal jurisdiction in the Diocese of Killala is not grounded on any alleged misconduct on his part, and that he retained the esteem of the Cardinal Prefect. But his Lordship is in possession of a still more conclusive document, dated May 11, 1838, proving that at the time when it was announced in the Dublin papers that his Lordship was *actually deposed*, the Secretary of the Sacred Congregation, Mgr. Cadolini, Archbishop of Edessa, who is in fact the acting official of the Sacred Congregation, quite as much as the Secretary of the Lord Lieutenant of Ireland is the acting official of the Government of Ireland, proposed to his Lordship to return to his See. The propositions, six in number, are in the hand-writing of the Secretary; but his Lordship felt it his duty to decline to accede to the two following.

(Copied from the Autograph.)

5º. Di confirmare tutte le collazioni delle parrochie conferite da Mgr. MacHale, abbandonando alla S. Congregazione la decisione intorno al danaro riscosso in occasione di dette collazioni da quel prelato.

6º. Di rinunziare con generosità tutta propria di un Vescovo Cattolico alle 500 lire sterline assegnategh per la male augurata lite.

(Translation.)

5º. To confirm all the collations to the parishes conferred by Mgr. M'Hale, abandoning to the Sacred Congregation the decision respecting the money received by that prelate on the occasion of such collations.

6º. To renounce with the characteristic generosity of a Catholic Bishop his claim to the £500 awarded to him in the ill-omened trial (at Sligo).

To the former of these propositions, Bishop O'Finan felt it his duty not to accede, because he knew that it referred principally to a priest of the name of Barrett, whose conduct had been such that his Lordship felt he could not in conscience be a *concurring* party to his having the care of souls.

The wretched man soon after terminated his turbulent career by a fall from his horse. The withdrawal by government of the £100. at first offered for his supposed murder, and the investigations which the most injudicious report of his having been murdered—a report apparently spread abroad to conceal the real facts of the case—rendered necessary, caused the circumstances of his awful death to become a matter of public notoriety. Those circumstances it is unnecessary to detail here.*

To the latter of these propositions Bishop O'Finan felt that he could not in honor or in conscience, or even in duty

---

* After these pages had gone to press, a letter signed "Tuamensis," appeared in the *Telegraph* Newspaper of February 16th, 1842, dated Feb. 8th. Boher-na-greine (Sun Street) Tuam, containing the following paragraph :—
"To this another question succeeds, who is better informed as to the circumstances of Mr. Barrett's death—whether the Priest of Killala, from the casual verdict of a Coroner's jury principally composed of his own adherents, or the special commissioner deputed by the government, to make a most full and searching enquiry into all the facts and circumstances connected with his death? Will the Killala Priest declare, for what reason his own boy, when carrying him home from the spot whereon he found him lying, so far from declaring him murdered to the groups of people who at short intervals succeeded each other upon the road passing home from the fair, used the utmost efforts to conceal both his condition and his name? After being brought home, if his friends conceived him murdered, why not alarm the neighbourhood? Why not intimate it to his friend and namesake from Newport Pratt, who slept in the house that night? Why not send for either of the two doctors to Crossmolina to attend him, instead of pouring melted butter down his throat, which they hoped would have the effect of an emetic? Why impose silence and concealment upon the inmates of the house respecting his condition, until they were certain of his being a rigid corpse? Whether is it more propable, that he fell from the vicious animal that repeatedly tumbled him previous to that night, or that he fell by the hand of an assassin in the midst of a parish where even the most lawless were at his command, and where a conspiracy in his defence was framed to assassinate Dr. O'Finan, should his Lordship come in person to open the chapel to the Rev. Mr. Murray? The Killala Priest therefore should be the last man to revive the memory of an assassin. Why did government withdraw the reward offered for the apprehension of the murderers? I could have propounded a few more pertinent interrogatories, but I am restrained by a friendly respect for the friends and memory of the deceased. I feel sorry at being obliged to make any allusion to the Rev. Mr. Barrett, but the blame rests on the Killala Priest, who, under the deceitful mask of friendship, 'with more than Vandal fury,' rakes from the grey stone and the narrow house the silent remains of an *ill-advised* friend —and by making them the second fact in a former letter, profanely exposes them to public gaze, in preference to his own name and wards off the provoked shafts of public opinion, with such a feeble, cadaverous shield."

to his Sovereign and in respect to the laws of his country, accede; because his Lordship was aware, that the Honble. Mr. Cavendish had been assured, in effect, that the verdict of a *civil* tribunal of his country would be set aside by an *order* to that effect from the Sacred Congregation at Rome, which would *oblige* him to renounce his *right* to damages awarded him by a jury in Ireland, in a suit brought by his Lordship for public defamation against a *Protestant layman*, editor of a public newspaper in Ireland. Bishop O'Finan considered, that he could not by any *voluntary act* of his, make himself a *concurring* party to what he considered a most *mischievous* as well as false assertion, namely, that the party who had given that assurance to the Honble. Mr. Cavendish, had interest enough at Rome to obtain an *order* from the Holy See, that his Lordship should renounce his *right* in such a case. But the moment the Honble. Mr. Cavendish had become persuaded of the falsehood of the assurance which had been made to him and had acknowledged the publication to be, what the jury as well as the judge at the trial at Sligo, and subsequently the whole bench on appeal to the Exchequer, had declared it to be, a gross calumny, Bishop O'Finan hastened to assure the Hon. Mr. Cavendish, that *it had never been his intention* to take a farthing of his money. So also, with regard to the collations, Bishop O'Finan *never* made that question one of *money ;* his objection was a conscientious one to the invalidity of those collations, and to the incapacity which that invalidity produced, as well in the collator as in the collated, of exercising their respective functions ; an evil of frightful extent as affecting the validity of all subsequent acts of jurisdiction of the guilty parties. Bishop O'Finan felt it his duty to refuse *his sanction* by his voluntary act to the uncanonical proceeding of the parties concerned.

No. IV.

[A.]

From the " Catholic Miscellany and Monthly Repository of Information," from January to June, 1826, volume the fifth. " In necessariis Unitas, in dubiis Libertas, in omnibus Charitas."—St. Augustine. London : Cuddon, 62, Paternoster-row.—Pages 114 to 121.

PASTORAL ADDRESS.

We feel great pleasure in laying before our readers the following Pastoral address, notwithstanding that we inserted some of the resolutions in our last number : it is a document worthy of the talents and piety of its venerable authors ; and whilst it breathes a spirit of conciliation, it is not wanting in firmness and strength of exprsssion.

Ed.

PASTORAL ADDRESS

Of the Roman Catholic Archbishops and Bishops, to the Clergy and Laity of their communion throughout Ireland.

Rev. Brothers, beloved children,

With a trembling sense of the obligations which the nature of our office imposes on us, we have come together after the example of our predecessors, to deliberate in common on the awful interests with which we are charged. We have taken into consideration various subjects which are intimately connected with the welfare of religion ; and whilst we have sought with jealousy to guard the sacred deposit " committed to our trust by the Holy Ghost " (2 Tim. i. 14) ; we have also esteemed it a duty to be " ready to satisfy every one that asketh us a reason of that

L

" hope which is in us " (1 Pet. iii. 15), that you, " dearly
" beloved, our joy and our crown, (may) stand fast in the
" Lord " (Phil. iv. 1); and " that he who is on the contrary
" part may be afraid, having no evil to say of us."—Tit.
ii. 8.

We know, dearly beloved, the filial duty with which you
are solicitous to hear the voice of those who " watch, as
" being to render an account of your souls."—Heb. xiii. 17.
We hasten therefore to make known to you our unanimous
decisions on such matters as are of common concern, that
you, on your part, may fulfil " our joy ; that being of one
" accord, you stand fast in one spirit, with one mind labour-
" ing together for the faith of the gospel."—Phil. ii. 2,
and i. 27.

1st Resolution,—Having considered attentively a plan
of national education which has been submitted to us—
Resolved, that the admission of Protestants and Roman
Catholics into the same schools, for the purpose of literary
instruction, may, under existing circumstances, be allowed,
provided sufficient care be taken to protect the religion of
the Roman Catholic children, and to furnish them with
adequate means of religious instruction.

2nd Resolution,—That in order to secure sufficient protection to the religion of Roman Catholic children under
such a system of education, we deem it necessary that the
master of each school, in which the majority of the pupils
profess the Roman Catholic faith, be a Roman Catholic;
and that in schools in which the Roman Catholic children
form only a minority, a permanent Roman Catholic assistant be employed; and that such master and assistant be
appointed upon the recommendation, or with the express
approval of the Roman Catholic Bishop of the diocese in
which they are to be employed ; and further, that they, or
either of them, be removed upon the representation of such

bishop. The same rule to be observed for the appointment or dismissal of mistresses and assistants in female schools.

3rd Resolution,—That we consider it improper, that masters and mistresses intended for the religious instruction of Roman Catholic youth, should be trained or educated by, or under the control of persons professing a different faith ; and that we conceive it most desirable, that a male and female model school shall be established in each province in Ireland, to be supported at the public expense, for the purpose of qualifying such masters and mistresses for the important duties which they shall be appointed to discharge.

4th Resolution,—That in conformity with the principle of protecting the religion of Roman Catholic children, the books intended for their particular instruction in religion, shall be selected or approved by the Roman Catholic prelates ; and that no book or tract for common instruction in literature, shall be introduced into any school in which Roman Catholic children are educated, which book or tract may be objected to on religious grounds by the Roman Catholic bishop of the diocese in which such school is established.

5th Resolution, — That a transfer of the property in several schools which now exist, or may hereafter exist in Ireland, may be utterly impracticable from the nature of the tenure by which they are, or shall hereafter be held ; and from the number of persons having a legal interest in them, as well as from a variety of other causes ; and that in our opinion, any regulation which should require such transfer to be made, as a necessary condition for receiving parliamentary support, would operate to the exclusion of many useful schools from all participation in the public bounty.

6th Resolution,—That, appointed as we have been by Divine providence to watch over and preserve the deposit of Catholic faith in Ireland ; and responsible as we are to God for the souls of our flocks, we will, in our respective dioceses, withhold our concurrence and support from any system of education which will not fully accord with the principles expressed in the foregoing resolutions.

7th Resolution, — Having taken into consideration the project of a provision to be made by law for the support of the prelates and clergy of the Roman Catholic church in Ireland, — Resolved, that no such legal provision for our support, and that of our clergy, will be acceded to by us until the Catholics of Ireland shall have been emancipated. And that at no period can we accept any such legal provision, unless our acceptance of it be found by us consistent with the independence of our church and the integrity of its discipline, as well as with the cordial union and affectionate attachment which has hitherto subsisted between the Catholic clergy and that faithful people, from whose generous contributions, we and our predecessors have, for centuries, derived our support.

8th Resolution, — Having learned with sorrow, that, notwithstanding the repeated expositions already given of our faith, some grievous misconceptions, regarding certain points of Catholic doctrine, are still unhappily found to exist in the minds of many of our fellow subjects, — Resolved, that we deem it expedient to remove the possibility of future misconception on those heads, by the following full and authentic declaration.

DECLARATION
Of the Archbishops and Bishops of the Roman Catholic Church in Ireland.

At a time when the spirit of calm inquiry is abroad, and men seem anxious to resign those prejudices through which they viewed the doctrines of others, the archbishops and bishops of the Roman Catholic church in Ireland, avail themselves with pleasure of this dispassionate tone of the public mind, to exhibit a simple and correct view of those tenets, that are most frequently misrepresented. If it please the Almighty that the Catholics of Ireland should be doomed to continue in the humbled and degraded condition in which they are now placed, they will submit with resignation to the divine will. The prelates, however, conceive it a duty which they owe to themselves, as well as to their Protestant fellow subjects, whose good opinion they value, to endeavour once more to remove the false imputations that have been frequently cast upon the faith and discipline of that church which is intrusted to their care, that all may be enabled to know with accuracy, the genuine principles of those men, who are proscribed by law from any participation in the honours, dignities, and emoluments of the State.

I.—Established for promoting the happiness of mankind, to which order is essential, the Catholic religion, far from interfering with the constituted authorities of any state, is reconcilable with every regular form which human governments may assume.—Republics as well as monarchies have thriven where it has been professed, and, under its protecting influence, any combination of those forms may be secure.

II.—The Catholics in Ireland of mature years, are permitted to read authentic and approved translations of the Holy Scriptures with explanatory notes ; and are exhorted to use them in the spirit of piety, humility, and obedience. The clergy of the Catholic church are bound to the daily recital of a canonical office, which comprises, in the course of a year, almost the entire of the sacred volume : and her pastors are required, on Sundays and on festivals, to expound to the faithful, in the vernacular tongue, the epistle or gospel of the day, or some other portion of the divine law.

III.—Catholics believe that the power of working miracles has not been withdrawn from the church of God. The belief, however, of any particular miracle, not recorded in the revealed word of God, is not required as a term of Catholic communion, though there are many so strongly recommended to our belief, that they cannot without temerity be rejected.

IV.—Roman Catholics revere the blessed Virgin and the Saints, and piously invoke their intercession. Far, however, from honouring them with divine worship, they believe that such worship is due to God alone, and that it cannot be paid to any creature without involving the guilt of idolatory.

V.—Catholics respect the images of Christ and of his saints, without believing that they are endowed with any intrinsic efficacy. The honour which is paid to these memorials, is reference to those whom they represent; and should the faithful, through ignorance, or any other cause, ascribe to them any divine virtue, the bishops are bound to correct the abuse, and rectify their misapprehensions.

VI.—The Catholic church, in common with all christians, receives and respects the entire of the ten commandments, as they are found in Exodus and Deuteronomy. The discordance between Catholics and Protestants on this subject, arises from the different manner in which these divine precepts have been arranged.

VII.—Catholics hold, that, in order to attain salvation, it is necessary to belong to the true church, and that heresy, or a wilful and obstinate opposition to revealed truth, as taught in the church of Christ, excludes from the kingdom of God. They are not, however, obliged to believe, that all those are wilfully and obstinately attached to error, who, having been seduced into it by others, or who, having imbibed it from their parents, seek the truth with a cautious solicitude, disposed to embrace it when sufficiently proposed to them; but leaving such person to the righteous judgment of a merciful God, they feel themselves bound to discharge towards them, as well as towards all mankind, the duties of charity and of social life.

VIII.—As Catholics in the Eucharist adore Jesus Christ alone, whom they believe to be truly, really, and substantially present, they conceive they cannot be consistently reproached with idolatry by any christian who admits the divinity of the Son of God.

IX.—No actual sin can be forgiven at the will of any pope, or any priest, or any person whatsoever, without a sincere sorrow for having offended God, and a firm resolution to avoid future guilt, and to atone for past transgressions. Any person who receives absolution without these necessary conditions, far from obtaining the remission of his sins, incurs the additional guilt of violating a sacrament.

X.—Catholics believe that the precept of sacramental confession, flows from the power of forgiving and retaining sins, which Christ left to his church. As the obligation of confession, on the one hand, would be nugatory without the correlative duty of secrecy on the other, they believe that no power on earth can supersede the divine obligation of that seal, which binds the confessor not to violate the secrets of auricular confession. Any revelation of sins disclosed in the tribunal of penance, would defeat the salutary ends for which it was instituted, and would deprive the ministers of religion of the many opportunities, which the practice of auricular confession affords, of reclaiming deluded persons from mischievous projects, and causing reparation to be made for injuries done to persons, property, or character.

XI.—The Catholics of Ireland not only do not believe, but they declare upon oath, that they detest, as unchristian and impious, the belief " that it is lawful to murder or destroy

" any person or persons whatsoever, for or under the pretence
" of their being heretics ;" and also the principle "that no
" faith is to be kept with heretics." They further declare,
on oath, their belief that " no act, in itself unjust, im-
" moral, or wicked, can ever be justified or excused by,
" or under the pretence or colour, that it was done either
" for the good of the church, or in obedience to any eccle-
" siastical power whatsoever ;" " that it is not an article of
" the Catholic faith, neither are they thereby required to be-
" lieve, that the pope is infallible ;" and that they do not hold
themselves " bound to obey any order in its own nature
" immoral, though the pope, or any ecclesiastical power,
" should issue or direct such an order ; but, on the contrary,
" that it would be sinful in them to pay any respect or
" obedience thereto."

XII.—The Catholics of Ireland swear, that they " will be
" faithful, and bear TRUE ALLEGIANCE, to our most
" gracious sovereign lord KING GEORGE THE
" FOURTH ; that they will maintain, support, and defend,
" to the utmost of their power, the succession to the crown
" in his majesty's family, against any person or persons
" whatsoever ; utterly renouncing and abjuring any obedi-
" ence or allegiance to any other person claiming, or pre-
" tending a right to the crown of these realms ;" that they
" renounce, reject, and abjure the opinion, that princes,
" excommunicated by the pope and council, or by any
" authority of the see of Rome, or by any authority what-
" soever, may be deposed and murdered by their subjects,
" or by any person whatsoever ;" and that they " do not
" believe that the pope of Rome, or any other foreign prince,
" prelate, state, or potentate, HATH, OR OUGHT TO
" HAVE, any temporal or civil jurisdiction, power, supe-
" riority, or pre-eminence, directly or indirectly, within
" this realm." They further solemnly " in the presence of
" God, profess, testify, and declare, that they make this

" declaration, and every part thereof, in the plain and ordi-
" nary sense of the words of their oath, without any evasion,
" equivocation, or mental reservation whatsoever, and
" without any dispensation already granted by the pope, or
" any authority of the see of Rome, or any person whatever,
" and without thinking that they are, or can be acquitted
" before God or man, or absolved of this declaration, or any
" part thereof, although the pope, or any persons or authority
" whatsoever, shall dispense with or annul the same, or de-
" clare that it was null and void from the beginning."

After this full, explicit, and sworn declaration, we are utterly at a loss to conceive on what possible ground we could be justly charged, with bearing towards our MOST GRACIOUS SOVEREIGN ONLY A DIVIDED ALLEGIANCE.

XII.—The Catholics of Ireland, far from claiming any right or title to forfeited lands, resulting from any right, title, or interest, which their ancestors may have had therein, declare upon oath, " that they will defend, to the
" utmost of their power, the settlement and arrangement of
" property in this country, as established by the laws now
" in being." They also " disclaim, disavow, and solemnly
" abjure, any intention to subvert the present church estab-
" lishment, for the purpose of substituting a Catholic
" establishment in its stead. And further, they swear that
" they will not exercise any privilege to which they are or
" may be entitled, to disturb and weaken the Protestant re-
" ligion, and Protestant government in Ireland."

XIV.—Whilst we have, in the foregoing declaration, endeavoured to state, in the simplicity of truth, such doctrines of our church as are most frequently misunderstood, or misrepresented amongst our fellow subjects, to the great detriment of the public welfare, and of christian charity; and whilst we have disclaimed anew those errors or wicked principles, which have been imputed to Catholics, we also avail ourselves of the present occasion, to express our readiness, at all times, to give, when required by the competent authority, authentic and true information upon all subjects connected with the doctrine and discipline of our church ; and to deprecate the injustice of having our faith and principles judged of, by reports made of them by persons either avowedly ignorant of, or but imperfectly acquainted with, the nature of our church government, its doctrines, laws, usages, and discipline.

This declaration we approve, subscribe, and publish, as well that those who have formed erroneous opinions of our doctrines and our principles may be at length undeceived, as that you, dearly beloved, be made strong in that faith which you have inherited as " the children of saints, who " look for that life which God will give to those that never " changed their faith from him."—Tob. ii. 18.

Reverend brothers, beloved children, " grace, mercy, and " peace," be to you, " from God the Father, and from " Christ Jesus our Lord."—1 Tim. i. 2.

Patrick Curtis, D. D.	Daniel Murray, D. D.
Oliver Kelly, D. D.	Robert Laffan, D. D.
Farrell O'Reilly, D. D.	J. O'Shaughnessy, D. D.
Peter M'Loughlin, D. D.	Thomas Costello, D. D.
James Magauran, D. D.	Kiaran Marum, D. D.
Geo. T. Plunkett, D. D.	Peter Waldron, D. D.
James Keating, D. D.	John Murphy, D. D.
Charles Tuohy, D. D.	James Doyle, D. D.
Edward Kiernan, D. D.	P. M'Nicholas, D. D.
Patrick Kelly, D. D.	P. M'Gettigan, D. D.
Cornelius Egan, D. D.	Edmund French, D. D.
William Crolly, D. D.	Thomas Coen, D. D.
Patrick Maguire, D. D.	Robert Logan, D. D.
Patrick M'Mahon, D. D.	Patrick Burke, D. D.
John M'Hale, D. D.	John Ryan, D. D.

Dublin, 25th Jan., 1826.

[B.]

*From a printed copy in the form of a placard printed in
1830, and forwarded to Lord Clifford from Dublin,
December 1841.—*

The ARCHBISHOPS and BISHOPS, whose names are un-
dersigned, to the Clergy and People of the Catholic Church
in Ireland, health and benediction.

Beloved brethren in Christ Jesus,

BEING assembled in Dublin to deliberate, as our
custom is, on our own duties and the sacred interests confided to our care, we are urged by the charity of God, and
the love we bear you, to address to you the following brief
instruction.

And first we give thanks to God and the Father of our
Lord Jesus Christ, that not only you continue to be of one
mind labouring together in the faith of the Gospel, but also
that this Gospel encreases and fructifies amongst you, so
that your improvement is manifest to all, whilst your faith
is spoken of throughout the entire world.   Be mindful,
however, that " neither he that planteth is any thing, nor
he that watereth, but God that giveth the encrease."—1
Cor. iii. 7.   As also, that " he that shall persevere unto
the end, he shall be saved."—Math. x. 22.

Indeed, beloved brethren, the present should be to us
and to you an acceptable time, not only on account of your
advancement in virtue, but also because our Divine Religion has of late been somewhat relieved, and your civil
rights greatly extended.   Since we last addressed you, a
great and beneficient and healing measure has been enacted
by the Legislature for your relief.

Only last year, and this country was agitated from end
to end, and from its extremities to its very centre.   The
dominion of the passions prevailed over the dominion of the

law—and men born to love each other, contended to almost the shedding of each other's blood; the public interests were neglected or forgotten; the ties of kindred were broken; the power of government was weakened—the laws themselves were paralysed, and Religion, which used to silence passion and consolidate the public peace, was unable freely to discharge her functions. It was at this time that HE, by whom Kings reign and Legislators decree just things, arose, and as it were, *said to the sea be still, and to the north wind do not blow.** Our gracious and beloved Sovereign, walking in the footsteps of his Royal Father, (whose memory be ever cherished,) commiserated the state of Ireland, and resolved to confer upon her the inestimable blessing of Religious peace. This great boon became the more acceptable to this country, because, among the *Councillors of his Majesty,* there appeared conspicuous the most *distinguished of Ireland's own Sons ; a Hero and a Legislator—a man selected by the Almighty to break the rod which had scourged Europe—a man raised up by Providence to confirm thrones—to re-establish altars—to direct the Councils of England at a crisis the most difficult, and to staunch the blood and heal the wounds of the country which gave him birth.†* An enlightened and wise Parliament perfected what the Sovereign and his Councillors commenced, and already the effects of their wisdom and justice are visible, and duly appreciated by all the wise and good. The storm which almost wrecked the country has subsided, whilst social order with peace and justice in her train, prepares to establish her sway in this long distracted country.

And is not the King, beloved brethren, whom by the law

---

* These Italics are so in the printed placard.
† Ditto.

of God we are bound to honour, entitled now to all the
honor, and all the obedience, and all the gratitude you can
bestow? And do not his Ministers merit from you a confidence commensurate with the labours and the zeal expended by them on your behalf? And that Legislature
which raised you up from your prostrate condition, and
gave to you without reserve all the privileges you desired
—is not that Legislature entitled to your reverence and
love? We confide that your feelings on this subject are in
unison with our own, and that a steady attachment to the
constitution and laws of your country, as well as to the
person and government of our most Gracious Sovereign,
will be manifested in your entire conduct.

Labour, therefore, in all things to promote the end which
the Legislature contemplated in passing this bill for your
relief, to wit, the pacification and improvement of Ireland.
Let religious discord cease, let party feuds and civil dissen-
tions be no more heard of, let rash, and unjust, and illegal
oaths be not even named amongst you; and if sowers of
discord or sedition should attempt to trouble your repose,
seek for a safeguard against them in the protection afforded
by the law,

Be sober and watch, so that no one may have evil to say
of you; give way to anger rather than contend with an
adversary, so that nothing on your part may be wanting to
promote peace and good will among all classes and descrip-
tions of the Irish people.

To our venerable brethren the Clergy, of whatsoever
degree, we propose, with reference to what here follows,
our own example; they will copy it into their lives, and
adhere to it as a rule of conduct. We united our efforts
with those of the laity, in seeking to attain their just rights,
and to attain them without a compromise of the freedom of
our Church. Success attended our united efforts, because

reason, and justice, and religion, and the voice of mankind were upon our side. We rejoice at the result, regardless of those provisions, in the great measure of relief, which injuriously affect ourselves, and not only us, but those religious orders which the Church of God, even from the Apostolic times, has nurtured and cherished in her bosom. These provisions, however, which were as we hope and believe, a sacrifice required, not by reason or policy, but by prejudices holding captive the minds of even honest men, did not prevent us from even rejoicing at the good which was effected for our country. BUT WE REJOICED AT THAT RESULT, NOT MORE ON PUBLIC GROUNDS THAN WE DID, BECAUSE WE FOUND OURSELVES DISCHARGED FROM A DUTY, WHICH NECESSITY ALONE HAD ALLIED TO OUR MINISTRY——A DUTY IMPOSED ON US BY A STATE OF TIMES WHICH HAS PASSED, BUT A DUTY WHICH WE HAVE GLADLY RELINQUISHED, IN THE FERVENT HOPE, THAT BY US OR BY OUR SUCCESSORS IT MAY NOT BE RESUMED. THESE ARE THE SENTIMENTS WHICH THE SPIRIT OF OUR CALLING INSPIRES, THEY ARE THE SENTIMENTS WHICH NEVER CEASED TO ANIMATE US, AND WHICH OUR CLERGY, ALWAYS OBEDIENT TO OUR VOICE, WILL CHERISH ALONG WITH US, THAT, AS THE APOSTLE COMMANDS, " ALL MAY SAY THE SAME THING, AND THERE BE NO DIVISIONS AMONGST US."*

As to the rest, beloved Brethren, Clergy and Laity, we charge you to be steadfast in the faith; preserve this faith unimpaired and unsullied, for it is " a best gift from above " ——James i. 17, and surpasses all whatsoever this earth or its rulers can bestow. Be not weakened by distress, or influenced by seduction. Guard from danger the children of your affection, whom our Father in heaven has confided

---

* These words are not in Capitals or in Italics in the printed placard.

to your care. Let no wild fanaticism, alike injurious to the Church and to the State, find access to your families, or be blended with the education of your children. Hope with us, that upon this subject of education our reiterated prayers, founded as they are upon justice and the public good, will be heard favourably by a Government and Legislature, anxious only to promote the public interest and consolidate the public peace.

Beloved brethren, farewell! And may the peace of God, which surpasseth all understanding, keep your hearts and minds in Christ Jesus.—Phil. iv. 7.

Given at Dublin, February 9th, 1830.

✠ *Patrick Curtis*, D.D.　　✠ *D. Murray*, D.D.
✠ *Oliver Kelly*, D.D.　　　✠ *Robert Laffan*, D.D.
✠ *W. Coppinger*, D.D.　　✠ *Michael Collins*, D.D.
✠ *Corn. Egan*, D.D.　　　✠ *Wm. Kinsella*, D.D.
✠ *P. M'Laughlin*, D.D.　　✠ *Wm. Higgins*, D.D.
✠ *John Murphy*, D.D.　　✠ *Edmund French*, D.D
✠ *John Ryan*, D.D.　　　✠ *James Brown*, D.D.
✠ *Patk. M'Mahon*, D.D.　✠ *Robert Logan*, D.D.
✠ *Patk. M'Gettigan*, D.D.　✠ *Edward Kiernan*, D.D.
✠ *James Keating*, D.D.　　✠ *John M'Hale*, D.D.*
✠ *James Doyle*, D.D.　　✠ *Thomas Costello*, D.D.
✠ *William Crolly*, D.D.　　✠ *P. M'Nicholas*, D.D.
✠ *Thomas Coen*, D.D.　　　*N. Foran*, D.D.V.C.
✠ *Thomas Kelly*, D.D.

---

* Extracts from a letter inserted in the *Freeman's Journal*, (Dublin,) December 20, 1841, and signed ✠ John, Archbishop of Tuam.

Col. 2, par. 5.—After my solemn approval of the spirit of those resolutions to which your Lordship refers. . . . . . Col. 3, par. 5.—Thirdly, *I was not at the meeting in 1832, at which those resolutions were adopted, either personally or by proxy, nor did I authorize any individual to attach my name to the resolutions or published exhortation.* My sentiments regarding the resolutions I have already stated; and as for the exhortation, I will candidly

[C.]

From a manuscript at the back of the preceding paper sent to Lord Clifford from Dublin; December 1841.

At a meeting of the Prelates of the Province of Connaught, convened at Loughrea, and held on the 23rd, 24th, and 25th of April, 1833. The Most Rev. Dr. Kelly, Metropolitan, presiding. Thirteen resolutions or statutes were adopted, of which the 12th was as follows, viz.:

Resolved 12th.—That, as the temples of Religion are peculiarly and specially the houses of Prayer, we prohibit

---

own there are passages in it which *never had, nor never would have, my sanction.* These objections, however, may be a matter of mere taste that do not affect the just principles of the resolutions. I refer to those terms of extraordinary eulogy that were lavished on the Duke of Wellington for his exertions on our emancipation, whom I consider to have been a mere instrument in the hands of Providence to achieve a measure to which the whole tenor of his political life and sentiments were in direct opposition. When one owns that he does a great national service, on account of the blessings of which it must be productive, then he is entitled to merit and thanks for his good actions, though he, too, is an humble agent in the hands of an over-ruling Providence. But when I find an individual confessing that nought but necessity would have induced him to consent to a measure to which his life was opposed, he may deserve the praise of prudence in yielding to that necessity, but he has just as much claim to public gratitude for positive benefits as many of those recorded in Scripture whom God made reluctant instruments in bringing about his own measures. The Duke of Wellington was such an instrument as some other powerful and influential politician may shortly in a crisis of great difficulties, dissipate all the small sophistries that now cloud the intellects of English lords regarding a Repeal of the Union, and restore her own parliament to Ireland in order to fix the stability of the throne and consolidate the strength of the Empire.

Fourthly.—*When that meeting was held to which your lordship refers, I was sojourning in the Eternal city ;* and allow me to add, that I had to labour to remove many erroneous and dangerous impressions which some officious gentlemen from your country endeavoured to fix there to the disparagement of the Irish Hierarchy.

m eetings, unconnected with religious purposes, to be held in the chapels, without the permission of the Ordinary of the Diocess,—and that we recommend to our Clergy not to become chairmen or secretaries of any purely political meetings.

Signed by all the Bishops of Connaught, and by JOHN M'HALE, BISHOP OF MARONIA.

[D.]

From the " Complete Catholic Registry, Directory, and Almanack," for the year of our Lord, 1836. *Compiled by W. J. B. Revised by a Catholic Priest, appointed for that purpose. Dublin : printed for the Proprietor, by John Sullivan.—p.* 66.

EXTRACT

From the minutes of the proceedings of the Roman Catholic Arch-bishops and Bishops of Ireland : assembled at the Parochial House, Marlborough-street, Dublin ; on the 28th of January, 1834. *The Most Rev. Dr. Murray, presiding.*

RESOLVED.—That we would view with the greatest alarm, and would visit with the severest chastisement that we could inflict, all or any interference of any Clergyman or Clergymen subject to us ; who, forgetful of his or their duty, unmindful of the obedience due to the Decree of the Sacred Congregation, bearing date the 19th of Oct. 1829, and regardless of the oftentimes expressed sentiments of the Irish Prelates, Clergy, and People, would seek to employ the influence of our own, or any other Secular Government, in the appointment of persons to Vacant Sees in Ireland.

RESOLVED.—That our Chapels are not to be used in future for the purpose of holding therein any public meeting, except in cases connected with Charity or Religion ; and

M

that we do hereby pledge ourselves to carry this Resolution into effect, in our respective Diocesses.

RESOLVED.—THAT WHILST WE DO NOT INTEND TO INTERFERE WITH THE CIVIL RIGHTS OF THOSE ENTRUSTED TO OUR CARE; YET, AS GUARDIANS OF RELIGION, JUSTLY APPREHENDING THAT ITS GENERAL INTERESTS, AS WELL AS THE HONOR OF THE PRIESTHOOD, WOULD BE COMPROMISED BY A DEVIATION FROM THE LINE OF CONDUCT WHICH WE MARKED OUT FOR OURSELVES, AND IMPRESSED UPON THE MINDS OF OUR CLERGY, IN OUR PASTORAL ADDRESS OF THE YEAR 1830; WE DO HEREBY PLEDGE OURSELVES, ON OUR RETURN TO OUR RESPECTIVE DIOCESS, TO REMIND OUR CLERGY OF THE INSTRUCTIONS WE THEN ADDRESSED TO THEM, AND TO RECOMMEND TO THEM MOST EARNESTLY, TO AVOID IN FUTURE ANY ALLUSION AT THEIR ALTARS TO POLITICAL SUBJECTS, AND CAREFULLY TO REFRAIN FROM CONNECTING THEMSELVES WITH POLITICAL CLUBS, ACTING AS CHAIRMEN OR SECRETARIES AT POLITICAL MEETINGS, OR MOVING OR SECONDING RESOLUTIONS ON SUCH OCCASIONS; IN ORDER THAT WE EXHIBIT OURSELVES IN ALL THINGS IN THE CHARACTER OF OUR SACRED CALLING, AS MINISTERS OF CHRIST, AND DISPENSERS OF THE MYSTERIES OF GOD.*

✠ D. MURRAY, ARCHBISHOP.

---

* These words are not in capitals in the Directory.—C.

No. V.

Printed from an autograph sent to Lord Clifford from Dublin, December 1841, *and supposed by Lord C. to be the autograph of the priest whose name is affixed to it. The reader will observe that there is no disavowal of the truth of the libels published in the " Mayo Telegraph " under the signature " Aladensis," against the Right Rev. Dr. O'Finan, Roman Catholic Bishop of Killala.*

My Lord,—As the trial, now pending in Sligo, between your Lordship and the Proprietor of the Telegraph, is likely, nay, certain to be the source of much scandal and injury to religion; and as I am sure your Lordship is not actuated by any vindictive feelings towards the press, and only anxious *to know* the author of the letter, which is the ground of the action; I do hereby acknowledge myself to be the author of the same letter, signed Aladensis ; and published in the *Telegraph* of the 15th of June, 1836. I sincerely regret to have written it, and to have caused it to be published. I make this avowal, and express this sincere regret, as a reparation to your Lordship; confidently trusting that it will induce your Lordship to abandon an action which cannot be proceeded with, without inflicting deep and lamentable injury on Religion. I am induced to adopt this course on account of the sincere regret which I have already expressed ; as also from a hope that your Lordship is anxious to leave to the decision of the Holy Father, the Ecclesiastical concerns of your Diocess, as far as relates to the Apostolical Visitation ordered by the Holy See.

I have the honor to be, My Lord,

Your Lordship's very obedient and humble servant,

PATK. FLANNELLY, P. P.,

Sligo, March 9th, 1837.　　and ARCHDEACON EASKY.

To the Rt. Rev. Dr. O'Finan.

M 2

LETTER V. ·

London, January 18, 1842.

MY LORD,

Whatever may be the result to myself
personally, of the venturous career in which I
have engaged, by addressing your Lordship as
I have done on the subject of your pamphlet
entitled "State of Ireland considered," this at
least seems certain to me, that I did not overrate
to myself last October, the degree of alarm
which my letters to your Lordship would occasion. I was perfectly aware of the existence of
men in Ireland, who saw or affected to see,
much more danger to public tranquillity in any
attempt to shake the credit, or even to call in
question the credit, which Archbishop M'Hale
enjoys, or is supposed to enjoy, with the See of
Rome, than in the continuation of that peculiar
species of clerical agitation, to which the assembled Catholic Hierachy of Ireland declared itself
so averse in 1830 and again in 1834. (a) This
view of the case bears directly upon the view
which your Lordship has taken of the present
state of Ireland. Your Lordship and I agree in

(a) See Appendix IV. B. C. D., to the fourth of these letters.

this—that the influence exerted by those Catholic clergymen in Ireland, who are of opinion, that the wise recommendations of the Catholic Hierarchy in Ireland in 1830 and 1834, are no longer wise in 1842, is highly to be deprecated; but unless I much mistake your Lordship, we greatly disagree on the *mode* by which that influence should be counteracted: my opinion is, that any admission, not warranted by the clearest evidence, of the truth of the assertion so boastingly and loudly made by Archbishop M'Hale and his adherents, that *they* are the organs of public opinion, or the leading members of the Catholic clergy in Ireland, is very bad policy. Honesty will in the end be generally, if not always, found to be the best policy; and they who know the truth must, I think, admit if they are honest, that the words of the Secretary for Ireland in the Commons' House of Parliament, Dec. 22, 1819, are as much applicable to the *great body* of the Catholic clergy in Ireland, and particularly to the *great body* of the Roman Catholic Prelacy in Ireland, at present, as they were twenty-three years ago.

Mr. Grant, Secretary for Ireland in 1819, now a member of the House of Peers, said, that " he felt he should not discharge the duty of one " connected with the government of Ireland, if " he did not bear testimony of the exertions of " that respectable class of men, the Catholic

" clergy of Ireland. He had no hesitation in
" saying, that the present tranquillity was owing
" to the exertions of those men, who went about
" from house to house, at the peril of their lives,
" to prevent the dissemination of the principles
" of the reformers. Such exertions were not
" confined to the lower orders, but extended to
" the Roman Catholic Prelacy. He confessed
" that the check which the wild doctrines of
" reformers had met in Ireland, might be attri-
" buted to the zealous, christian-like, and patri-
" otic exertions of that respectable class of
" men."(*b*)

(*b*) The above report is taken from the *New* " Times " newspaper, December 23, 1819. No mention of it is made in Hansard's Parliamentary Debates, Vol. XLI., pages 1446 to 1515.
It is *briefly* given in p. 1, col. 4 of the *Times* newspaper, on a
Parliamentary Report, headed " Irish Roman Catholic Clergy."
The only speakers on the occasion were Sir Henry Parnell and
the Right Hon. C. Grant. Sir Henry Parnell, on the occasion
of postponing a motion for leave to bring in a bill to enable
Catholics to provide residences for their clergy, observed, " he
" thought it his duty to state, without going at all into the
" question of Catholic Emancipation, that there was no body of
" men who deserved a more kind consideration at the hands of the
" legislature than the Roman Catholic Clergy and Hierarchy of
" Ireland. (Hear, hear.) A more highly respectable, intelligent,
" and useful body of men did not, he was persuaded, exist in the
" United Kingdom ; and he said this, not less with reference
" to them as individuals, than to the moral and political good
" produced by the effects of their character and conduct. (Hear,
" hear.) He had the pleasure of being acquainted with some of

Knowing this character of the Roman Catholic Prelacy in Ireland to be the true one, I certainly cannot agree with the Earl of Roden,

---

" the Prelates of that body, and he could state, that on every
" occasion, they were the most strenuous advocates and sup-
" porters of loyalty and good order in their several districts.
" He felt it his duty to state thus much of them; but he had
" risen chiefly for the purpose of postponing his motion till after
" the holidays."

That the Vicars Apostolic of Great Britain deserve equally with the Roman Catholic Hierarchy in Ireland the commendation bestowed on that venerable body by the Secretary for Ireland, may appear from the two following extracts from pastoral letters issued at different times by those Vicars Apostolic, and selected from among several others of similar import.

From the pastoral letter of the Right Rev. Dr. Poÿnter, V. A. addressed to the Catholics of the London District in 1813 :—

" Dearly beloved brethren—We cannot conceal the consolation we experience, when we reflect on the temperate, peaceful, and consistent conduct of the British Catholics, in seeking the relief which we so earnestly desire. If we deem it unlawful to invade the spiritual rights of our supreme Pastor, the visible Head of the Catholic Church, we are guided by a general spirit of subordination in government, and by the same principle as would deter a British subject from invading the acknowledged prerogative of the Crown. ' Let every soul be subject to the higher powers.' —(Rom. xiii. 1.) In order to enforce this duty of respect and submission to the civil government of our country, we are emphatically charged by the Apostolic See to inflict the severest ecclesiastical censures in our power, on such of our subordinate pastors as should speak with disrespect of the government of our country ; because, says the Apostolic See, ' their duty is not to

in p. 6 of his Lordship's observations, where he
says :—" That the bishops have not been the
" *passive* spectators of the turbulent scenes that

' excite discord and disturbances, but to employ themselves dili-
' gently in the spiritual functions of their pastoral charge.' "
From the pastoral letter of the Right Rev. Dr. Baines, V. A.
addressed to the Catholics of the Western District—dated Prior
Park, February 24, 1840 :—

" We have witnessed, beloved brethren, with excessive grief,
the events that have recently taken place in one portion of our
extensive district (South Wales), and we have not ceased to
pray that God would give wisdom to our rulers to avert the
evils that threaten us. In the mean time, one subject has
afforded us inexpressible consolation : it is, that none of our
beloved flock have been involved in these rebellious proceedings.
No, not a single Catholic, thank God, we are assured, has risen
up in rebellion against the lawfully constituted authorities.....
Such precisely was the conduct of the early Christians.....They
entered into no nice disquisitions about the quantum of oppression which justifies resistance to authority ; but adhered literally
and rigorously to the Apostle's advice : ' Let every soul be
subject to the higher powers ; for there is no power but from
God : therefore he that resisteth the power resisteth the ordinance
of God ; and they that resist, purchase to themselves damnation.'
—(Rom. xiii.)   They had also before their eyes a striking proof
how resistance to authority only increases the evil it aims at
redressing, and that the poor are always the victims whom
revolution sacrifices on her ensanguined altars.   They knew that
God, the Supreme Ruler of the world, can alone effectually
redress grievances resulting from national oppression, and that
He never fails to do so in His own good time.

" Do you, my beloved brethren, continue to act upon these
wise and sublime principles.   Never attempt to correct human
laws by violating the divine.   Employ, as far as truth, justice,

" have been of late years enacted by the priest-
" hood, is too evident to require any lengthened
" proof; with them the tithe-agitation origi-
" nated, and by their means it was prosecuted
" and sustained (vide Dr. Doyle's Letters). (c) In
" every society that has been formed for keeping
" up incessant agitation, whether under the name
" of Precursors, Repealers, or others, we find
" some of the bishops have been eminent contri-
" butors; and under them many of the priests
" active agents in procuring funds for their
" objects, and encouraging through the country
" that political agitation which has been so great
" a bane to its happiness and prosperity."

I do not think I am in error in asserting, that
Archbishop M'Hale could not wish for a better
ally than the Earl of Roden. If indeed there
were but a slight shade of difference in opinion
or in action, between Archbishop Murray, together with the great body of the Roman

---

and prudence permit, that powerful moral agency which has
been so strikingly developed in modern times, to procure the
redress of public grievances; but never listen to those wicked or
deluded men, who would urge you to break the laws of your
country, and offend God, for any purpose whatsoever."

(c) The readers of Appendix IV. to the third of these letters,
will have seen that Mr. de Beaumont does not *quite* agree with
the Earl of Roden—see p. 74 at the bottom and p. 75 at the
top.

Catholic Hierarchy of Ireland which adhered
to his Grace on the National Education question,
and Archbishop M'Hale, I might possibly admit
that it would have been a wise policy in Archbishop Murray to have allowed in perfect pas-
siveness Archbishop M'Hale to take the lead,
which he evidently wished to take, among the
Catholic clergy in Ireland; and to plume him-
.self, to his heart's content, upon being the special
nominee of Gregory XVI. in opposition to the
wish of the British government, declared, as
openly as the Whig cabinet dared to do so,
having due fear of the law of Elizabeth before
its eyes, through Sir Henry Seymour. The
virulence of Archbishop M'Hale and of his
adherents *might* have been diminished—the dislike entertained towards the Catholic clergy by
the Earl of Roden, and by the Orange party,
could not, if I am to judge from his Lordship's
" Observations," have been increased—by such
a course. But nevertheless, had such a course
been pursued by Archbishop Murray, so great
in effect would such an abandonment of principle
and such a change of conduct on his part have
produced, and so fatal would such a mistaken
course of policy on his part have been to the
interests of public tranquillity in Ireland, that
I doubt much whether, in such case, any coercive
measures on the part of Great Britain could
have preserved Ireland from irremediable anar-

chy and from torrents of bloodshed, in which
the Earl of Roden might 'ere now have been
swept away with the whole mass of the present
proprietors in Ireland, Catholic as well as Protestant. The truth is, however unpalatable it
may be to the Earl of Roden, that he holds his
lands much more by the tenure of the christianity
and loyalty of the Roman Catholic Hierarchy in
Ireland, as a body, than by his title-deeds.

Now the College of Maynooth is confessedly
the seminary of the great body of the Catholic
Hierarchy in Ireland; and your Lordship would
have (State of Ireland considered, p. 32,) " the
" reformation of the College of Maynooth, and
" the revisal of the whole system of that institu-
" tion," as the third of the " measures proposed
" for restoring tranquillity to that country."   I
shall be perfectly satisfied with any improvement in that College, which the Catholic Bishops
in Ireland may think proper to recommend; and
I am equally satisfied, that the College of Maynooth will readily accede to any measure proposed by the Catholic Bishops in Ireland for its
improvement; but I should be very sorry that
it should accede to any measure *not* proposed by
that prelacy, whether that measure be called a
measure of reform or of improvement.   Of this
I am quite certain, that my friends of Clongowes
College, and especially the present Head of that
College, would most decidedly refuse to be par-

ties to any alteration in the direction of Maynooth College, whether spiritual or literary,
unless at the clear wish and urgent request of
those, who now have that direction. To what
then does the third measure proposed by your
Lordship reduce itself? To the wildest chimera
that ever entered the brain of any man.—
And why has this wildest of extravagances
entered your Lordship's head? Because the
discipline of Maynooth is too severe!!! Were
your Lordship to try it for six months, perhaps
you might not find it so over-severe as you seem
at present disposed to consider it, even for a
British Peer. But for the sake of argument let
us suppose it to be really too severe for your
Lordship; let us, nevertheless, before we absolutely condemn the direction of Maynooth College under the Catholic Prelacy of Ireland for
rigorism, take into consideration the opinions of
a man, in speaking of whom, I am sure I mean
no disparagement to your Lordship in saying,
that he was as anxious for the tranquillity and
welfare of Ireland as your Lordship can be;
and as sincere and able an advocate and champion of the people of Ireland as Archbishop
M'Hale can be; who, by the bye, if I am not
misinformed, would have been inevitably expel-
led Maynooth College, for grievous violation of
its statutes, had it not been for the able advice
of Chief Remembrancer Blake, whom his most

rev. client has so ungratefully rewarded by falsifying his printed evidence before Parliament.——
If your Lordship wishes for further information on this subject, I beg leave to refer you to the Chief Remembrancer himself. The advocate and champion of Ireland to whom I allude, is the Right Hon. Edmund Burke, who wrote thus in 1782 to Lord Kenmare :——

" When we are to provide for the education
" of any body of men, we ought seriously to
" consider the particular functions they are to
" perform in life. A Roman Catholic clergy-
" man is the minister of a very ritual religion ;
" and by his profession subject to many restraints.
" His life is a life full of *strict* observances, and
" his duties are of a laborious nature towards
" himself, and of the highest possible trust towards
" others. The duty of confession alone, is suffi-
" cient to set in the strongest light the necessity
" of his having an appropriated mode of educa-
" tion. The theological opinions and peculiar
" rites of one religion, never can be taught pro-
" perly in universities founded for the purposes
" and on the principles of another, which in
" many points are directly opposite. If a Ro-
" man Catholic clergyman, intended for celi-
" bacy (d) and the·function of confession, is not

(d) I may be pardoned, I hope, for indulging here in a smile at an *aged* priest, who writes in the Dublin University Magazine for November and December, 1841, a most pathetic lamentation on

" *strictly* bred in a seminary where these things
" are respected, inculcated, and *enforced*, as
" sacred, and not made the subject of, derision
" and obloquy, he will be ill-fitted for the for-
" mer, and the latter will be indeed in his hands
" a terrible instrument."

     * * * * " The Council of Trent has wisely
" introduced the *discipline* of seminaries, by
" which priests are not trusted for a clerical
" education *even* to the *severe* discipline of their
" colleges; but after they pass through them,
" are frequently, if not for the greater part,
" obliged to pass through peculiar methods,
" having their particular ritual function in view.
" It is in a great measure to this, and to similar
" methods used in foreign education, that the
" Roman Catholic clergy in Ireland—miserably

---

the hardship which celibacy imposes on his *younger* clerical
brethren, in a strain which proves him to be, not indeed exactly of
the same mind as old Cato in Cicero *de Senectute*, but on one
point at least, something of the same kidney as the old harper,
who sung the " Lay of the Last Minstrel " before the Duchess
of Buccleugh :—

         "And said I that my limbs were old," &c.

     The Catholic clerical correspondent of the Dublin University
Magazine recalls to my mind the lines of Horace :—

         " Iliæ dum se nimium querenti
         Jactat ultorem, vagus et *sinistra*
         Labitur ripā Jove non probante
         Uxorius amnis."

" provided for, living among low and ill-regu-
" lated people, *without any discipline* of sufficient
" force to secure good manners—have been pre-
" vented from becoming an intolerable nuisance
" to the country, instead of being, as I conceive
" they generally are, a very great service to it."

How says your Lordship ? Would you have
a more talented, a more courtly Catholic clergy
in Ireland,—a clergy more gifted with fluency
of speech, more ready with the pen, than Archbishop M'Hale ? I may be tempted to wish that
his Grace had had less talent,—that he had been
less courtly at Rome,—that his tongue had been
far less smooth,—that even at the price of our
never having been able to read " Hierophilos,"
or the " Evidences " of " John, Bishop of Maronia," we had never been scandalised by the newspaper productions of " ✛ John, Archbishop of
Tuam." But I do most heartily wish, that either
he had never violated the *severe discipline* of Maynooth College, so as to have *run any risk* of expulsion from that great object of your Lordship's horror, or that the talents of my learned friend, the
Chief Remembrancer, had not rescued him from
his otherwise inevitable disgrace. I rather suspect
that the Chief Remembrancer thinks now much
as I do on this point, though, less " flippant " (e)

(e) See letter of " ✛ John, Archbishop of Tuam " to " The
Honourable Lord Clifford," in the *Freeman's Journal*, Dec. 20,
1841.

than myself, he may not think it advisable to *say* so, unless perhaps your Lordship should be able to obtain a private hearing. To prevent, however, any injurious suspicion against the *morality* of Archbishop M'Hale, which I believe to be above suspicion, I think it necessary to observe here, that the infraction alluded to was, of having, contrary to the statutes, published *Political* Essays, without the knowledge of the President. Your Lordship may I think satisfy yourself upon this point, should you have any doubt upon it, by referring, in the Eighth Report of the Commissioners on Irish Education Inquiry, ordered to be printed by the House of Commons, June 19, 1827, pp. 461. folio, to the Statutes of Maynooth College, page 39, to pages 100 to 104, containing the examination of the Very Rev. Dr. Crotty, D.D., President of the College; and pages 298 to 303, containing the examination of the Right Rev. Dr. M'Hale. (*f*)

The Earl of Roden observes, p. 5, that your Lordship "states, p. 5 of your pamphlet, that "*you cannot believe* that the scenes which have " lately taken place in Ireland have been sanc- " tioned by the higher classes of the Irish clergy, " or (if they had the authority) that they would- " have abstained from interfering to prevent

(*f*) It will be seen by reference to the Letter in the *Freeman's Journal* of December 20, 1841, quoted in the note p. 175 of these letters, that the present Catholic Archbishop of Tuam was appointed Coadjutor Bishop of Killala in March 1825. (Report, p. 103,) "At the time when that pamphlet (Letter to Mr. Canning,) was published . . . . we considered him as "about to "be appointed Coadjutor Bishop, and consequently to leave the "house."—Answer of Dr. Crotty, Nov. 9, 1826, Report, p. 103.

N

" the great scandal that has been occasioned
" by them to the Roman Catholic ministry."
The noble Earl proceeds to observe, that your
Lordship " is much mistaken if you think that
" the Romish priest is not in complete subjection
" to his bishop, who has the strongest coactive
" authority to enforce obedience, not only in
" the exercise of his spiritual functions, but in his
" daily conversation. His authority, instead of
" being too little, is only too great, (g) and such
" as is inconsistent with the enjoyment of the
" liberties of a British subject. No state rela-
" tion into which we could be brought with the
" Court of Rome, could give greater force to
" this authority than is already given ; and
" instead of such a relation making the exercise
" of it safer for our liberties or our peace, it will
" only tend the more to endanger both."

I am in error greatly, if the great majority of
those who may take the trouble to read the
Appendix No. IV. to my last letter, do not
decide in favour of your Lordship in the matter
here at issue between the Earl of Roden and
your Lordship. The wishes and THE FEELINGS
of the Irish Catholic Hierarchy *as a body* are
clear from the resolutions of 1830 and 1834 ; the
power and the determination of Archbishop
M'Hale to set those resolutions and THOSE

(g) The noble Earl appears to me evidently to have fallen
into this, to me, palpable error, on account of his being a member of the Church of England.—See in Appendix No. II. to this
letter, the passage which I have caused to be printed in capitals,
p. 324.

FEELINGS at defiance are, I think, equally clear from the letter signed " ✠ John. Archbishop of Tuam," in the *Freeman's Journal* of Dec. 20, 1841. The influence he has over the clergy in his Archdiocese, and even, in some instances, over priests not under his Archiepiscopal jurisdiction, is also, I think, clear.— But to what cause do I attribute this baneful power ? To this cause *alone*,—that an *open* state relation between the See of Rome and the government of this United Kingdom, did not exist at the death of Archbishop Kelly, the predecessor of Archbishop M'Hale. On occount of the non-existence of such state relation, the cabinet of Earl Grey committed in 1831 the *immense mistake*, which it did commit, and of which Austria naturally took advantage, (*h*) by sending Sir Henry Seymour to Rome, in an *utterly untenable position;* and which in 1835 the cabinet of Lord Melbourne again committed, if possible, in a still greater degree, by *absolutely courting a refusal* from Gregory XVI. of the wish intimated to the Holy See through Sir Henry Seymour, whom it had been the interest of Austria to blacken as much as possible

---

(*h*) Austria in 1831 was alarmed at the *early* recognition by England of Louis Philippe, dreaded the politics of Count Sebastiani and Lord Palmerston, and was in apprehension of a war with France; in which case it was important to Austria that Gregory XVI. should not be swayed by the counsels of France or England, but that Austria should have military possession of Italy.—See note *(m)* p. 205 of these letters.

and but too successfully in the eyes of Gregory
XVI. in 1831, and through Mr. Aubyn, whose
position at Rome the present or late Secretary
for Foreign Affairs in Downing-street is better
able to explain to your Lordship than I am.—
What was that wish ? It was this,—that the
Catholic Bishop of Killala should not be promoted to the Catholic Archbishoprick of Tuam.—
Really, my Lord, if the British Cabinet has
reason to complain of the baneful influence of
Archbishop M'Hale, every Catholic and Non-
Catholic in Ireland who wishes for the tranquillity of that country and who deplores that baneful influence, has much more reason to complain
of the existence of the law, which prevented the
British Cabinet from expressing its wish to the
Holy See, in any other manner than such as
must in fairness be called, *courting a refusal.*

I beg your Lordship to consider attentively
the first of the resolutions in Appendix No. IV.
(C) to my last letter ; and to ask yourself the
question—whether it was possible for Gregory
XVI. to suppose, that the writer of the letter of
Hierophilos, App. No. I. to my second letter to
your Lordship, or of the " Evidences," App.
No. II. to my second letter, could be justly
objectionable on *political* grounds to the British
Government ? It may be quite true that the
British Government had discovered in 1835, that
the successor of Bishop Waldron in the See of
Killala had, since the decease of his predecessor,

developed sentiments very different from those expressed in the resolutions of the Catholic Hierarchy in Ireland in 1830 and 1834; and that it did not wish that the Archiepiscopal character should increase the influence of a prelate, so evidently determined, as the successor of Bishop Waldron had shewn himself, to exert whatever talents God had given him, and whatever influence his station in the Catholic Church in Ireland might give him, in opposition to the spirit, if not to the very words, of the resolutions of 1830 and 1834; but it is no less true, that the law of Elizabeth placed the British Government in a position of inability to acquaint Gregory XVI. with the discovery it had made; and placed Gregory XVI. in the inability of acting upon that wish. To the operation of the law of Elizabeth, which, whatever may have been its political expediency in reference to that Queen, and to England and Ireland under her government, is a monstrous absurdity and a most pernicious statute-law at present; to that law chiefly, if not solely, must be attributed whatever detriment to public tranquillity in Ireland has arisen, from the elevation of Archbishop M'Hale to his present power. Such, at least, is my opinion; and I think I am entitled to say, that my position in Rome, at the time of that promotion, enabled me to form as correct an opinion upon this point as any man could form. No alteration whatsoever in the discipline or direction of Maynooth

College ; no payment of the Catholic clergy by the State,—even were it possible, which I much doubt, in the present temper of public opinion in Great Britain and Ireland,—can give the government any adequate security for public tranquillity in Ireland, so long as the law of Elizabeth exists, in direct opposition to the interests of Queen Victoria, her heirs, and successors. To those interests, it is the duty of the Earl of Roden, of your Lordship, and of myself, and of every British and Irish Legislator, to look ; to Her Present Majesty, and to Her heirs and successors, and not to Queen Elizabeth, have we sworn allegiance ; that is to say, we have recognized on oath that duty, which was imposed upon us by our Creator at our birth—a duty, so paramount and sacred, that no subsequent obligation *can* be contracted by any of us, by any act of our own, in violation of that duty. The consent of our Sovereign alone can absolve us from its obligation. This I understand to be the doctrine taught at Maynooth College, as well as at Clongowes College ; (*i*) and which, as far as I have been able to ascer-

---

(*i*) See in Appendix to this letter, No. II, the words printed in capitals in the 186th of the answers *selected* from the evidence given by the late Rev. P. Kenny, superior of Clongowes College, before the Commissioners appointed by Parliament to enquire into the state of Education in Ireland. Eighth Report, ordered by the House of Commons to be printed 19th of June, 1827, containing 461 pages folio, entirely on Maynooth College.

tain, is, and always has been, made a rule of conduct by the eléves of that great seminary of the Irish Catholic priesthood. In such an education of the Irish Catholic clergy,—in such a spirit as breathes in the episcopal resolutions of 1830 and 1834,—IN THE ABOLITION OF THE LAW OF ELIZABETH forbidding intercourse between the See of Rome and the Government of the United Kingdom; *not* in the payment of the Roman Catholic clergy in Ireland by the State,—*not* in relations with the Holy See similar to those of Russia or Prussia,—*not* in any relaxation of the severity of the discipline of the College of Maynooth,— *not* in any alteration of its direction ; must your Lordship seek tranquillity for Ireland, and Earl Roden seek security for his landed estates in Ireland.

I have now to take leave of your Lordship ; and I do so with a feeling of sincere respect and esteem ; because your Lordship has honorably laid your opinions before the public, with a sincere wish for the welfare of our common country. You have written nothing of which you need be ashamed, though I do not think your opinions are, perhaps with the sentiments with which your education as an English Protestant has inspired you respecting the Catholics of Ireland, they could not be, correct. But as I have been in some degree identified, in consequence of my two first letters to your Lordship, with others who have thought fit to lay before the public, during the course of last year, their opinions on the state of Ireland, although I have had no correspondence or connexion with them, I may perhaps be permitted, ere I lay down my pen, to add a few words upon a subject, on which I consider myself fully as much entitled to hold my opinions, without being denounced as an enemy to Ireland, as Archbishop M'Hale is entitled to hold his. There is not perhaps in the whole of the United Empire, any man less disposed than myself to admit, that an Archbishop's mitre, whether on the head of a christian in communion with the See of Rome, or on the head of a christian not in communion with the See of Rome, does or can give its wearer the right to accuse a Peer of the United Parliament of Great Britain and Ireland in the newspapers, of that of which I have been publicly accused in the *Freeman's Journal* of December 20, 1841, in these words, by a writer signing himself ✠ John, Archbishop of Tuam :—

" It would be more in accordance with that
" ingenuous and lofty bearing, which your Lord-
" ship affects so much to admire, to announce to
" the world those feelings of enmity to Ireland,
" which cannot be disguised, than to be screening
" them under the cloak of a friendship in which
" it is impossible we should any longer confide."

It is rank nonsense that any Archbishop, whether professing himself a Catholic, or professing himself a Protestant, can without personal risk publish in a newspaper, or can screen from the penalties of libel in this country, whatever he may be able to do elsewhere, any editor of a newspaper, for publishing such an accusation against any Peer of the United Parliament of Great Britain and Ireland, in consequence of any sentiments expressed by him, such as I have expressed in any of the letters which I have taken the liberty of addressing to your Lordship. It is equally rank nonsense to say, that that which is vulgarity and defamation, when spoken or written by a layman, ceases to be vulgarity and defamation, when spoken or written by an Archbishop, whether Catholic or Non-Catholic. I have not the most remote intention of taking the trouble to institute an action for libel against the editor of the *Freeman's Journal,* for publishing, or against the writer who has signed himself " ✠ John, Archbishop of Tuam," for writing, the four columns and a half of absurdities, which appeared in the *Freeman's Journal* of December 20, 1841; but I say that it would be a great benefit to Ireland, that Archbishop M'Hale should cease to be a member of the Irish Catholic Hierarchy in Ireland, exercising jurisdiction in that country; *because* it is utterly impossible, after the publication, I do not say of the fourth of these letters to your Lordship, but of the public declaration of the Hon. Frederick Cavendish in the *Telegraph,* or *Connaught Ranger* of December 22, 1841, and of the letter signed "✠ John, Archbishop of Tuam," in the *Freeman's Journal* of December 20, 1841, that Archbishop M'Hale can be respected in Ireland ; and it is highly important to the tranquillity of Ireland, that the Catholic Bishops, and especially the Catholic Archbishops, in Ireland, should be respectable and respected by all. There is no service which I can do to Ireland, (and there are none of her sons more desirous of doing her service than I am,) greater than that which I wish to do, by impressing upon *all men* in Great Britain and Ireland, that in order to be, either with advantage to Christianity, or with credit to themselves, members of the Irish Catholic Hierarchy, they MUST BE HONOURABLE MEN. I beg to be understood as meaning by these last words, not merely, or principally, men having by their station in life the *title of Honourable* before the world ; on the contrary, no one wishes more than myself, to see in the Prelacy of that Church which was founded by Him, who, " not having where to lay His head," S. Matt. viii. 20, chose twelve poor men for his Apostles, a constant proof that the Divine Founder of that Church " has " chosen the weak things of this world that " He may confound the strong," 1 Cor. i. 27 ; and that the true children of that Holy Mother, venerate and obey *in spirituals*, not the Prince but the Pastor. I mean that in Ireland *particularly*, where, above all other countries, the conduct of the Catholic Hierarchy stands prominently in *comparison* with that of the Hierarchy of the Church established by law, the Catholic Hierarchy must be a living example of the words of St. Paul to Titus, ii. 7, " in ex-" ample of *good works*, in doctrine, in *integrity*, " in gravity," and *ib*. i. 8, " gentle, sober, *just*."

Such *were*, to the last moment of their lives, Archbishop Curtis, my old friend at Salamanca in 1811, and Archbishop Kelly, my late brother Robert's (*k*) friend. Such *are* my venerable friend, Bishop O'Finan, and last, not least, my invaluable (though if I could find any fault in his character, *over cautious*) friend, Archbishop Murray, — beyond all doubt one of the most meritorious men in the British Empire, as well as one of the most amiable. Such in one word are, and have always been, whatever the Earl of Roden may have imagined to himself, or may have been told by others to the contrary, the Catholic Hierarchy of Ireland, with hardly a single exception, furnished by history to the contrary. The great cause of error and mischief in the O'Finan case, appears to me to have been, a persuasion in the mind of Archbishop M'Hale, that it was *possible* effectually to shelter *fraud*

(*k*) Lieutenant in the 83rd Regiment. He died at Limerick, June 10, 1833, aged 26, and in gratitude for the kindness shewn him by Archbishop Kelly, left him his gold watch. His venerable friend died soon after, in Italy, in ignorance of this mark of gratitude and respect from his young friend.

and *tyranny* in the oppression of a *British* or *Irish* Catholic Prelate, by throwing the mantle of an Archbishop's or a Cardinal's robes over that fraud, or that tyranny, and then saying:— " *Respect the Mitre, or the Pallium, or the Sacred " Purple."* I will not dispute upon *possibilities ;* but the *odds* against a *British* or *Irish* Catholic, playing that desperate game, are tremendous— especially if he meddles with newspapers. Had Archbishop M'Hale been possessed of as much common-sense and fore-thought, as he unques- tionably is of talent, he would have foreseen, that in patronizing the *Telegraph* newspaper, during the publication of the letters signed " Aladensis," still more in making to the Hon. Mr. Cavendish the disgraceful proposition which that ill-treated Editor indignantly rejected (see the *Telegraph* of December 22, 1841), he placed himself entirely in the power of the Editor of that paper, from the moment that *that Editor* had discovered the truth. Had he known the Italian character as well as I know it, he would never have at- tempted to *compromise the reputation* of Mgr. Cadolini, of Cardinal Franzoni, and even of Pope Gregory XVI., in the silly attempt of impressing upon the priests of Connaught, that he himself was omnipotent at Rome.

Archbishop M'Hale has to blame himself, not me, for the public disgrace which he has *brought upon himself* at Sligo, (*l*) and in Dublin. I may eventually have contributed by these letters to disabuse, the Earl of Shrewsbury having failed in his attempt (see p. 100 of these letters), that Sacred Congregation, in which my lamented father-in-law for six years, from 1830 to 1837, did good and honest service to his religion and to his country, and proved himself a faithful and useful member of the Sacred College to Pius VIII. and Gregory XVI., without ceasing to be a loyal and dutiful subject to King George the Fourth and to King William the Fourth, of the erroneous and mischievous impressions produced upon that Sacred Congregation after his death ; impressions which could not have been produced during his life.(*m*) I may be the humble instrument in

---

(*l*) See in Appendix No. III. to my third letter, and in App· No. I. to this fifth letter, the declarations on this point of the Hon. Mr. Cavendish, Editor of the *Mayo Telegraph.*

(*m*) I owe it, as a sacred duty, to the memory of my lamented father-in-law, publicly to contradict, as I intend to do by this note, an imputation upon his conduct as a member of the Sacred College, of which I only became aware, after I had commenced this fifth letter. I have observed, p. 194, that, in my humble opinion, *a great mistake* was committed in 1831, in sending Sir Henry Seymour to Rome, where he failed in his mission, not at all on account of any want of ability on his part, for there was none ; nor, as far as I can judge, on account of any intrinsic unreasonableness in the propositions he was directed to make (See Annual Register for 1832, Public Documents, pp. 379 to 387,) *to such quarters as the law of Elizabeth would allow him to make*

the hands of Divine Providence, for opening the eyes of Gregory XVI., in spite of those who have attempted to keep them closed, to the

them, without compromising himself and the British Government, *under that law*. I have also observed, that a still greater mistake was committed in 1835, in the *method* taken to acquaint Gregory XVI., *under that law*, with the wishes of the British Government, respecting the promotion of the Catholic Bishop of Killala to the Archbishopric of Tuam. It is only since the commencement of this present month of January, 1842, that I have learnt from a quarter which I am quite sure would not deceive me, that Cardinal Weld, not Sir Henry Seymour, or Mr. Aubyn, was said to have been selected by the British Government to acquaint the Sacred Congregation and Gregory XVI. with its wishes. Such was the information *given in Rome* in 1841 to the quarter to which I allude. I can pledge my honor, as a Peer, to the public, that Cardinal Weld *never received any intimation whatsoever from the British Government*, of its wishes respecting the appointment of Archbishop M'Hale, either to the See of Killala, or of Tuam; nor have I any reason for believing that he became acquainted from *any quarter whatsoever*, that it would be *agreeable* to the British Government, that he should intimate any such wishes, either to the Sacred Congregation, or to Gregory XVI., until *a fortnight after* the Sacred Congregation had recommended the appointment of Bishop M'Hale to the Archbishopric of Tuam, to which he had been elected by the Bishops of the Province, and Gregory XVI. had confirmed the election, and had ordered the bulls to be sent off. But if the *mis*-information, given at Rome in 1840, to the quarter to which I allude, was sent in 1835 or 1836 to Archbishop M'Hale, it is much easier for me to explain the hostility of that Archbishop to the Grey and Melbourne administrations and to myself, than I otherwise could; and perhaps the intimation made to myself in November 1841, see p. 22 of these letters, may be similarly explained.——C

wrongfulness of the advice given him to suspend Bishop O'Finan, and not Archbishop
M'Hale, from all exercise of Episcopal jurisdiction in Ireland in 1839; but if Archbishop M'Hale's existence in Ireland, as *an
influential character*, is, as he seems to think
by the letter published in the *Freeman's Journal*,
Dec. 20, 1841, to cease, (*n*) he will have fallen
in atonement of the crime he has committed
AGAINST THE PUBLIC PRESS in Ireland, by first
deceiving and then persecuting the Hon. Mr.
Cavendish. By his hand in reality, rather than
by mine, Archbishop M'Hale must fall, if he falls.
Of these letters, I may with truth say to the
voluntary witness of March 20, 1837, at Sligo :

> Pallas te hoc vulnere, Pallas
> Immolat et poenas * * * sumit.
> *Virgil, Eneid*, B. 12.

Had Archbishop M'Hale not chosen to act
since 1830 and 1834 in opposition to the resolutions of the Catholic Hierarchy in Ireland in
those years, he would never have brought
himself into his present unenviable position ;
nor should I have come forward, in justification of the character of that Sacred Congregation, of which my lamented father-in-law was
for six years an honest and laborious member,

(*n*) " Yes, the destiny of the Archbishop of Tuam is disposed
" of "—words of the letter signed ✠ John, Archbishop of Tuam,
in the *Freeman's Journal*, December 20, 1841.

with no other remuneration than the testimony of his own conscience, that he was promoting the interests of Christianity in all those countries whose Catholic Bishops are under the jurisdiction of the See of Rome, acting through the Sacred Congregation called *De Propaganda Fide.* I distinctly and emphatically deny the *truth* of the imputation cast upon that Sacred Congregation, in the evidence *upon oath* of Archbishop M'Hale, as reported in the *Mayo Constitution* (4th of these letters, p. 105.) I distinctly and emphatically protest against the *fairness* of *that* evidence, as reported in the *Telegraph* or *Connaught Ranger*, then known by the name of " Lord John's newspaper," or Archbishop M'Hale's newspaper *(ibid).*—I must leave to your Lordship and to the public in Great Britain and Ireland to decide, whether, possessing the information of which I have shewn myself in the three last of these letters possessed, I was justified or not justified in writing to your Lordship last October, in p. 13 of my second second letter, that " I agreed " with your Lordship, " that some *new* and *more efficient* line of " policy must be adopted which shall repress " and put under control irresponsible power"— words which *appear* to have been the chief cause of the indignation vented against me by the writer, signing himself ✚ John, Archbishop of Tuam, in the *Freeman's Journal* of December 20, 1841. I deny that in these words I have expressed, and I equally deny that I entertain, any wish to place the Catholic Hierarchy of Ireland under control from *any* quarter, other than such as Gregory XVI. himself would wish it should be placed. I think however that I have shewn from the conduct of Archbishop M'Hale since he became Archbishop of Tuam, that under the *present* system of intercourse with the Holy See, a much greater facility is afforded to a Catholic Archbishop, choosing to set at defiance the unanimous wish and feeling of the Catholic Hierarchy of Ireland, as expressed in the resolutions of 1830 and 1834, in reference to clerical interference in political agitation, than is consistent with the tranquillity of Ireland; I have also candidly expressed my conviction, that the remedy for this great and *increasing* evil is to be found in the Repeal of the Law of Elizabeth, prohibiting "*open*" or *avowed* state-relations between the Holy See and the British Government; and that a Repeal of the Legislative Union, without a repeal of that law, will not remedy that evil. In what I have written in reference to the case of my venerable friend Bishop O'Finan, and to the deeply-to-be-lamented trial *O'Finan versus Cavendish*, which came before the *Civil* Court at Sligo, on the 20th and 21st of March, 1837, I am not aware of having written any thing, and *I expressly declare that I have not intended to write any thing* cal-

o

culated to impress upon your Lordship's mind,
or upon that of the public in Great Britain
or Ireland, that Archbishop M'Hale was the
author of the letters signed " Aladensis," which
appeared in the newspaper called the *Telegraph*
or *Connaught Ranger*, in 1836, or that that
Archbishop ever *expressly told* the Hon. Mr.
Cavendish, that he was able to oblige, or that
he was desirous of obliging, by his influence at
Rome, Bishop O'Finan to renounce his right
to the 500*l.* damages awarded him by the verdict of the jury on that occasion.

Finally, I most positively and emphatically
deny, that by calling the attention of your
Lordship and of the public to the trial in the
Civil Court at Sligo on the 20th and 21st of
March, 1837, and to the proceedings taken at
Rome to misrepresent as a *criminal* action
brought by a Catholic Bishop against one of his
own priests before a Protestant lay tribunal,
that *civil* action brought by Bishop O'Finan by
the advice of his friends, and not merely or
principally at the instigation of any attorney,
still less at the instigation of any one who wished
thereby to cast discredit upon the Catholic
religion or the Catholic Hierarchy in Ireland,—
brought against a *Protestant* Editor for *publishing*, not against any one, whether Catholic or
Protestant, for *merely writing*, what the Publisher himself, when his eyes became open to the

infamous deception practised upon him, unhesitatingly and publicly declared in the *Telegraph* newspaper of the 20th of April, 1839, to be " unfounded calumnies against a pious and ex- " emplary prelate," and " freely admits it a libel " which had not a shadow of truth to rest " upon,"(*o*)—I have either adverted to any *long since forgotten subject,* to which it would have been better for the credit of the Catholic religion not to have adverted, or have given any just cause of regret to the friends, or of triumph to the enemies, of Catholicity in Ireland.

What I *have wished* to impress upon the mind of your Lordship and of the public in Great Britain and Ireland is, that the *general* conduct of Archbishop M'Hale in his conduct towards my venerable friend Bishop O'Finan ; and that his *public* conduct at Mr. Sharman Crawfurd's dinner, in 1836, at the Sligo trial in 1837, and at the Galway dinner in 1839, affords strong ground for believing, that such characters as Archbishop M'Hale cannot be *restrained* or *prevented* from acting contrary to the wishes and feelings of the Catholic Hierarchy in Ireland as expressed in the Resolutions of 1830 and 1834, to the great detriment of public tranquillity in Ireland in

(*o*) See declaration of the Hon. Frederick Cavendish. Appendix III. to the third of these letters, pages 57, 58, and 59.

every possible supposition, to the great dismay
of the Christian, peaceable, and loyal subjects of
Queen Victoria in Ireland, whether Catholic
or non-Catholic, and to the great affliction of
Gregory XVI. ; unless such "a *new* and *more*
" *efficient* line of policy," as in my humble
opinion can only be effected by the repeal of
the law of Elizabeth, and is not, in my humble
opinion, likely to be effected by a repeal of the
Legislative Union, be speedily adopted. I think
that until the law of Elizabeth be repealed,
Archbishop M'Hale will continue to enjoy
"irresponsible power" in Ireland, and that he will
exercise that power injuriously to the interests
of Christianity and social order in Ireland, and
injuriously to the reputation of the Holy See.

On the question of the Repeal of the Union,
to which I have been represented as *decidedly*
opposed, in opposition to the wish of the great
majority of the People of Ireland, who, it is alleged, consider such repeal essential to their
interests, but on which, I have not expressed any
opinion in any of these letters, other than that
I do not think it is *of itself* a measure which can
secure tranquillity to Ireland (page 119), I wish
to draw the attention of your Lordship and of
the public to the following words of Mr. Burke,
in his letter to Sir Hercules Langrishe in 1792.

" You mention that the minds of some gentle-
" men are a good deal heated ; and that it is

" often said, that, rather than submit to such
" persons (the Catholics) having a share in their
" franchises, they would throw up their inde-
" pendence, and precipitate an union with Great
" Britain. I have heard a discussion, concerning
" such an union, amongst all sorts of men, ever
" since I remember any thing. For my own
" part, I have never been able to bring my mind
" to any thing clear and decisive upon the sub-
" ject. There cannot be a more arduous ques-
" tion. As far as I can form an opinion, it
" would not be for the mutual advantage of the
" two kingdoms. Persons, however, more able
" than I am, think otherwise."

I confess to your Lordship, that were the
question at present the *enactment* of a legislative
union between Great Britain and Ireland, I
should be very loth to give an opinion; and
were I compelled to do so, I should be inclined
to follow the generally safer rule, in very difficult cases,—not to alter the actual state of things.
But the question now is not, whether a legislative union, which has never existed, should be
created by statute; but whether a legislative
union, which has existed forty-one years, should
be *dissolved* by statute. During the existence of
that union, Catholic Emancipation *has been* carried; and the consequence has been, that Ireland
has had, ever since 1829, the services of the present Lord Mayor of Dublin, with greater benefit

to *herself*, as well as to Great Britain, than I think she could possibly have derived from any services which that extraordinary man could have rendered her in an Irish Parliament in College Green, Dublin ; and the services of several other most valuable advocates of her interests, in the House of Commons at Westminster ;—an advantage which Ireland must forego, in the event of a dissolution of the legislative union. Some Municipal Reform *has been* effected ; a system of National Education, which, though far from being faultless in principle, has worked well in practice, *has been* carried into effect, in lieu of the system of the Kildare Street Society ; and, in spite of the immense efforts of Archbishop M'Hale, it has given the youth of Ireland, generally, the idea, so admirably expressed by Queen Victoria, in her own words, to the Lords of the Council of Committee on Education in England : " IT IS MY " WISH THAT THE YOUTH OF MY KINGDOM SHOULD " BE RELIGIOUSLY BROUGHT UP, AND THAT THE " RIGHTS OF CONSCIENCE SHOULD BE RESPECTED." It has taught Ireland, that the Government of England takes an interest in the *Christian* education of its youth, without wishing to interfere with the rights, either of their parents, or their pastors, or with the children's own, if possible, still greater civil unalienable right and conscientious duty, to profess and practise, as the *true* profession and practice of the christian religion, that which in their consciences, after sufficient instruction, they *believe to be* the true profession and practice of that Religion.(*p*)

When I apply to the question of an attempt to dissolve by statute this legislative union, after forty-one years, the consideration of the maxim of Cardinal Consalvi,—"Calculate the resistance," —which I have endeavoured to impress upon your Lordship (p. 118 of these letters), I feel that I would rather cling, to the last moment, to the hope, that full justice *will* yet be done to Ireland, than have to reproach myself with having hastily voted for the abolition of a system, under which so much *has been* done for Ireland—either on the problematical assertion, that more *would have been* done, if that union had not taken place; or upon the equally problematical assertion, that more *will be* done, if it be dissolved, than if it be preserved. By the law of nature, we cannot stand still in human affairs: the probability in my mind is, that we shall go forward if the Legislative Union be preserved; (*q*) and your

---

(*p*) It is almost equally a subject of astonishment and confusion, how little the Catholics of Great Britain and Ireland have reflected upon the immense benefit to *Christianity*, which Queen Victoria has conferred, by causing to be carried into effect by Parliament Her own principles upon National Education in England. See App. III. to this letter.

(*q*) A still stronger expression of opinion on this point will be

Lordship's pamphlet is no small assurance to me on this point.

I intended to have terminated, with this last observation, a public correspondence with your Lordship, on which it will give me real pleasure to be assured *by you*, that *your Lordship* is not disposed to be as severe a critic as the honorable and learned barrister and his lay and clerical friends, alluded to in p. 5 of the second part of these letters; and that *your Lordship* does *not* think that " they are not written in the

---

found at the top of p. 34 of a pamphlet which, while this page was printing, has been put into my hands by my bookseller, entitled, " The Repeal of the Union would be SEPARATION, and " must lead either to the Re-conquest of Ireland, or the Destruc-" tion of the British Empire; in which the question of Irish " Grievances and Justice to Ireland is incidentally discussed. " By M. J. Fagan, Esq., Barrister-at-law. Dublin ; Machen, " 1841." This pamphlet is well worth the perusal of those who are disposed to take for granted, that Repeal of the Union is the *deliberate wish*, as well as the *popular cry* of the PEOPLE OF IRELAND. I do not feel competent to pronounce any opinion upon its general merits, still less to assert the correctness of *all* the views expressed in it by the learned writer. I will only observe, that the passage relating to the Duke of Wellington, p. 38, is not only more in unison with the resolutions of the Irish Catholic Hierarchy of Ireland in 1830, but more in analogy with the feelings of many influential *lay* members of the Catholic body in Ireland, than are the sentiments published in the *Freeman's Journal* of December 20, 1841, signed ✠ John, Archbishop of Tuam.

" language adapted to a peer of the realm, or in
" such language as ought to be addressed by one
" peer to another." The public of course will
form its own opinion.

But at the moment of receiving from my
printer the proof sheet of what I intended to be
the last page of my fifth and last letter to your
Lordship, on your important pamphlet, entitled
" The State of Ireland considered, and measures
" proposed for restoring tranquillity to that
" Country," I also received by post from Ireland,
a smaller pamphlet of seventy-two pages duo-
decimo, in type rather small for eyes as much
fatigued as mine have been with writing and
reading since the first of the present month, (and
it was on the 18th that I received the pamphlet
in question,) which has induced me again to take
up my pen.

This little pamphlet appears, by the title page,
to have been printed and published at Castlebar,
by John Henry Doyle, Editor of the *Mayo
Telegraph*, price one shilling and six-pence, and is
entitled " An ample report of the important
" Libel record, tried before Baron Richards at
" the Galway Assizes, on the 5th and 6th of
" August (1841), the Rev. Michael Gallagher,
" R.C.C. Islandeady, being Plaintiff, and the
" Honorable Frederick Cavendish, proprietor of
" the *Mayo Telegraph*, being Defendant."

It appears from page 1 of this pamphlet, that—

The counsel for the Plaintiff were—Mr. Charles O'Malley,(r) Mr. Matthew Baker, Mr. Gerald Fitzgibbon, Mr. Thomas Jennings, and Mr. James Kilne O'Dowd; agent, Mr. William Thomas Kelly, solicitor, Mountjoy-square, Dublin: and that the counsel for the Defendant were—Mr. Richard Keating, Q.C., Mr. James H. Monahan, Q.C., and Mr. Armstrong; agent, Mr. Richard Prendergast, solicitor, Marlborough-street, Dublin.

It appears from the same pamphlet, p. 2, that the names of the jury were—

James Lynch, Winfield
Peter Blake, Hollypark
Thomas Lynch, Oatfield
James P. Comyn, Ballinderry
John W. H. Lambert, Aggard
Anthony O'Kelly, Creran
Daniel H. Smith, Newgarden

Thomas Tully, Jun. Rathfarn
William Usher, Kilgeran
John Burke, Lisbrien
Edward Brown, Coloo
James Kerwan, Gardenfield,
Esquires.

It appears from the same pamphlet, p. 2, that after the jury had been sworn, the following conversation took place between the Court and counsel:

Mr. Keating, Q.C.—My Lord, I am anxious that the witnesses on both sides should retire from court.

(r) By reference to the *Mayo Constitution* and *Telegraph* newspapers, of March, 1837, I find Mr. O'Malley counsel for Hon. Mr. Cavendish, Defendant, Mr. O'Dowd opening the pleadings on the side of Bishop O'Finan, Plaintiff; Mr. Gerald Fitzgibbon counsel, and Mr. William Thomas Kelly solicitor for the plaintiff.—C.

Baron Richards.—Certainly. I will not take down the evidence of any witness who remains in court.

Mr. Keating, Q.C.—Let all the witnesses be removed.

His Grace the Archbishop of Tuam, who occupied a seat near the Plaintiff's Counsel, was about retiring, when one of the learned gentlemen asked the Court would his Lordship's remaining in court be deemed objectionable?

Mr. Keating, Q.C.—Certainly. We will make no distinction on the present occasion between the Archbishop and the Curate.

Doctor M'Hale then withdrew.

Baron Richards.—Is there any possibility of the parties arranging this case before the record is opened.

Mr. Keating, Q.C.—If the Plaintiff, my Lord, withdraws the record, we shall not ask any costs.

Mr. O'Malley.—Vastly civil, Mr. Keating.

It appears from the same pamphlet, p. 2, that—

Mr. O'Dowd then opened the pleadings. The Rev. Michael Gallaher, Roman Catholic Curate, was the Plaintiff, and the Honorable Frederick Cavendish, the Defendant. The action was one for libels, printed and published in the *Mayo Telegraph* newspaper, of which the Defendant was the Proprietor. The declaration contained the prefatory averment, that the Plaintiff was a person in holy orders, discharging the duties of a Roman Catholic Curate, in the parish of Islandeady, Archdiocese of Tuam; and that Tobias Burke, and his son, John Burke, were residents of the same parish. The first count of the declaration averred that the Defendant, well knowing that the Plaintiff was a person of good temper, moderation, and benevolence, did publish in the *Telegraph*, of the 24th of March last, a false, scandalous, and malicious libel, headed " Undue Clerical Influence."

Baron Richards.—A printed sketch of the libel has been handed up to me, Mr. O'Dowd.

Mr. Keating, Q.C.—Oh, my Lord, they do not scruple printing and publishing what they allege to be a libel.

Mr. O'Dowd.—The second count charges the Defendant with publishing another libel in the *Telegraph*, of the 31st of March, reiterating the former scandalous statements, and further contriving to injure and vilify the Plaintiff's character. Mr. Cavendish pleaded the general issue in his first plea, and justification in his second and third pleas, and averred that the libel was true. Damages were laid at £1,000.

It appears from the opening speech to the jury of Mr. O'Malley, p. 3, that—

The Rev. Michael Gallaher, a Roman Catholic curate, of a remote parish, came forward into a Court of justice to seek at their hands, reparation from the Honourable Frederick Cavendish, the proprietor of the *Mayo Telegraph*, for having scandalously and maliciously inserted in his journal charges affecting the character of the Reverend Plaintiff as a man and a christian clergyman, and calculated from their intense malignity to degrade him in the eyes of his fellow-men."

It appears from p. 7 of this pamphlet, that Mr. O'Malley in his opening charge states, that —

On Sunday the 14th of March, the Rev. Michael Gallaher addressed the congregation assembled in the chapel of Islandeady, on the subject of the then ensuing election for Poor-law guardians, and without relation to Protestant or

Catholic,(s) he extolled the conduct of the late guardian, Mr. Conroy, as most exemplary, and called upon those qualified to vote to re-elect him, in preference to a mere stranger who cared not for their interests or welfare; but never for one moment did the Rev. Plaintiff contrast the religion of the candidates,(s) never for one instant did he attempt to excite a prejudical feeling against Mr. Brown (the other candidate) because of his being a Protestant.

Mr. O'Malley further states, according to this pamphlet, page 8, in his opening charge, as follows :—

On the 24th of last March, the Defendant, impelled by a sense of what he modestly terms public duty, published in the *Telegraph* an editorial article, from which I take the following libellous extract, headed " Undue Clerical Influence : Parish of Islandeady"— " Conduct of a most atrocious nature was resorted to in this electoral district by the Rev. Michael Gallaher, R. C. C., for the purpose of intimidating the voters. On last Sunday week, after offering up the adorable sacrifice of the Mass, this gentleman, from the altar of the Islandeady chapel, dressed in his clerical robes, called on the congregation to vote against the Protestant candidates, as they could not possess sufficient honesty to discharge the duties of Poor Law Guardians. This in itself was a pretty specimen of disgusting bigotry and intolerant sectarianism, but not at all sufficient to gratify the voracious appetite of the gall-hearted minister. It so happened that Tobias Burke, Esq., an

---

(s s) It will be seen presently that on this point, as well as upon the *very material* point, whether the curse was conditional or absolute, and followed by a prayer for the amendment of the party on whose head the curse was invoked, the witnesses *swear* in direct and irreconciliable opposition to each other; both parties *agreeing in the fact*, that the priest spoke with a loud voice in by no means a large chapel.—C.

extensive Roman Catholic landed proprietor, and a magistrate of this county, beloved by his tenantry, and respected by all who know him, had the unparalleled impertinence and presumption, in defiance of the Rev. Mr. Gallagher's admonitions, *to express a wish* to those voters resident on his property to record their votes in favor of a Protestant candidate. His son, a kind-hearted and excellent gentleman, was guilty of a similar offence. The rabid intolerance of the Roman Catholic Curate spurred him on to notice the interference of the Messrs. Burke; (*t*) *he invoked the curse of the Almighty God on their heads, and proclaimed aloud that his curse would rest on them* (*t*) *for ever.* A general murmur of indignation ran through the congregation—the daughter of Mr. Burke, who was present, fainted, (*u*) and altogether the scene was one of the most appalling ever witnessed in the house of God. But Mr. Gallagher continued giving vent to his wicked imprecations and blasphemy on the very spot where, but a few minutes before, *he partook of the blessed Eucharist.* Frightful reflection! Our flesh creeps at the idea, and we actually freeze with horror. Painful is the task of a Journalist, in the conscientious discharge of his duty, to arraign at the bar of public opinion the conduct of some few Roman Catholic Clergymen; but, when we find them actually polluting and debasing the religion of which they are ministers, we cannot avoid particularising the guilty members, in order that the exemplary body at large may *not be censured*

(*t t*) It will be seen presently, that the curse was invoked on the head of *only one person.* These observations are by no means unimportant, as shewing the *natural irritating effect* on Protestants of a non-compliance on the part of Catholic priests, with the injunctions of the resolutions of 1830 and 1834—see pages 174 and 178 of these letters.—C.

(*u*) Of this alleged fact, no evidence appears to have been given in court. If the fact were not so, the misinformation given on this point is another proof of the *excitation* of the parties.—C.

for their demon fury and bigot revilings." That is the publication, gentlemen, which the Defendant in his plea thinks proper to tell you is a fair and *bona fide* comment on the proceedings in the chapel of Islandeady on the 14th of March last. For you, gentlemen, will it be to consider whether the comment is fair or otherwise. For you, and for you alone, will it be to declare whether it was within his duty as a Newspaper Proprietor to publish such an atrocious libel. Was such a production the emanation of momentary reflection—was his object to ensure the success of the Protestant candidate, Mr. Henry Browne, or, gentlemen, for the more malignant purpose of turning the whole (*v*) Roman Catholic priesthood of Ireland into disrepute and heaping obloquy on them? The learned Counsel proceeded to comment on the above quoted extract at some length, and then alluded to the publication of the alleged libellous article in the *Telegraph* of the 31st of March:—" In the *Freeman's Journal* of the 27th instant, we find a most offensive epistle addressed to the Editor, and bearing the signature of ' A Mayo Layman.' We know not who the correspondent of our cotemporary may be, but as he has deemed it prudent—not only to animadvert on the conduct of the Hon. Mr. Cavendish, and considered it advisable deliberately to publish most unfounded assertions, but also to misrepresent, in the grossest manner possible, the principles of the *Mayo Telegraph*, we feel ourselves imperatively called upon to enter into a refutation of the base and malignant calumnies, as well as to expose the repre-

---

(*v*) I should say, and I think every impartial reader of these pages *must* say, " neither the one nor the other." The *object* of the editor clearly was, to discountenance political invective and defamation under false pretences, by Catholic priests, of political opponents, from the altar during divine service. He seems in one or two *expressions*, to have committed himself; but of his object, in which he is fully warranted by the resolution, p. 178 of these letters, there can be no doubt.—C.

hensible insinuations in which he has indulged. The subject is very irksome and unpleasant in itself—but more so is the recrimination which it necessarily involves. But a ' Mayo Layman' has only himself to blame, if his character suffers in the conflict. If he considers it honourable, under a feigned signature, to impute the basest motives to a high minded man,—if he holds himself justified in studiously distorting and misrepresenting facts, why, then, if he contradicts his unpalatable (*w*)—if it is harsh—for truth is sometimes harsh—he can only censure his own conduct, which has rendered such unqualified contradiction and consequent exposure, absolutely indispensable. In the conscientious discharge of our duty as public journalists, we commented, in our last publication, on the indecency and injustice of some few members of the Roman Catholic clergy exercising their sacerdotal rights over the secular acts of their flocks, by traversing the Electorial districts of this Union—visiting the houses of the qualified voters—possessing themselves of several voting papers by force and fraud —and actually filling them up in favour of the Catholic candidates, without the consent or even knowledge of the voters themselves. We also exposed the disgusting bigotry and intolerant sectarianism of the Rev. Michael Gallagher, Roman Catholic Curate of the parish of Islandeady, who, in the presence of Tobias Burke's daughter, invoked the curse of the almighty God on his head and that of his son, *because* (*x*) this kind-hearted gentleman and excellent Catholic landlord had the unparalleled presumption

---

(*w*) Query ! Should not the text stand thus—if the contradiction with which he meets be unpalatable ?

(*x*) If this word which is in Italics in the pamphlet, was *so* in the *Telegraph*, it must surely be admitted by the editor that his zeal has carried him beyond the bounds of what *fact* would justify. The reason *given* by the priest was not that here assigned. The editor should have left to his readers to judge whether the reason *given* was the *real* one.—C.

to favour the Protestant candidate in his Electoral division, by *merely expressing a wish* that his tenantry should vote for him. We certainly blushed to find so bigoted and sectarian a spirit prevailing in Connaught, and we felt not a little annoyed that the Roman Catholic priesthood of Ireland—the great majority of whom are a credit to old Erin, and a source of the most profound comfort to her people(*y*)—should be contaminated by the adhesion of such " *gall-hearted member*." Hence the cause of our *exposé* ; but we took particular care, when levelling our animadversions against the Rev Mr. Gallaher and other ministers, " to distinctly name the object of our indignation that no stigma or foul blot might be attached to the exemplary body at large, and that they should not be censured for the demon fury and bigot revilings of a few unworthy members." Here we have the identical charges, but not in the same language, preferred against the Rev. Michael Gallaher. Is it a fair or *bona fide* comment on Mr. Gallaher's conduct, such as the editor of a journal should put forward? Counsel, after some further observations on the verbiage of the libels, made allusions to the pleas of justification put upon the record by the Defendant, in which he stated and advisedly affirmed, that the Plaintiff was fairly and truly designated " a gall-hearted minister ;" that he gave vent to wicked imprecations and blasphemy on the very spot where, but a few moments before, he partook of the blessed sacrament, that his conduct was bigotted and arrogant, and that the supposed libel contained nothing but a fair and accurate report of the blasphemous words spoken by the Plaintiff in the chapel of Islandeady, with a fair and *bona*

(*y*) The reader will not fail to remark how *pointedly*, in this and in other passages, the editor of the *Telegraph* has endeavoured to preclude the *possibility* of the imputation put upon his article by Mr. O'Malley.—See p. 223. —C.

fide editorial commentary, published by the Defendant with no scandalous, malicious, defamatory, or unlawful motive, but in the discharge of his duty as a public journalist. Mr. Cavendish avers that every scintilla of what he put forward touching Mr. Gallaher's conduct is true, and when he attempts to place on the record a plea of justification, the learned judge will tell you that, in point of law, should he fall short of substantiating every one of his averments, it will be your bounden duty to return a verdict for the Plaintiff ; and I must say that in doing so, his having failed to prove every statement should be a presumption in your mind of his malicious intent in publishing the libel, and a strong inducement to increase the damages instead of reducing them. Gentlemen of the Jury, a more ingenious or clever attempt to stab and vilify, and defame a great and venerated body through the medium of a poor Curate, I never recollect to have heard ; but, gentlemen, we shall prove to your satisfaction, if necessary, that greater falsehoods were never penned or published. Mr. Gallaher, my client, it is most true, expressed a wish to his flock to record their votes in favor of Mr. Conroy, but to declare that he invoked the curse of the Almighty God on the heads of Tobias Burke and his son, John Burke, because they presumed to favor the Protestant candidate in their electoral district, is as absurd as it is malicious, as malicious as it is unfounded ; and, should my learned friends so far violate the bounds of common decency as to go into such a gross case, I, gentlemen, and those with me, will be able to give it a most complete and triumphant denial. Many of you, gentlemen, are aware that it is not unusual on the part of Roman Catholic Clergymen to allude before their flock to any gross violation of public morality. This was precisely what my client did. This is the crime which the *Mayo Telegraph* insidiously terms " invoking the curse of the Almighty God on a kind-hearted Roman Catholic gentleman and excellent landlord." After having given his advice in the chapel of Islandeady on the subject of the Poor Law Guardians, the Rev. Michael Gallaher turned round to the Altar and took from it a paper, and again addressing the congregation, he stated that he had now to speak on a different subject altogether. When private remonstrance had failed to correct gross immorality, he stated it to be his duty, and the duty of every Catholic minister anxious for the eternal happiness of those confided to him, to hold up the perpetrators of such immorality to the observation of the people, with a view to deter others from following the bad example. This my client did in the discharge of his clerical duties, and he named three persons on whose misconduct, with regard to the seduction of female virtue in the parish, he commented at some length. Having animadverted on the malpractices of individuals moving in an humble sphere of life, he observed that he could not pass over the conduct of a person who was called, or supposed to be a gentleman, namely, Mr. John Burke, the son of Tobias Burke, who seduced a servant girl named Kitty Walsh. Mr. Gallaher stated that Mr. Burke was the more culpable person of the two, the poor female being an ignorant, uninstructed person, while he had received an education which should have prevented him from committing such an outrage upon public morals; but what added to the enormity of the offence was, that the poor female had been with her child in misery and poverty, in another part of the parish without any provision for her support, or that of his child.(z) Now, gentlemen of the Jury, it was Mr. Gallaher's

---

(z) See the evidence *on oath* on this point of Mr. John Burke, infra p. 225. It may appear surprising to some that the girl herself was not subpœnaed *by either party.*—C.

P 2

duty to have so spoken; he would have been highly culpable had he not taken every means in his power to prevent the bad example which had been given, from operating injuriously on the minds of his parishioners. He spoke, it may have been strongly, and with severity, of the several persons upon whose conduct he had animadverted; but certainly neither the Proprietor nor the Editor of the *Mayo Telegraph*, had any right to outrage the rules of decency by calling him for so doing—" a gall-hearted minister"—" a demon bigot "—a person whose adhesion to the body of the Catholic Clergy of which he was a member, would be contamination to them. No curse was invoked by Mr. Gallaher on the day in question upon any man, but he expressed his hope in the great God that the four individuals would repent of their sins, and not put off the day of penance until the vengeance of the Almighty had fallen on them. I indignantly deny that any curse whatsoever was used. There was nothing but a christian imploration to turn the wicked ones from their evil ways to the paths of justice and morality.

It appears from p. 13 of this pamphlet, that *Michael Quin*, a resident parishioner of the parish of Islandeady, *states on oath*, that the Rev. Richard Henry is parish priest, and has two curates, Mr. Gallaher and Mr. Gill; the Plaintiff generally officiates at Glanisland Chapel until lately, since Mr. Gill came ; he sometimes used to officiate before that at Islandeady ; his residence was nearer to Islandeady than Glanisland ; that—

Mr. Browne's estate is considered very trifling; he holds it all in his own hands, and has no tenants. Mr. Browne is called a Protestant; does not know if he is one. Mr. Browne does not go to mass, nor to Church either, as witness believes; witness was never in Church, nor does he intend going there. Mr. Conroy, the other candidate, has no property in Islandeady; he lives in Castlebar; believes he kept a shop there some time ago; he was elected Guardian last year, and this year also.

It appears from p. 15 of this pamphlet, that Archbishop M'Hale *states upon oath* that he—

Has read the paragraph pointed out to him before now; read it about the time of its publication; cannot say that he read it in the county of Galway; believes the *Telegraph* newspaper is circulated in this county; knows it only as a matter of notoriety which cannot be disputed, unless in a legal sense.

Cross-examined by Mr. Keating. — Knows the Rev. Richard Henry. Mr. Henry is Rector of the Parish of Islandeady; that is the correct parlance, not as put by Mr. Keating—rector of the Rev. Mr. Gallaher. Cannot be accurate as to date, but thinks Mr. Henry has been rector about two years, since the death of the Rev. Mr. M'Mahon. The Plaintiff, the Rev. Michael Gallaher, has been Curate of Islandeady for three or four years, and was so before Mr. Henry became rector; witness as diocesan had given general instructions, that where there were two chapels and two curates, the curates should attend each chapel on Sundays alternately; has not heard particularly as regards Islandeady as to the practice, whether these instructions have been observed or not.

Mr. Keating asked his Grace, did those paragraphs on perusal lower Mr. Gallaher in his estimation?

Mr. Fitzgibbon objected to the question, as the fact of the Plaintiff's character having suffered, was the issue for the jury, and that issue did not depend on the individual opinion of his Grace.

After some discussion the question was allowed to be put, and his Grace said—that they did not lower the Rev. Plaintiff in his estimation, the attention he paid them was very slight; he is not disposed, nor is he in the habit to form his estimate of his clergy by paragraphs in newspapers; he should be very sorry to depend on such publications for means of judging of the merits or demerits of his clergy; anything appearing in certain journals could have no weight with him as to the credit or discredit of Catholic clergymen.

Mr. Keating asked, if the statements made in the alleged libels were true, would they be consistent with the discipline and duties of the Catholic clergy?

His Grace was about to answer, when Baron Richards said, that he could not permit such a supposition to be a question in a court of law in a Christian land; he could not, by allowing the question to be put, sanction the supposition that it could be a question in a Christian land.

It appears from the same pamphlet, p. 16, that—

Christopher Birmingham was next produced and examined by Mr. Baker.—He deposed that the *Telegraph* circulated in the county Galway; read the publications of the 24th and 31st March, containing the libellous articles.

Mr. Monahan, Q.C.—Pray when did you read them?

Witness.—*About five minutes since*, in the Criminal Court, at the solicitation of Mr. Conroy.

The learned Judge stated, that it was highly improper for Mr. Conroy to pursue such a line of conduct. Have you any other witnesses to produce?

Mr. Fitzgibbon.—Oh! yes, my Lord.

Baron Richards.—If you do not produce one immediately, I must nonsuit the Plaintiff instantly.

Michael Mannion was next tendered; but he having been in court during a part of the trial, the Judge ruled that his evidence was inadmissible.

It appears from the same pamphlet, p. 16, that it was stated *on oath* by—

The Rev. Richard Henry the next witness.—That he knew the *Telegraph* newspaper; he had read a good many numbers of that paper in the county Galway, and at different periods; it was eight or nine years ago since first he read the *Telegraph* in Galway county, and from that time he has occasionally read it in Galway up to the present time; lives in the parish of Islandeady, in the county Mayo; was not in the county Galway in March last; was in the county Galway in last January; certainly read the *Telegraph* in this county in January last; cannot speak from his own knowledge of the circulation of the *Telegraph* in this county.

Cross-examined by Mr. Keating.—The Plaintiff, Rev. Michael Gallaher, is one of witness's Curates; the practice was, that the curates should officiate alternately in the two chapels; has not been absent many Sundays since appointed to the parish; has seen Mr. Gallaher officiating at the chapel of Islandeady about two Sundays in the month; knows Mr. Tobias Burke and his sons; is not aware that he ever heard Mr. Gallaher express himself unkindly respecting Mr. Tobias Burke, or his sons, or any of them. Mr. John Burke has been intimate with witness until lately; they were intimate in March last. Mr. John Burke has dined at witness's house, not very often, perhaps twice; he dined with witness some days before the 14th of March last; cannot say how many clergymen were of the company on that occasion, about four or five; thinks the Reverend Plaintiff was one of those clergymen; recollects an evening party at witness's house, but cannot say whether it was before or after the dinner-party alluded to; hopes it will not be the last dinner or evening party he will give, and he will be glad to see Mr. Keating at his house if he should pass that way (laughter); his house is four miles from Castlebar, and four from Westport, just the half-way, and he would feel most happy if Mr. Keating would make it a half-way house (continued laughter); is always glad to see friends, and entertains them as well as he can; he might have given two or three evening parties since he went to Islandeady; remembers the particular evening party to which Mr. Keating alludes, when the fiddler played and danced; there were ladies at the first party; there were six at the evening party; Mr. John Burke was at that party; did not introduce Mr. John Burke to a lady that evening, as there was no necessity, he having been introduced to her long before; Mr. John Burke danced with *the* lady; Mr. O'Malley, another guest, danced with a child; witness did not dance that evening; considered Mr. John Burke fit company for respectable ladies, and respectable clergymen; thought him as a gentleman, a fit companion; had got notice to produce the register of his parish; the book is now in court, and can be produced; has seen in that book the baptism of the child before alluded to, registered in the handwriting of the Rev. Mr. Whelan, who was Curate of Islandeady; cannot exactly say when the child was baptized.

The registry-book was here produced, and the entry pointed out by the witness, which he stated was written by his Curate, Mr. Whelan, not at the time it bore date, but some months afterwards, when he was settling accounts with his Curate.

It appears from the same pamphlet, p. 18 to

p. 28, that Mr. Keating, Q.C., addressed the Jury for the Defendant, and p. 28 that—

When the eloquent and learned gentleman sat down, after a speech of nearly two hours' duration, the people who crowded the court house—and whose attention was so charmed by the eloquence which they had been devouring, that they forgot the place in which they were, expressed their admiration in loud applauses, as if the court house had been a theatre. It was with difficulty that the officers of the court could obtain a cessation of demonstration so unwonted.

It appears from the same statement, p. 28 to p. 33, that Richard Grady, Esq.

Was the first witness called and examined *(on oath)* for the defence by Mr. Monahan, Q.C.—Knows Mr. Tobias Burke, who is my father-in-law; that gentleman resides at Woodville, in the parish of Islandeady, county of Mayo, and is to my knowledge a Roman Catholic; his family consists of two sons and five daughters; the sons' names are Joseph and John; Joseph is the eldest; I cannot say what John's age is, but he has arrived at maturity, and is a grown-up man; three of the daughters are married; Mrs. O'Grady and two Mrs. Sheridans, the former being my wife; I have a perfect recollection that I heard mass in Islandeady chapel on Sunday, the 14th of last March.

Mr. Monahan, Q.C.—What members of Mr. Burke's family accompanied you to chapel?

Witness.—Mr. Joseph Burke, Mrs. Sheridan, Miss Ellen Burke, and Mrs. O'Grady; some of the nephews and nieces of Mr. Tobias Burke, and the O'Malleys of Cloonane, were also present; in fact the congregation was much larger on that day than I have seen it before.

Mr. Monahan, Q. C.—Who was the officiating clergyman?

Witness.—The Rev. Michael Gallaher, one of the Rev. Richard Henry's curates, who is the plaintiff in the present action.

Mr. Monahan, Q.C.—Was that clergyman in the habit of attending the chapel of Islandeady to celebrate mass?

Witness.—I do not recollect to have seen him officiating at the altar during the months of January or February last.

Mr. Monahan, Q.C.—Now state shortly and distinctly what occurred.

Witness.—During the service the reverend gentleman addressed the congregation in the Irish language, and announced that an election for poor law guardians was to take place in the following week, for certain districts in the Union of Castlebar, which he named; but he alluded more particularly to the divisions of Islandeady and Castlebar. Lord Lucan, he observed, had the presumption to nominate four candidates of his own choosing for Castlebar; he mentioned the names of these four persons, and their religions—George Ormsby, John Larminie, William Kearney, and James Malley, all of whom were Protestants. Reference was then made by him to the electoral district of Islandeady, and the candidates for the office of poor law guardian; for that district he stated there were two candidates, Mr. James Conry and Mr. Henry Browne, the latter of whom he termed " *Honrie na Prehawn*," that is " Henry of the Crows," and spoke of him in very disparaging terms. He made use of other expressions relative to this gentleman, but I cannot at this moment recal them to mind. He recommended Mr. Conry to the consideration of his flock in the strongest terms possible, and called upon those qualified to vote to re-elect him. He then went back, and adverted to the electoral district of Castlebar, where he stated Lord

Lucan supported four Protestant candidates for his own purposes and objects.

Mr. Monahan, Q.C.—Did he state what his motives or objects were?

Witness.—Yes: to take taxes off his own shoulders and place them on the poor people.

To Mr. Monahan, Q.C.—The Plaintiff mentioned the candidates nominated in opposition to Lord Lucan—Messrs. Remmy Carney, Henry Murphy, William Walsh, and Richard Morris—and observed that they were Roman Catholics and most worthy men, on whom the people could rely for protection from enormous and unnecessary taxation. Besides, continued Mr. Gallaher, they have my support and that of the rest of the clergymen.

Mr. Monahan, Q.C. — Did he make any, and what remarks as to the difference of religions professed by the respective candidates?

Witness.—Mr. Gallaher said that the persons on whom they could rely were of the Catholic creed : at least that is the construction I put upon what he uttered in the Irish language. I think he also remarked that the other candidates, who professed the Protestant religion, could not be relied upon.

Mr. Monahan, Q.C.—What did he say about those persons who supported the Protestant candidates?

Witness.—Lord Lucan's conduct, he observed, did not much surprise him, when he found such Roman Catholic gentlemen—if gentlemen they were—as Tobias Burke, and his son, John Burke, going on the same side with his Lordship.

Mr. Monahan, Q.C.—What were the Plaintiff's observations on the propriety or impropriety of having Protestant guardians?

Witness.—He spoke about the danger of electing such

men, as they would throw heavy and oppressive taxation upon the people.

Mr. Monahan, Q.C.——Now proceed to narrate the concluding portion of the reverend gentleman's observations on the election of poor law guardians.

Witness.——The Catholic gentlemen he accused with supporting my Lord Lucan's candidates were Tobias Burke, and his son, John Burke; who, he stated, went to the tenants on a farm called Graffymore, and told them to give their votes to Mr. Larminie, one of Lord Lucan's nominees, all because Larminie was in the habit of giving them loan money to pay their rack-rents, the profit of which their miserable holdings could not otherwise afford. He hoped the tenants would not attend to Mr. John Burke's arbitrary directions—that he was well aware of the persecution practised on them, and he would give an instance of it, namely, that the Graffymore tenants were in the habit of going a great distance to do Tobias Burke's work and business throughout the year, and were obliged to bring their own buttermilk with them. He also said something else about Mr. Burke and his tenantry which I do not recollect; it was in a strain of invective, to the effect that he was a harassing and oppressive landlord. Mr. Gallaher having enlarged considerably on the subject of the poor law guardian elections, concluded by calling on the tenants of Mr. Burke not to do the bidding of their master. He then commenced speaking of the immorality of some of his parishioners, whom he charged with having taken away girls, and then refusing to marry them until they succeeded in exacting from their parents a marriage portion which they could not, consistently or honestly, towards either themselves or the rest of their children, attempt to give. After abusing these immoral characters, he called them several opprobrious epithets, *which created considerable merriment and laughter.*

Baron Richards.——In the chapel?

Witness.——Yes, my Lord.

Mr. Monahan, Q.C.——What were the opprobrious epithets?

Witness.——Why he called them *loragnie brac, loragnie dhothy*, the English translation of which is " spotted shins, or burned shins."

Mr. Monahan, Q. C.——Did Mr. Gallaher curse any of those persons charged by him with immorality?

Witness.——Most positive am I that he did not.

Mr. Monahan, Q. C. —— Did Mr. Gallaher make any further observations?

Witness.——There was another case, he observed, to which he considered it his duty to refer; Mr. John Burke, one of his parishioners, having seduced a servant girl, Kitty Walsh, living in his father's house. The girl, he stated, had a female child by him, and was christened Biddy Walsh. She now resided at the lower end of the parish in a state of misery and destitution, without any means of support for either herself or child.

Mr. Monahan, Q.C.——Did the reverend Plaintiff make use of that observation?

Witness.——The words he used were " that she now resided in the lower end of the parish in misery and wretchedness, without any means of subsistence whatsoever either for herself or child."(*aa*) He also added that she was highly culpable, but he was more so——she being an illiterate uneducated person; that he ought to know better, if he had any information, which he believed was very little indeed. After commenting and eulogising a good deal on this topic, he called out in a loud tone, " *Bherimshe gho Shaun O'Bourka molacht Dhia agus molacht en pubil shoh.*" The literal translation of which is, " I give him the curse of God and the curse of this flock or congregation."

(*aa*) See note (*z*) on p. 227.

Baron Richards.—Who did he allude to?

Witness.—Mr. John Burke. In fact he named him distinctly.

Baron Richards.—Repeat the precise words he used in the Irish language.

Witness.—" *Bherimshe gho Shaun O'Bourka molacht Dhia agus molacht en pubil shoh.*"

Mr. Monahan, Q. C.—Did Mr. Gallaher conclude his statement concerning the immorality of the other three persons with a curse?

Witness.—Certainly not.

Court.—Where was Mr. Gallaher standing at this time?

Witness.—On the altar, with his back to the tabernacle, and dressed in his clerical robes.

Mr. Monahan, Q.C.—What impression did Mr. Gallaher's conduct make upon the congregation?

Witness.—They did not join in the malediction or imprecation, but the sensation created by the denunciation was of an awful and painful character. The usual method of giving expression to feelings of dissent was adopted, and several persons behind me in the gallery cried out " *nar dhug a Dhia ard ar*," "God don't hear him." The expression from the congregation was one of horror: they gave vent to their feelings by a noise made with the lips and tongue—a sort of smacking. My wife was beside me in the chapel: at the time of the execration she rather cheered up and smiled, evidently endeavouring to conceal her indignation. From my own observation I did not perceive any other effect, but she told me—

Mr. Fitzgibbon.—Never mind, sir; what she told you.

Witness.—Well, I'm content.

Mr. Monahan, Q.C.—Did you observe anything else?

Witness.—Yes: Miss Ellen Burke appeared much agitated, and cried from the commencement of the imprecation to the conclusion. When this subject was over, Mr. Gallaher announced that there would be a collection for crosses, when Mass was over, at the chapel door. He then pointed to one of the doors that was open, and directed it to be closed—finished reading Mass (*bb*)—read the prayer for the dead, the *De profundis*, and went to superintend the collection. I and my wife, on going out, gave sixpence each ; when the Plaintiff, who was next to the collector, smiled, and thanked us for it.

Mr. Monahan, Q.C.—What property has your father-in-law, Mr. Burke ?

Witness.—I was always under the impression that it was upwards of £400. a year ; indeed, I heard it was more. He is a man of extremely benevolent disposition and charitably disposed. I have frequently heard his tenants remark upon his kindness of heart towards them.

Cross-examined by Mr. O'Malley.—The *De profundis* or prayer for the dead generally follows the last gospel. Mass concludes at that time when the priest says *Ite missa est.* The priest unrobes himself previous to the *De profundis.* The people do not immediately leave the chapel after that prayer.

Mr. O'Malley.—You stated that there was merriment in the chapel when Mr. Gallaher spoke about the three persons guilty of immorality, and you added that the crying

---

(*bb*) This statement, if correctly reported, indicates the existence of a practice in Ireland peculiar to that country, of which any one who has attended mass as celebrated in a Catholic chapel in any country according to the Latin rite, must be instantly persuaded. It is almost incredible that the Rev. Mr. Gallaher *could* have addressed his congregation till the mass was finished by the words *Deo gratias, after* the reading of the last gospel ; though, *before* the reading of the last gospel, the priest turns round and says to the congregation *Ite missa est*, the meaning of which is, You may depart, mass is finished.

did not commence until after *the curse* was invoked on Mr. John Burke's head.

Witness.—Just so.

Mr. O'Malley.—Did your sisters-in-law join in that merriment?

Witness.—I cannot say that they did. I did not observe them.

Mr. O'Malley.—Did you observe Mr. Gallaher, after he had concluded his observations on the subject of the poor law guardians, turning round to the altar, and taking any paper off it, before he commenced speaking about the immorality of his parishioners?

Witness.—I cannot recollect that I observed him doing any such thing.

Mr. O'Malley.—How long did you remain in the parish of Islandeady after Sunday, the 14th of March?

Witness.—About three days, I should think.

To Mr. O'Malley.—My father-in-law holds a good deal of land—he is a grazier. Sir Roger Palmer, Lord Sligo, and Lord Kilmain, are his landlords. His leases, I believe, are all determinable. Mr. Gallaher did not accompany the curse by any qualification. He did not call on the flock to pray for the conversion of Mr. John Burke.

Mr. O'Malley.—You stated that the people joined in a prayer at the conclusion of Mass; now, was not that prayer for the conversion of the three parishioners, guilty of immorality, from their evil ways?

Witness.—No. The prayer was the usual one for the repose of the dead.

Juror.—Did it appear to you that Mr. Gallaher cursed Mr. John Burke from motives of hostility towards that gentleman or his family?

Mr. Baker.—I must object to the witness answering that question on the ground of its illegality. The jury have been empanelled to try the very matter a juror wishes to have from Mr. O'Grady.

Baron Richards.—Just so, Mr. Baker. I cannot allow the question to be answered.

Mr Keating, Q.C.—We have not the slightest objection to that question or any other Plaintiff's counsel may be pleased to put the witness.

To Mr. O'Malley.—Mr. Tobias Burke derives his principal interest from lands let to tenants : I do not think he holds any fee simple property in the county Mayo.

Mr. O'Malley.—Did Mr. Gallaher accompany his curse on Mr. John Burke with any qualification ?

Witness.—None, whatever.

Mr. O'Malley.—Did he not call on the congregation to pray for his conversion ?

Witness.—Certainly not. (*cc*)

Mr. O'Malley.—What distance were you from the Altar ?

Witness.—About the breadth of the Court-house.

Mr. O'Malley.—Was your attention closely fixed on the clergyman during the entire of the scene you have described ?

Witness.—Particularly so.

Mr. Keating, Q.C.—The learned counsel for the Plaintiff require not your presence any longer, Mr. O'Grady.

It appears from the same statement, p. 33 to p. 35, that—

Mrs. J. O'Grady, wife to the former witness, and daughter to Mr. Tobias Burke, was next *examined on oath* by Mr. Armstrong—I was in the chapel of Islandeady on Sunday

---

(*cc*) See conclusion of Mr. O'Malley's address to the Jury. — Supra p. 228, and Michael Quin's evidence, infra p. 269.—C.

Q

the 14th of March last, in company with my sisters, two of whom are married ; the congregation was unusually crowded on that day ; I am personally acquainted with the Rev. Michael Gallaher, the Plaintiff in the present action, who officiated at the Altar.

Mr. Armstrong.—Do you recollect Mr. Gallaher, on that Sunday, having made use of some observation unconnected—totally unconnected—with the religious service?

Witness.—Perfectly.

Mr. Armstrong.—At what time did he make use of those observations ?

Witness.—After the last Gospel. (*dd*)

Mr. Armstrong.—Previous to, or before the termination of, the service ?

Witness.—At the conclusion of the Mass.

Mr. Armstrong.—Can you repeat the substance of what he said ?

Witness.—He stated, in the Irish language, that an election for Poor-Law Guardians would shortly take place, and mentioned the day on which they were to be elected.

Baron Richards.—Do you understand the Irish language ?

Witness.—Yes, my lord, but I do not speak it well.

To Mr. Armstrong.—Mr. Gallaher spoke about the election of Poor-Law Guardians, and alluded to those Protestant Candidates for whose success Lord Lucan was anxious ; he mentioned their names but I do not recollect them.

Mr. Armstrong.—Did he state whether he wished the people to vote for the Protestant or Catholic Candidates ?

Witness.—He expressed a wish that the Catholics might be returned, and assigned as a reason something about oppression and the payment of heavy taxes. He also spoke

---

(*dd*) See note (*aa*) p. 229.—C.

about my father, who, he stated, was influencing his tenantry to vote for the Protestant candidate, Mr. Larminie, in order that they may get loan money from him to pay their ruinous rack rents.

Mr. Armstrong.—What was the next topic of his conversation ?

Witness.—He spoke about my brother John, and brought an unpleasant charge against him—that he had seduced a girl who had a child by him.

Mr. Armstrong—Did he say anything about baptism ?

Witness.—The child, he stated, was christened Biddy Burke. (*ee*) I do not remember that he mentioned the woman's name, but he made use of very strong language towards my brother, abused and cursed him.

Baron Richards.—What do you mean by abusing him? What were the precise words he used ?

Witness.—He said that John Burke was influencing my father's tenants to vote for the Protestant candidates, and added a great deal more to which I did not pay particular attention until he commenced cursing.

Baron Richards.—How did he curse him ? What were the words he used ?

Witness.—" I give John Burke the curse of God and the curse of the congregation."—(Sensation.)

Baron Richards.—Repeat that in Irish.

Witness.—" *Bherimshe gho Shaun O'Bourka molacht Dhia agus molacht en pubil shoh.*"

Mr. Armstrong—What happened to you in consequence of hearing your brother cursed ?

Witness.—I felt quite weak, and became sick, and much agitated.

(*ee*) Vide supra, p. 237, l. 21. The *name* of the child *may* appear no immaterial point *to a magistrate*, as evidence of the *intention* of the father to support his child and its unfortunate mother.—C.

Mr Armstrong—How were you affected ?   Did the male-diction produce any subsequent disappointment ?

Baron Richards—Allow the lady to tell how she felt.

Witness.—I was but badly able to walk out of the chapel.

Mr. Armstrong.—Had you any disappointment or mishap ?

Mr. Baker objected to the question.   Mrs. O'Grady could not, he contended, be examined as to her after condition, as the plea did not extend to it.   The defendant merely alleged that she fainted *at the time.*

Baron Richards concurred in Mr. Baker's opinion.   The question was illegal and should not be answered.

Mr. Armstrong.—Now, Mrs. O'Grady, can you recollect whether Mr. Gallaher cursed any other persons on that day ?

Witness.—I am quite satisfied that he did not.

Mr. Armstrong.—What was the sensation produced in the chapel when he invoked the curse of God on Mr. John Burke's head ?

Witness.—I heard many people exclaim that it was a great shame for him to do so.

Cross-examined by Mr. Baker.—I observed a bit of paper in Mr. Gallaher's hands at the time he was speaking from the Altar, but I do not know what it was, nor am I aware it was sent to Mr. Gallaher by Mr. Henry, directing him to denounce from the Altar certain persons guilty of immorality.   I saw the girl, Kitty Walsh, on two or three occasions, but until that Sunday I never heard of the occurrence made mention of by Mr. Gallaher.   It was never stated, to my knowledge, that the Rev. Mr. Henry had interfered to put an end to the connection.

Mr. Baker.—Well, ma'am, you may go down.

It appears from the same pamphlet, p. 35, that—

Joseph Burke, Esq. was next *sworn and examined* by Mr. Armstrong.—Is son of Mr. Tobias Burke, of Woodville, in the county Mayo, and recollects having been at the chapel of Islandeady, on Sunday, the 14th day of March last, in company with his three sisters and brother-in-law, Mr. O'Grady; Mr. Gallaher, the Plaintiff, officiated on that day; that reverend gentleman was in the habit of attending at the chapel; the congregation was particularly large on the occasion referred to. Previous to the conclusion of the service, the Plaintiff spoke of the elections of Poor-Law Guardians for the electoral districts of Castlebar and Islandeady, and named the day on which they were to take place; he made allusion to the Earl of Lucan, and said, that his Lordship was using his influence to have persons of his own persuasion—Protestants, returned as guardians for Castlebar; he named the persons, among them Mr. Larminie, and animadverted a great deal on Lord Lucan's conduct in presuming to have persons of his own choosing nominated as Poor-Law Guardians; Mr. Gallaher then spoke of the persons he wished to have returned, namely—Mr. Henry Murphy, Richard Morris, Redmond Carney, and William Walsh, all of whom, he said, were good Catholics; he named the candidates for the electoral district of Islandeady —Mr. Henry Browne and Mr. James Conry, and mentioned their religions. They all, he stated, knew who Mr. Henry Browne was—*Honrie na Prehawn*—and a Protestant, while Mr. Conry was one of their own persuasion—a Roman Catholic, and lauded him to the highest, saying, that he was a person who would see justice done them; is acquainted with Conry; he is not at present in any business; he was not at that time in any business, but he had been before when he kept a shop in Castlebar.

Mr. Armstrong.—Is Conry, or was he at the time of the election, a landholder in the electoral district of Islandeady?

Witness.—He did not hold as much as a foot of land to

my knowledge. Mr. Henry Browne has a very nice property in that parish, and resides on it. The name of his place is, Rehins.

Mr. Armstrong.—Now, state everything that took place in the chapel of Islandeady on the 14th of March last.

Witness.—Mr. Gallaher said, that if Mr. Henry Browne was elected as Guardian, he would throw the taxes off his own shoulders and place them on the poor people. He then made allusion to Lord Lucan, and stated it was not to be wondered at that his Lordship should support Protestant candidates, when there were persons in the parish of Islandeady, bearing the name of Catholics and gentlemen—if gentlemen they were—who were acting the same part, aiding and assisting him. He then named my father and brother as the individuals to whom he alluded, and added, that John went through the tenantry using undue influence with them to support the Protestant candidates. He hoped, however, that the unfortunate harassed tenants would not be led or said by him. My brother, he said, had stated to the tenantry that he was their master, and that they should vote as he directed them.

Mr. Armstrong.—Can you recollect any other expression which he made use of ?

Witness.—He repeatedly charged my brother with coercing the tenants to vote for the Protestant candidate ; but, said he, thank God, he has very little influence with his own poor, half-starved, miserable, wretched creatures. My father he denounced as a harsh and cruel Landlord, whose tyranny and oppression could not be equalled ; that he set his land so high, they could not possibly pay the rent but by getting loan money from Mr. Larminie, one of the Protestant Poor-Law candidates, whom he supported.

To the Court.—Mr. Larminie is Secretary or Agent to a Charitable Loan Fund.

Examination continued by Mr. Armstrong.—Mr. Galla-

her then stated that he would give an instance of my
father's cruelty and harshness, to the tenantry, namely—
that they were obliged to come great distances throughout
theyear to do his work, and to bring their own butter-milk
for their consumption; he expressed a hope that they would
support the Catholic candidates, and stated that he would
arrange a day to meet them and sign the voting papers; he
was confident they would act right, and refuse to give any
support whatsoever to the Protestant candidates as the
Catholics were the men who would keep down heavy and
oppressive taxation. Having concluded his lecture on the
election of Poor-Law Guardians, he then turned to another
subject, that there were persons in the parish who had taken
away girls, and were living with them, not consenting to
marry them, in the hope of extorting fortunes from their
parents, to which they were not by any means entitled.
He called these persons opprobrious names, that caused
laughter—such as " burned shins"—" spotted shins "—and
others which I cannot, at the present moment, recollect.
He abused them heartily for not marrying the women they
had taken off.

Mr. Armstrong.—Did Mr. Gallaher state anything about
your brother?

Witness.—Yes; he said there was another person in the
parish who brought a servant maid, residing in his father's
house, to misfortune; that she had a child by him, and that
she was residing in the lower part of the parish in the
greatest poverty, my brother refusing to give her any support; he named the girl, Kitty Walsh, and mentioned
distinctly John Burke, Tobias Burke's son, as the immoral
person to whom he alluded, He then said, in the Irish
language, " *I give, or I invoke on John Burke, the curse of
the Almighty God, and the Catholic congregation.*" This
imprecation caused very great excitement and sensation in

the chapel ; there was smacking of the tongue, and a general cry of " *oh Dhia ! Dhia !* " I did not hear any of the congregation say anything more. Shortly after Mr. Gallaher concluded, I observed my sister, Eleanor, crying, and, apparently, very much affected ; Mrs. O'Grady, my married sister, was in a tremor ; in fact, all the family appeared very uneasy and annoyed. I was near enough to Mrs. O'Grady to observe her minutely. Mr. Gallaher did not curse any of the other persons he named about the girls. During the time of the discourse and imprecation, Mr. Gallaher was standing on the Altar, dressed in his clerical robes ; he did not preach any sermon on that day, and I am not quite certain whether he read the Gospel of the day or not ; but he certainly gave no exposition, explanation, or discourse on it.

It appears from the same pamphlet, p. 38, that Mr. Joseph Burke was cross-examined by Mr. O'Malley, as follows—

Mr. O'Malley.—Had you any conversation with the Rev. Richard Henry about your brother and this girl, Kitty Walsh ?

Witness.—Mr. Henry, without mentioning names, alluded one day in the chapel of Islandeady, to a case of immorality, similar to that in which my brother had unfortunately been engaged ; and I told him that I suspected who the person was that he had hinted at, and I hoped he would not expose him, as I was sure he, my brother, had repented of his conduct, and ceased to have any connection or intercourse, for some time past, with the girl. (*ff*)

(*ff*) This evidence *on oath* is very material, when compared with the evidence also *on oath* of the same witness in line 14 of page 247.—C.

Mr. O'Malley.—When did you make that communication to Mr. Henry?

Witness.—About one month or so before the 14th of March.

Mr. O'Malley.—Did Mr. Henry communicate with you or your brother, before allusion was made in the chapel by him to the illicit connection?

Witness.—I am quite sure that he did not.

Mr. O'Malley.—Had you any communication with any member of your family before you went to speak to Mr. Henry about not calling out or exposing your brother? (*gg*)

Witness.—Upon my oath I had not.

Mr. O'Malley.—What was the allusion made to your brother by Mr. Henry, without mentioning names, on a former Sunday in the chapel of Islandeady?

Witness.—He said, that there was an unfortunate girl living in the parish, who, he had heard, was in the family-way, and he would curse her if she did not leave it immediately.

Mr. O'Malley.—Did you not take that as a friendly hint?

Witness.—I did not.

To Mr. O'Malley.—My father's house is about one quarter-of-a-mile distant from the chapel of Islandeady; I cannot say whether Mr. O'Grady has a better right to know what went on in the chapel than I have; it is not customary for the Clergyman to leave the Altar without first giving an exhortation; Mr. Gallaher, I am quite positive, read the last Gospel, if at all, and the *De profundis* after (*hh*) the discourse related; I cannot say whether the

---

(*gg*) The object of this question is evident, on comparing the answer to it with those given by the *sister of the witness* in her *cross*-examination. (See p. 244.)—C.

(*hh*) A positive contradiction given by the witness to his sister's evidence (see note (*dd*) p. 242); unless it can be *explained* by the last words of this

boys and girls spoken of were afterwards married or not ; Mr. Gallaher might have had a paper in his hands when he was commenting on the immorality of the men who took off the women, but I did not observe it ; I did not see him take anything off the Altar when he concluded his discourse on the Poor Law Guardians ; I intend paying my own expences ; my father has not, I am positive, indemnified Mr. Cavendish.

Mr. O'Malley (angrily)—Have any of your family, upon your oath.

Witness—I am quite sure they have not.

Mr. O'Malley—Did you relate to Mr. Cavendish what happened in the chapel.

Witness.—Upon my oath I did not, nor am I aware of any person having done so.

Mr. O'Malley.—Had you any conversation with him.

Witnes.—I might have conversed with him after the publication of the alleged libellous article.

Mr. Armstrong.—Now, Mr. Burke, you stated that you heard Mr. Browne had been dismissed from the magistracy ; can you assign any reason for that dismissal ?

Witness.—I heard he was dismissed because he wrote some letters to Lord Sligo, and not for any improper conduct, as he is a very good magistrate and a well conducted man.

To Mr. O'Malley.—Never heard that he was dismissed, for any other reason ; it was never stated, to my knowledge, that he was dismissed because he made use of violent inflammatory language in a speech at a Tithe meeting, for

---

witness, previous to his cross-examination.—p. 248, lines 13 and 14. It is customary in some chapels, after reading the *last* Gospel *in Latin*, to read again, *in the language of the country*, the *first* Gospel, called the Gospel *of the day*, and to explain *that* Gospel to the Congregation. In other chapels it is customary to do so after the *first* Gospel.—C.

which the Attorney General threatened to take an action
against him,

To Mr. Armstrong.—Two Gospels are read in Latin
during the service of the Mass.

Baron Richards—Are they read in Latin ?

Witness.—Yes, my Lord, and then the first one is translated into the English or Irish language and explained.

Baron Richards.—Were the two Latin Gospels read
before Mr. Gallaher spoke in the manner alleged ?

Witness.—The first Gospel only had been read, my
Lord. (*ii*)

Juror.—Did the curse come upon you very unexpectedly ?

Witness.—Very much so.

Juror.—Was the smacking of lips, which you described
on your direct examination as having been used by the congregation, indicative of horror at the crime upon which the
clergymen had been commenting, or disapprobation towards
him for his comments ?   What was your impression ?

Witness.—That it proceeded from horror at the priest
cursing and invoking the curse of the Almighty on a parishioner.

To another Juror.—On the day that I had a conversation
with the Rev. Mr. Henry, when I assured him that my
brother, to my certain knowledge, had no connexion or intercourse with the girl since she left my father's house, he
promised that there should be no more about it ; from the
day, on which I had that conversation, Mr. Henry never
alluded to the subject, and my impression was that he had
forgotten and forgiven it. (*kk*)

To Mr. O'Malley.—My brother dined with Mr. Henry
after that interview.

(*ii*) This evidence *on oath* appears to me to be utterly irreconcileable with
the evidence, p. 242, l. 12.—C.

(*k k*) See p. 256, l. 6.—C.

To Mr. Armstrong.—The girl received ample pecuniary compensation from my brother; whenever she required money he gave it to her.(*ll*)

To a Juror.—Never complained to Mr. Henry of Mr. Gallaher's conduct. Mr. Gallaher and another curate alternately officiated in the chapel of Islandeady. Understands that the girl came to reside within one mile of his father's house.

Another Juror.—Did she give any public scandal about your brother, or go to the chapel publicly and complain of his leaving her in a state of destitution?

Witness.—Certainly not, to my knowledge. Indeed I never even heard that she did so.

Mr. O'Malley submitted to the Court that after the examination of the last witness, the justification could go no further. It should have been set forth on the pleadings in the Irish language, and then translated.

Baron Richards.—You raise a very serious objection, Mr. O'Malley, of which I shall take a note, but I will not now stop the proceedings on the part of the defendant.

Mr Armstrong.—There would be a great difficulty, my Lord, I think, in getting a pleader who understood the Irish language so thoroughly as to be able to draw up a plea in it. Mr. O'Malley's point might be a very good one if the libel were written in the Irish language.

It appears from the same pamphlet, p. 40, that Mr. James Nolan was examined (on oath) by Mr. Monahan, Q.C. and stated as follows—

Resides in the parish of Kilfian; *is no relative or connexion whatsoever to the family of the Burkes ;* was at the chapel of Islandeady on the 14th of March last, when the

---

(*ll*) See note (z) p. 227.

Rev. Michael Gallaher, the plaintiff in the present action, officiated ; he addressed the congregation in the Irish language, after offering up the sacrament but previous to the public thanksgiving.

Mr. Monahan, Q.C.—Was that before or after the last Gospel ?

Witness.—Before the Gospel according to St. John ;(*mm*) he commenced by enlarging on the subject of the Poor-Law elections.

Baron Richards.—Had the sacrament been offered up before this discourse commenced ?

Witness.—Yes it was.

To Mr. Monahan, Q.C.—It is quite in my recollection that Mr. Gallaher read the Gospel of the day in Irish, but he did not expound or explain it ; there was a contrast made between the Protestant and Catholic guardians ; Mr. Gallaher stated that Lord Lucan and others of the party, termed the Tory party of the county, were, in their anxiety to have Protestant guardians returned for that electorial district, putting forward their nominees, but that the Catholics could not expect justice from Protestants, or the nominees of the Tory party, as they could from people of their own persuasion, and recommended by him ; if the Tories were elected, the poor people would have to pay more unnecessary taxes ; when he concluded speaking of the elections for Poor-Law guardians, he turned to another subject about persons taking away young girls and refusing to marry them until their parents gave an exorbitant marriage portion.

Baron Richards — What did he say about Mr. John Burke ?

Mr. Nolan—He stated that there was a girl in Mr.

(*mm*) See notes (*a a*) (*d d*) (*h h*) (*i i*).—C.

Tobias Burke's house, who had become pregnant by Mr. John Burke, and given birth to a child, of which that gentleman was the father ; he spoke a good deal on the enormity of Mr. John Burke seducing a young girl, and then leaving her in a state of indigence and destitution ; he could make no reparation as he had given much scandal ; she was at that time, he stated, living convenient to the chapel, and he invoked the curse of God and the curse of the congregation or Catholic Church on Mr. John Burke ; he said that twice.

Mr. Monahan, Q.C.—What effect did his malediction produce on the congregation ?

Witness.—The people appeared to feel it greatly, and there was a general murmur of indignation through the whole chapel.

Cross-examined by Mr. Baker.—I am sub-agent to Sir Roger Palmer ; I do not speak the Irish language very well ; I had no conversation with Mr. Cavendish before the publication of the alleged libellous articles in his journal ; indeed I never was in the habit of conversing much with him ; I know Mr. Gallaher very slightly ; I believe that he was introduced to me, but I never much admired him ; I may have said to others that he was a person I did not like over well.

Mr. Baker—Is there any difference between you ?

Witness—None, that I am aware of. I entertain no hostile feeling towards the man, but I do not admire him ; I did state that neither of the parties in this record were much liked by me : the Rev. James Hughes was present when I stated so ; I am quite disinterested in the matter ; I never told what happened in the chapel to Sir Roger Palmer.

Mr. Baker—I believe you paid more attention to what bore on the political question than to the other portions of Mr. Gallaher's discourse. ?

Witness—Indeed I did not.

Mr. Baker—Did you mention to your uncle the occurrence in the chapel?

Witness—I stated to him every thing that occurred.

Juror—Was the observation made by Mr. Gallaher, about Protestants not doing justice to the people, intended to reflect on Protestants in general, or confined merely to the Protestant candidates for the office of poor law guardians?

Witness—He alluded to Protestants in general; that is the impression on my mind.

Juror—That is not the way in Galway.

Mr. Baker—Will you, Sir, undertake to swear that Mr. Gallaher said from the altar that *Protestants* generally were not to be trusted, as they would not do justice to the people?

That is the substance of what he stated.

Mr. Baker—You do not understand the Irish language well?

Witness—I do not speak the language well; and I dare say many of the plaintiff's congregation understand it much better.

Mr. Baker—Then your knowledge of it is merely superficial?

Witness—By no means.

Juror—State in Irish what Mr. Gallaher said on the subject of Protestants not doing justice to the people.

Witness—I cannot well do so.

Juror—No matter; we can well understand a person being able to translate the language, and at the same time unable to speak it fluently.

To Mr. Baker—I served a latittat once at Tierena, but I did not know at the time what it was.

It appears from the same pamphlet, p. 42, that—

John Burke Esq. was examined *(on oath)* by Mr. Armstrong.—I am a son of Tobias Burke; I knew a servant girl, named Kitty Walsh, by whom I had, unfortunately, about Christmas last, a child; she was a servant in my father's house about twelve months; had no intercourse or connection with, nor did I ever see her, since she left my father's house about the end of August last, or the commencement of September;*(nn)* from that period, up to the present time, she has been supported by me.*(oo)*

Mr. Armstrong—Did you ever leave her in a destitute, unprovided state?

Witness—No. Whenever she required money, or sent for it, I gave it to her.

Mr. Armstrong—Are you acquainted with the Rev. Richard Henry, Parish Priest of Islandeady?

Witness—Yes, I was acquainted with him.

Mr. Armstrong—Did he ever remonstrate with you on the subject of seducing that girl?

Witness—He never did. Had he or any other clergyman given me their advice, I would have done any thing they desired me, consistent with reason; but neither the parish priest or his curates ever conversed with me on the matter.

Mr. Armstrong—Were you on good terms with Mr. Henry?

Witness—Particularly so. Up to the 4th of March last, I visited him and enjoyed the hospitalities of his table.

Mr. Armstrong—The 14th of March was the day on which the occurrence took place in the chapel of Islandeady?

Witness—Yes.

Cross-examined by Mr. Baker—I do not know where the

(nn) See note *(k k)* p. 251.   *(oo)* See note *(z)* p. 227.

poor girl is now, (*pp*) not having heard of her within the last month, when she sent to me for money ; gave her various sums of money at different times ;   since Christmas, I gave her upwards of £5. ; the girl is between twenty and thirty years of age ; and I have heard that her parents are dead.

Mr. Baker—You said that y u dined with Mr. Henry about a fortnight before the 14th of March ?

Witness—I did.

Mr. Baker—Now was there not a station some time before that in your father's house?

Witness—I believe there was, but having been from home at the time, I cannot state positively.

Mr. Baker—Were you at chapel on the 14th of March last ?

Witness—I went there rather late ; but finding the people on their knees and the crowd very considerable, I knelt outside, as I did not wish to disturb them.

Mr. Baker—Then you did not go into the chapel ?

Witness—I did not.

Mr. Baker—At what part of the service was it that you went to the chapel and knelt outside ?

Witness—I could not tell, I did not see the Priest on the altar, the crowd was so great.

Mr. Baker—Could you form an opinion at what time the Priest commenced speaking about secular affairs ?

(*p p*) Namely, in the month of *August*, 1841. In *March*, 1841, she appears from p. 254, l. 7, to have recently *returned* to the vicinity of the chapel of Islandeady.   Since Christmas, *to the time when witness gave his evidence*, he *swears* to have given the girl five pounds at *different times*.   It might have been more satisfactory to the court if he could have sworn that he gave her *between Christmas*, 1840, *and March*, 1841, five pounds.   This observation is made, not invidiously or ill-naturedly to the witness, whose error, as well as that of the unfortunate girl, by whom he publicly confesses himself to have " had unfortunately a child," has *unnecessarily* as many may be inclined to think been published to the world, but to shew the *possibility* of the truth of Mr. O'Malley's assertion in p. 227 (note *z*).   The probability is, that the money was given *previous* to the 14th of March, 1841.—C

R

Witness—I could not.

Mr. Baker—Did you hear the priest on that day making any allusions to your conduct?

Witness—I neither heard nor saw the officiating clergyman.

Mr. Baker—Do you attend your duty regularly?

Witness—Yes; I generally go to communion twice-a-year.

Mr. Baker—What time might have intervened between the period of your communion and the last time you dined with Mr. Henry?

Witness—Six months might possibly have elapsed, but I cannot state precisely.

Mr. Baker—Had you been at communion from the time that the girl left your father's house to the day on which you dined with Mr. Henry?

Witness—I cannot recollect.

Mr. Baker—How soon after the 14th of March had you any conversation with Mr. Cavendish, the defendant?

Witness—I had no conversation with him, directly or indirectly, until after the publication of the articles alleged to contain libellous matter.

Mr. Baker—Was Mr. Cavendish, or any of his family, in the chapel of Islandeady on the 11th of March?

Witness—He was not.

Mr. Baker—Were any of his printers?

Witness —Not that I know of.

Mr. Baker—You may retire, Sir.

Mr. Monahan, Q.C.—We close, my Lord.

It appears from the same pamphlet, p. 43, that the following conversation took place between the Court and Counsel—

Mr. O'Malley—I do not wish, my Lord, to keep the

defendant's justification from the jury, but your Lordship will be pleased to take a note of my objections. Firstly, I contend that the justification set forth on the pleadings by the defendant has not been supported by the evidence. Secondly, I maintain that justification was not open to him at all, he not having put the words on which he sought to justify, on the pleadings in the Irish language.

Baron Richards—You contend that the justification, as set forth on the pleadings, has not been proved.

Mr. O'Malley—Precisely so, my Lord. The evidence has failed in many points. They have not proved, as alleged in the libellous article, that Mr. Gallaher called on the people to vote against the Protestant candidates, as they could not possess sufficient honesty to discharge the duties of poor law guardians. There is no evidence whatever of his having invoked the curse of the Almighty God on Tobias Burke's head, nor did the Plaintiff, I am instructed, do so. They have failed to show that a general murmur of indignation ran through the congregation.

Baron Richards—There is evidence sufficient to go to the jury that there was a murmur of indignation.

Mr. O'Malley—They have not proved that Mrs. O'Grady fainted at the time, nor is there any evidence that Mr. Gallaher continued giving vent to his blasphemy and wicked imprecations. In fact, it has not been proved that he blasphemed at all.

Baron Richards—Several witnesses have deposed that he invoked the curse of the Almighty God on Mr. John Burke's head.

Mr. O'Malley—A curse, my Lord, is not blasphemy.

Baron Richards—I do not know what else it is.

Mr. O'Dowd—A celebrated and eminent clergyman has defined blasphemy as " something said in derogation of the attributes of the Deity."

Baron Richards—If all the clergymen in the world were to swear that blasphemy means not a curse, but something said in derogation of the attributes of the Deity, I would not believe them. Mr. O'Malley, you say, I think, that the defendant has failed to prove that "Mr. Gallaher invoked the curse of God on *their* head."

Mr. O'Malley—He has, my Lord.

Mr. Baker—The entire *gravamen* of the accusation contained in the libellous articles is this, that Mr. Gallaher cursed and invoked the malediction of the Almighty on Mr. John Burke, because of his having interfered with the votes of his tenantry previous to an election for poor law guardians. The defendant repeats this inuendo on his plea of justification; but the evidence goes directly to prove that the curse was invoked, if invoked at all, on account of Mr. Burke's immorality.

Mr. Monahan, Q.C.—That is the question for the jury to determine on.

Baron Richards—Just so, Mr. Monahan.

Mr. O'Malley—I must press my objection—that the defendant has failed to prove his justification.

Baron Richards—Draw up, in any form you please, your objections, and I will take them down in my book.

Mr. Baker—Meanwhile, my Lord, we will go on with our rebutting case.

It appears from the same pamphlet, p. 43, that in the rebutting case—

The Rev. Richard Henry, Roman Catholic Rector of Islandeady, was first called and examined *(on oath)* by Mr. O'Malley.—Recollects the 14th of March last; was not in the chapel of Islandeady on that day; knows Mr. Gallaher, the plaintiff; he is one of my curates; knows Mr. Cavendish; read the libellous publications in the *Tele-*

graph ; Mr. Gallaher officiated in Islandeady on the Sunday in question.

Mr. O'Malley—Why did he perform the service on that day in Islandeady?

Witness.—He officiated at my request, as I went to Glan Island chapel to offer up mass.

Mr. O'Malley.—What caused you to go to Glan Island?

Mr. Monahan objected to the question.

Baron Richards.—I think it is quite sufficient for you, Mr. O'Malley, to know that Mr. Henry is rector of Islandeady; and, of course, he has ample power over his curates, and is fully entitled to direct them to officiate at either of the chapels in that parish.

Examination continued by Mr. O'Malley.—There was a collection to be made on the 14th of March in both chapels for the purpose of repairing them.

Mr. O'Malley.—When you told Mr. Gallaher to officiate at Islandeady on the 14th of March, what directions did you give him?

Mr. Monahan.—Surely, Mr. O'Malley, you do not mean to say that the answer to such a question would be evidence.

Baron Richards ruled that the question was admissible from the nature of the defence gone into.

Mr. O'Malley.—Now, state what were the directions that you gave Mr. Gallaher, on the subject of certain immoral conduct?

Witness.—I directed him to expose and rebuke four persons; three for seducing females, and a fourth for immorality. The names of the three persons were Needham, Butler, and Maguire; two of them farmers' sons, and one a shoemaker by trade.

Mr. O'Malley.—What was the species of immorality to which you directed Mr. Gallaher's attention?

Witness.—I told him there was a more glaring case than that of the three men who took off young girls, and refused

to marry them ; and I then made allusion to Mr. John
Burke's business, saying that one of them resided in the
very next house to the residence of the girl, Kitty Walsh, (*qq*)
and that it would appear strange to the people if he would
only expose poor persons, and spare the gentlemen ; therefore, it was that I directed him to expose John Burke's
conduct, as well as that of the other persons already named.
I gave him a list of the four persons whom I ordered him
to rebuke, and I mentioned, at the same time, that Mr.
Burke's female, who left the neighbourhood three months
previous, had come back again, and now resided quite close
to the chapel. I authorised Mr. Gallaher to *reprove* the
four persons, whose names I gave him; and I would have
done so myself, had I officiated there. It was Mr. Gallaher's duty to rebuke and reprove as I directed him. Mr.
Gallaher did not know that he was to officiate at Islandeady
on the Sunday alluded to, until about half-past five o'clock
on the previous evening. Had I not given directions to
Mr. Gallaher to officiate in Islandeady, he would, in all probability, have gone to a distant station in the parish, held
for the convenience of the poor people in a remote district,
during the severe months, when they are but badly clad,
Some time, about three months, before the Sunday on which
Mr. Gallaher animadverted on Mr. Burke's conduct, I had
a conversation with Mr. Joseph Burke, who called on me,
about Kitty Walsh. He stated that, having heard I was
determined to expose his brother, and being solicited by his
mother, he waited on me for the purpose of inducing me
not to denounce or expose any member of his family ; he
stated that his father and mother were old and delicate, and
that public exposure of their child might, probably, shorten
their days ; that his brother had become penitent, and re-
gretted having acted as he did. My reply was, " That I

(*qq*) See note (*nn*) p. 256. The reader, however, will observe that the two
depositions do not *absolutely* contradict one another.—C.

had a sacred duty to perform, but as John Burke repented of his conduct, I should not expose him, but merely allude without mentioning names, to the subject. The girl, I insisted, should leave the parish."

Mr. O'Malley.—Did Kitty Walsh immediately quit the parish?

Witness.—On the very evening of the day on which this conversation took place she left the neighbourhood altogether, but she subsequently returned and took up her residence near to the chapel where she remained up to the Saturday preceding the 14th of March. I sent three or four times to direct her to remove, but she persisted in remaining, and in consequence I gave the directions already mentioned to Mr. Gallaher. I saw Mr. John Burke at communion on the day of a station in his father's house. After that I received him as a visitor at my residence, as I conceived he had become truly penitent.

Cross-examined by Mr. Monahan, Q.C.—The interview between Mr. Joseph Burke and myself, took place on the morning of the day on which I alluded to the occurrence in the chapel of Islandeady. So far as I can bring to recollection, I think it was in December last that Kitty Welsh left the house of Mr. Tobias Burke. I cannot recollect when the child was baptised, but you will find it in the registry book. [The registry book was here produced.] It appears that the child was baptised on the 10th day of January—so the entry sets forth, but whether that was the day on which it took place I cannot undertake to say. The child was baptised, so far as I can judge from the handwriting of the entry, by Mr. Wheelan. The entry was made not at the time of the baptism, but on the day very we settled accounts, the 3d of March last. I was in the habit of visiting Mr. Tobias Burke's house, but I never particularly noticed the girl, Kitty Walsh.

Mr. Monahan, Q.C.—Allow me to ask you, on your

solemn oath, do you consider it to be the duty of a Christian minister to invoke the curse of the Almighty God and the Catholic congregation on the head of a Catholic parishioner?

Witness.—Very seldom. It is never done except in extreme cases. Such a proceeding is never resorted to unless when the person against whom a serious charge is preferred does not turn from his evil ways. My own impression is that a curse is never invoked.

Mr. O'Malley.—Do you mean to convey to the court that Mr. John Burke lived in a state of sin with the girl, Kitty Walsh, up to the time of the denunciation?

Witness.—When I heard that the girl had returned to the neighbourhood, I was impressed with the conviction that she was determined to have recourse to her bad practices, and persons residing in the neighbourhood told me that Mr. John Burke visited her frequently.

Mr. Monahan, Q.C.—Who told you that?

Witness.—Many people. (rr)

Mr. Monahan, Q.C.—Name one of them.

Witness.—A person named Butler told me.

Mr. Monahan, Q.C.—Is he here?

Witness.—Not to my knowledge.

Mr. Monahan, Q.C.—Did Mr. John Burke dine at your table?

Witness.—He did when I considered him fit company for my guests.

Mr. Monahan, Q.C.—Supposing him to be a fit subject for denunciation, would you consider him fit company for respectable society?

Witness.—I would not, unless he repented.

Mr. Monahan, Q.C.—Did you ever hear who it was that turned the woman, Kitty Walsh, out of the house in which she resided at the lower end of the parish?

(rr) See next note.

Witness.—I never did.

Mr. Monahan, Q.C.—Do you know that it was in her sister's house she lived at the lower end of the parish?

Witness.—I do not know who the owner of the house is.

Mr. Monahan, Q.C.—Do you know where she lived after she left Mr. Burke's house in the family way?

Witness.—She resided for three or four days in the very next house to the chapel.

Mr. Monahan, Q.C.—Whose house is that?

Witness.—A family named Barrett lives in it.

Mr. Monahan, Q.C.—Are they related to this unfortunate girl?

Witness.—I cannot say that she is any relation of the Barretts.

Mr. Monahan, Q.C.—You stated that Mr. John Burke was in the habit of visiting at your house and dining at your table before Mr. Gallaher cursed him?

Witness.—He visited and dined with me up to the 2nd of March, I think.

Juror.—Did you go the length of desiring Mr. Gallaher to curse Mr. John Burke, when you directed him to allude to his immoral conduct?

Witness.—Certainly not.

Juror.—Did you desire or give him any directions to speak about the election of poor law guardians?

Witness.—I did not.

Baron Richards.—About what time did you hear that the girl came back to live near the chapel?

Witness.—She returned from the lower end of the parish about the 3rd or 4th of March.

Baron Richards.—When did you hear that she came back?

Witness.—At the very instant; because I stated publicly some time before, that if she happened to return to the neighbourhood, I would feel obliged to my parishioners for the earliest information on the subject.

Baron Richards.—Did you ever remonstrate with Mr. John Burke before you gave Mr. Gallaher directions to rebuke him from the altar?

Witness.—I never did.(*ss*)

Juror.—Was he residing in his father's house?

Witness.—I should suppose so.

Another Juror.—When you heard that Mr. Gallaher cursed and denounced Mr. John Burke, did you speak to him on the subject?

Witness.—I never uttered a syllable to him, approving or disapproving of his conduct.

Juror.—And you heard that he cursed one of your parishioners!!

Witness.—Yes, I did.

Mr. Monahan, Q.C.—Go down, sir.

It appears from the same pamphlet, p. 48, that—

Martin Quin, a *simple* looking country lad, was the next witness produced, and examined on oath by Mr. Baker. His demeanour on the table, mode of answering the questions put to him, and the very *fine* language in which he indulged with the most apparent self-satisfaction, created considerable laughter and amusement. "On my examination here yesterday," stated this simpleton, "I observed, without prejudice to either party in this important record now pending, that I knew the Rev. Michael Gallaher, Roman Catholic curate, and I remarked that I saw him in the chapel of Islandeady on the 14th of March.

(*ss*) From this answer it would appear, that on the assurance of the persons alluded to by the witness—see note (*rr*)—the witness directed his curate to *denounce*, and that the curate *denounced on March* 14, either by an absolute or conditional *curse*, the parishioner of witness, to whom witness swears he made no remonstrance after the return of the girl about the *third* or *fourth* of March till the fourteenth.—C.

Mr. Baker.—Did he speak about secular matters before the chalice was veiled and mass concluded?

Quin.—After the mass was over, but before the concluding prayer, or *requiem* for the eternal repose of the faithfu departed, the reverend clergyman turned round to the assembled congregation, and said that an election for poor law guardians would shortly take place, when those persons liable to pay cess would be called upon to exercise their franchises in the selection of fit and competent persons to represent them at the board of guardians. Mr. Henry Browne and Mr. James Conry, he observed, my lord, were the contending candidates for the parish of Islandeady, and in his opinion he considered Mr. Conry was in every respect highly competent and qualified to discharge the duties of that important office. (Laughter.) Mr. Conry was the guardian for the previous year, and it was the reverend gentleman's decided opinion that he should be re-elected.

Mr. Baker.—Did the Plaintiff speak about any persons who offered themselves as candidates for the electoral district of Castlebar?

Quin.—He commented that landlords and other gentlemen, if gentlemen they were, should allow their tenants to elect whomsoever they pleased; as the most they could possibly expect in justice or in reason was their rent, and that they should get. For his own part, he held no land in the division, and no matter who was in or who was out, he would not be at any loss, but he deemed it his duty to give them the soundest advice.

Mr. Baker.—Why did Mr. Gallaher advise the people to vote against Mr. Browne?

Quin.—Because Mr. Brown would lay a heavy portion of the tax on the poor villagers resident in Derryoushe and other places convenient to Rehins. With reference to the family of the Burke's, residing at Woodville, in the county of Mayo, Mr. Gallaher remarked that in addition to their rent, the father and son required days' work from the tenants. His Reverence then turned to the Altar and took a piece off it, having, as he said, to refer to a different case altogether There were three lads in the parish, he stated, who had seduced young girls, in the hopes of getting little fortunes, which the parents were unable to give unless they beggared themselves and the rest of their children. One of the men (Needham) was a shoemaker, and Mr. Gallaher said—" the next pair of shoes he makes for himself may he not be able to wear them." As for Maguire, " he was a pretty object, a handsome creature, to want a marriage portion with his wife." He was not so severe on the third delinquent. Then, my Lord, he alluded to a worse case by far—a case of great immorality, in which Mr. John Burke was concerned, and narrated the history of his having a child by a servant girl in his father's house. The reverend gentleman considered that young Mr. Burke, who had received some education, and professed the Roman Catholic religion, was highly culpable ; and instead of leading his ignorant, uneducated servant from the paths of virtue and morality, he should have impressed on her mind the necessity of leading a good life, and advised her when he saw any *tendency* on her part to go astray. Mr. Galaher then said—" *Beremshe gho Shaun O'Bourka mha molachtsa, molacht Dhia, agus molacht en pubil shoh, mur neenie shea phenuas,*" which being translated into English is—" *I give John Burke my curse, the curse of God, and the curse of the congregation, unless he does penance.*" After concluding his malediction, he called upon the people to " go down on their knees and pray to God for the conversion of such people who were in a state of mortal sin to a state of grace ; and also to implore the intercession of the ever Blessed Virgin Mary, and the saints in Heaven with the Almighty God, for it was more

powerful than ours, to reclaim them." That was all Mr.
Gallaher said concerning Mr. Burke's conduct.

Mr. Baker.——Did Mr. Gallaher state anything about the
girl, Walsh?

Quin.——All he said about her was, that she was a very
poor servant girl.

[During this witness's examination the quietude of the
Court was frequently disturbed with loud peals of laughter,
in which the grave and sober gentlemen of the bar and the
learned Judge joined most heartily, doubtless not a little
tickled at his high flown language, and most *accurate*
memory.]

Cross-examined by Mr. Armstrong.——I hold about two
sums and one quarter of land in the parish of Islandeady;
there was a large congregation and a vast number of respectable people in the chapel on the 14th of March; the chapel
is in the form of a T, and I stood fornent the Altar; I cannot
recollect that Gallaher said anything about the religion of
Henry Browne or James Conry, indeed I am firmly of
opinion that I can lawfully swear neither of their religions
were referred to; Mr. Gallaher did not say that the people
might expect more justice from Catholics than from Protestants.

Mr. Armstrong.——Will you swear that he did not speak
anything about Mr. Larminie?

Witness.——I will not swear anything about it.

Mr. Armstrong.——Nor about Lord Lucan?

Witness.——No; unless he made mention of his Lordship's name in his own mind. Pardon me, counsel; however, he spoke about loan money, and Mr. Burke's tenants
getting money, but I cannot swear to it; he did not say one
word about bad landlords.

Mr. Armstrong.——What mention did he make of Mr.
Burke's tenants in reference to certain work they performed?

Witness.—All he observed was, that those people who were in the habit of working for him should bring their own butter-milk to *feed* themselves.

Mr. Armstrong.—What happened after Mr. Gallaher gave the curse on Mr. John Burke?

Witness.—His reverence called upon the congregation to pray for the conversion of Mr. John Burke, and the entire flock *simultaneously responding to the request,* fell upon their knees, and prayed a prayer which lasted for about five minutes.

Mr. Armstrong.—Did Mr. Gallaher repeat the prayer aloud?

Witness.—He did not.

Mr. Armstrong.—Now, was it not to join in the *De profundis* that the people knelt down?

Witness.—No; but to pray for the conversion of Mr. John Burke.

Juror.—Repeat the curse in English.

Witness.—I give John Burke the curse of God, and the curse of the flock, for the scandal and bad example he has given, and the injury he has inflicted on the poor girl, unless he does penance.

Juror.—Repeat it in Irish, now.

Witness.—" *Beremshe gho Shaun O'Bourka molacht Dhia agus molacht en pubil shoh gnal err ea sconul agus drough vass hug shea, agus err gnal err an eagour rhin shea err ea Cauleen bhought shoh, mur neenie shea penuas,*"

Mr. Armstrong.—Did he say one word about doing penance?

Witness.—I am quite sure that he said the words I *narrated.*

Mr. Armstrong.—Did he speak very audibly?

Witness.—What do you mean?

Mr. Armstrong.—Did he speak very loud?

Witness.—Oh, now I comprehend (laughter); he discoursed in a full toned voice; every person in the chapel could hear him.

Mr. Armstrong.—When did you first tell this story?

Witness.—We often repeated it among ourselves, but I told it to Mr. Kelly, the attorney, last Saturday after I was served with the test; there are five others here in attendance who will fully corroborate my evidence.

Mr. Armstrong—Did Mr. Kelly read any paper for you?

Witness— I heard read an extract from the libel.

Mr. Armstrong—Who was aware of what you could swear here to day?

Witness—I told Mr. Kelly what I could depose to in Castlebar; we all told him the same.

Mr. Armstrong—How much are you to get for coming here to-day to give your evidence?

Witness : I only got my bare expenses.

It appears from the same pamphlet, p. 51, that the next witness was Samuel Quin, examined (on oath) by Mr. Jennings. He—

Recollects having been in the chapel of Islandeady on the day in question, shortly before St. Patrick's day; Father Michael Gallaher officiated and said Mass, and made a discourse to the assembled congregation on the subject of the ensuing elections, naming Mr Conry and Mr. Henry Brown, as persons who intended contesting the district of Islandeady; Mr. Conry, he stated, was more suitable, but if they elected Mr Henry Browne, he would throw the burden of taxes off his land on the shoulders of the poor people resident in the adjacent villages; Mr. Tobias Burke, he also remarked, had given a part of his property to his son, Mr. John Burke, who was influencing his tenants to vote for Mr. Browne; he then turned round to the altar, took off it a bit of paper, and mentioned the name of three men who had seduced girls; he also spoke of Mr. John Burke as a gentleman, and a man of learning, if he was so, who had seduced a female servant living in his father's house, and then left her in a state of destitution; he then said in Irish, " my curse, the curse of the flock, and the curse of God on John Burke, the son of Tobias Burke, for the scandal he has committed, *unless he repent*—and for keeping this woman so near to the house of God."

Mr. Jennings.—State in Irish the nature of the curse?

Witness.—" *Mha molacht molacht en pubil shoh, agus molacht Dhia err Shaun O'Bourka, moc Tuboad O'Bourka, gnal err en sconal tau shea err eas a yeanu, mur neenia shea phenuas—agus gnal err ea vhea counal en bhan shoh nhar to Taugh Dhia.*"

Mr. Jennings.—Is there any other John Burke but the one residing in the parish.

Witness.—There is another, the son-in-law of Mr. Jos. Burke.

Mr. Baker.—We wish to show, my Lord, that Mr. Tobias Burke's name was introduced into the curse not for the purpose of denouncing or rebuking him, but to distinguish his son from another person of the same name.

Baron Richards.—So I understand, Mr. Baker.

Mr. Jennings to witness.—Did he speak entirely in the Irish language?

Witness.—Oh, Yes, all his sermon.

Juror.—Repeat some of his observations on the election of poor law guardians, as he spoke them, in the Irish language, I just wish, my Lord, to find out whether the witness has a perfect understanding of the Irish language.

The witness proceeded to relate what he declared to be a *verbatim* account of the " poor law guardian's discourse."

Mr. Jennings.—After the curse, what took place?

Witness.—There was a prayer offered up for the conversion of the persons guilty of immorality, and Mr. Gallaher said, " I hope you will fall on bended knees, and invoke the Almighty God to convert those persons to a state of grace, from the mortal sin they are in, and pray to the ever blessed Virgin Mary to intercede with her beloved son, and to all the saints, for their intercession is very efficacious." That, my Lord, is *substantively* the prayer offered up.

[The methodistical manner and assumed gravity with which the witness answered the last question convulsed the court with shouts of laughter.]

Cross-examined by Mr. Monahan, Q.C.—I am a cousin of the last witness. A greater number of gentlemen than usual were in the chapel on the Sunday in question. Mr. Charles O'Malley, wife and family were there. His two sons were in the chapel, as well as I can recal to mind.

Mr. Monahan, Q.C.—Do you know Mr. Joseph Burke of Greenhill ?

Witness.—I am not personally acquainted with the gentleman, but I know him.

Mr. Monahan, Q.C.—Was he in the chapel ?

Witness.—Well, you see now I cannot recal that to mind either. He and his family probably might have been in the gallery, but as it is contrary to the rules and regulations of our church to gaze about, or allow our thoughts to be distracted from the sacred service, I did not take any particular remark of him. (Loud laughter.)

Mr. Monahan, Q.C.—You state that you were not gazing ?

Witness.—I certainly took a little bit of an observation now and again, but the most of my attention was fixed on the clergyman who officiated at the altar. (Continued laughter.)

Mr. Monahan, Q.C.—Did Mr. Gallaher speak about Lord Lucan ?

Witness.—He did not speak of any Lord that I can bring to mind, neither did he mention Mr. Larminie's name ; but from his speaking about loan money, the people considered he referred to Larminie. Mr. Gallaher did not speak of any sect or religious persuasion whatsoever ; he stated nothing about the difference of religions professed by Mr. Browne or Conry. There was no necessity for him to do so, for every member of the congregation must have been fully aware of their *respective tenets* (laughter). I am as sure of that as of everything else I swore to day.

Mr. Monahan, Q.C.—Now, are you quite positive ?

Witness.—Sir, I have said so.

Mr. Monahan, Q.C.—Did Mr. Gallaher curse these three young men who ran away with the girls ?

Witness.—No ; concerning Needham, a shoemaker, he said " may he not be able to wear the next pair of shoes he makes for himself, unless he marries the girl." Maguire, he stated, was a nice object to want a property with his wife ; " if you observe his legs minutely," remarked the Priest, " you will find them stroked like bracket stars."

Mr. Monahan, Q.C.—Do you consider that proper language for a minister of the Roman Catholic religion to use in the house of God ?

Witness.—My consideration is that a priest should entertain more suitable notions of propriety than I possibly could, and, therefore, I did not, nor would I, form any opinion in *contradistinction* to him. (*ss bis*) (Laughter.) Very frequently matters similar to those take place in the house of God, and, therefore, I did not marvel much. (Renewed laughter.)

Mr. Monahan, Q.C.—When were you first asked what you knew about the occurrence in the chapel?

Witness.—Sometime since by a schoolmaster, named Kenny, who is also clerk to an attorney. I was a scholar of his whenever an opportunity presented itself. All he

(*ss bis*) This observation of this " simple" witness is, perhaps, one of the *most important* of the whole trial, in exemplification of the *wisdom which dictated the resolutions* of the Catholic Hierarchy of Ireland in 1830 and 1834, and the *public danger which must result* from the Catholic Clergy in Ireland acting in opposition to them.—C.

asked me was simply whether I had been in the chapel of Islandeady on the 14th of March, and I replied that I was. "What can you prove?" said he : "Only what happened," said I.

Mr. Monahan, Q.C.—How long is it since the schoolmaster asked you all those questions?

Witness.—About one fortnight before the assizes of Castlebar. I then gave a brief sketch of what had occurred.

Mr. Monahan, Q.C.—Who did you give it to?

Witness.—I cannot recal to mind, but I am positive that I never spoke to Mr. Gallaher or Mr. Henry on the subject good or bad.

Mr. Monahan, Q.C.—Did you speak to Mr. Kelly, the Plaintiff's attorney, about it?

Witness.—Since I came to Galway I conversed with him on the subject. He read a paper for me, which he stated to be an extract from the libellous article.

Mr. Monahan, Q.C.—Did he tell you to prove anything about the priest having said " unless he does penance "?

Witness.—Not a solitary word.

Mr. Monahan, Q.C.—But he read a paper, and said, " Boys, that's the libel; mind and swear no such thing took place."

Witness.—He read a paper, surely; but he never said what we were to swear, right or wrong.

Mr. Monahan, Q.C.—Now, when the priest cursed Mr. Burke was there a murmur of indignation through the congregation?

Witness.—There was no murmur or noise, further than when the people, with elevated eyes, looked up to heaven, and implored the Divine Saviour for forgiveness. There was a noise as of all uttering the exclamation of prayer, and crying out, " Oh God, oh Lord!"

Mr. Monahan, Q.C.—None of the congregation expressed feelings of horror and indignation ?

Witness.—Not that I could hear, and if it did take place I am confident I would have remarked it.

Mr. Monahan, Q.C.—Was the prayer offered up solely for the conversion of Mr. Burke, or for the other three men who went against the rules of the church ?

Witness.—For the entire flock and the entire world.

Michael Cusack, another of the frieze-coated parishioners, was next produced, and examined by Mr. James O'Dowd. —He deposed that he attended the chapel of Islandeady on Sunday, the 14th of March, when Mr. Gallaher officiated, and spoke about the ensuing elections of poor law guardians. He recommended Mr. Conry as a fit and proper representative for the electoral district of Islandeady, and said he had been guardian for the past year; that he had discharged his duty honestly, and he thought that it would be their interest to re-elect him for the ensuing year. Having enlarged a good deal and at considerable length on this subject, Mr. Gallaher referred to certain immoral persons among the parishioners who took away women, and refused to marry them until they had exacted from their parents exorbitant marriage portions. Here the witness detailed the observations made use of by Mr. Gallaher, and corroborated, in this respect, word for word, the evidence of the preceding witnesses.

Mr. O'Dowd.—What did Mr. Gallaher say about Mr. John Burke ?

Witness.—That he had seduced an innocent young female girl, and left her in indigence and destitution after she gave birth to a child. He was ashamed of a person who had an education being guilty of such conduct, and he gave " the curse of God and the curse of the flock on his head, unless he did penance and made reparation."

Baron Richards.—Repeat the curse in Irish.

Witness.—" *Beremshe gho Shaun O'Bourka molacht Dhia agus molacht en pubil shoh, mur neenie shea phenuas.*"

Cross-examined by Mr. Keating, Q.C.—I was at the house of Mr. William Thomas Kelly, at Castlebar, and the libel which appeared in Mr. Cavendish's paper, the *Mayo Telegraph*, was read for me. It contained matters and assertons quite contrary to what Mr. Gallaher either did or said. Nothing was said in the chapel by the Plaintiff about Protestant guardians not doing justice to the people. Mass was over before the discourse on secular matters commenced, but the priest kept on his robes.

It appears from the same pamphlet, p. 54, that—

Patrick Ryder was next examined on oath by Mr. O'Malley.—He corroborated the evidence of the witnesses produced by the counsel for the Plaintiff, in the rebutting case, with regard to Mr. Gallaher's observations on the election of poor law guardians, and on the immorality of three or four of the parishioners. The curse invoked on Mr. J. Burke's head was conditional. It was substantively to this effect, " I give John Burke, the son of Tobias Burke, my curse, the curse of God, and the curse of the Catholic flock, for the bad example he has set, and the scandal he has given, unless he repent." Witness *believes* there was a prayer at the conclusion of Mass for the conversion of the people guilty of immorality.

Cross-examined by Mr. Armstrong: The words used by Mr. Gallaher at the end of the curse were "if he repents not;" I am quite positive he did not say—" unless he does penance;" Cusack and the two Quins were present in the office of Mr. Kelly when the libellous paper was read for us. Mr. Gallaher made no distinction whatsoever between the creeds or religious persuasions of the candidates for the office of poor law guardian. There was something said about loan money, in reference to Mr. Burke's tenants paying their rents. Mr. Gallaher stated that the rent was sufficient for the landlord, the tenant should be allowed liberty of conscience.

It appears from the same pamphlet, p. 55, that—

Richard O'Grady, Esq., at the desire of some of the jury was re-called and re-examined.

Juror—You have heard all the witnesses produced by the plaintiff's counsel swear that the curse was a qualified one, invoked only in the event of Mr. John Burke not doing penance, now is that true ?

Mr. O'Grady—Upon my solemn oath there was no qualification whatsoever.

Juror—Repeat the curse in Irish.

Mr. O'Grady—*Beremshe gho Shaun O'Bourka mha molachtsa, molacht Dhia, agus molacht en pubil.*

Juror—Did he conclude the curse with the words " unless he does penance ? "

Mr. O'Grady—Upon my oath he did not.

Another Juror—Was any prayer offered up for the conversion of the four persons who had been rebuked for their immorality ?

Mr. O'Grady—No prayer was publicly said at the conclusion of the Mass but the usual one for the repose of the faithful departed.

Juror—Are you positive that Mr. Gallaher did not conclude the service with any prayer but the one usually offered up ?

Mr. O'Grady—I am quite sure.

Juror—You state, Mr. O'Grady, that Mr. Gallaher did

not conclude his curse with the words "unless he does penance." Now, might he not have commenced it that way? Might he not have said "unless Mr. John Burke does penance, I give him the curse of God and the curse of the Catholic flock?"

Mr. O'Grady—He did not. Neither at the commencement or the conclusion did he use the words "unless he does penance, or unless he repent of his conduct."

Juror—What distance were you from the altar?

Mr. O'Grady—About the same distance as there is between the jury galleries.

Juror—You were in the gallery?

Mr. O'Grady—Yes, I was.

Juror—Were the persons on the floor nearer to the altar than you were?

Mr. O'Grady—Yes, they were.

Another Juror—Did you mention the nature of Mr. Gallaher's curse to any person after you left the chapel?

Mr. O'Grady—Oh yes, to several.

Juror—It was sworn by one of the witnesses that Mr. Gallaher had observed from the altar that Protestants generally would not do justice to the rate-payers; now, Sir, do you consider that observation was intended merely to reflect on the Protestant candidates for the electoral districts of Islandeady and Castlebar, or on the entire body of Protestants?

Mr. O'Grady—Having spoken largely on the subject of electing the Protestant guardians who offered themselves to the considerations of the rate-payers, he said that the people could not get justice from Protestants.

Another Juror—Did Mr. Gallaher pray aloud for the conversion of Mr. John Burke?

Mr. O'Grady—He certainly did not.

Juror—Had you as great a facility of hearing him, had he done so, as any other person in the chapel ?

Mr. O'Grady—I had.

Juror—The four witnesses produced by the plaintiff's counsel, in the rebutting case, concurred in swearing that no allusion whatsoever was made to the four guardians for Castlebar electoral district ; now did such take place?

Mr. O'Grady—Mr. Gallaher alluded to Lord Lucan's nominees and to the Catholic candidates. He named them distinctly.

Juror—Do you understand the Irish language well ?

Mr. O'Grady—Particularly so. I have read some Irish, and, as a very extraordinary coincidence, I must mention that the first work I read was written by Doctor Gallaher. (laughter.)

Juror—Does your knowledge of the Irish language justify you in swearing positively contrary to what was sworn by the four witnesses produced by the plaintiff?

Mr. O'Grady—Yes, positively.

Mr. Baker—Did you mention anything of what occurred in the chapel to the defendant ?

Mr. O'Grady—On the very next day, the 15th of March, in the course of conversation I mentioned the matter to Mr. Cavendish when we were chatting on the steps of Foy's hotel. The fact of Gallaher having cursed my brother-in-law was town-talk at that time.

Mr. Baker—Can you say that Mr. Cavendish published the libellous articles in consequence of the information you conveyed to him ?

Mr. O'Grady—No, I cannot.

Baron Richards—The inference is a natural one that he did.

Counsel for the plaintiff tendered other witnesses for

cross-examination, but the learned gentleman for the defence did not deem it necessary to avail themselves of the privilege.

Mr. Baker——We close, my Lord.

It appears from the same pamphlet, p. 56, that Baron Richards *immediately* addressed the Counsel for the Defendant as follows——

Baron Richards——Allow me now, Mr. Monahan, to call your attention to those portions of the libellous articles which counsel for the plaintiff affirm have not been covered by the plea of justification which has been placed upon the record, in order that you may direct your observations to them in your reply to evidence. In the first place it is alleged, that no evidence has been adduced to sustain the averment, that Mr. Gallaher stated Protestants did not possess sufficient honesty to discharge the duties of poor law guardians. Secondly, it is contended that the defendant has not proved that " Mr. Gallaher invoked the curse of God on their heads "——meaning Tobias and John Burke—— " and proclaimed aloud that his curse would rest upon them for ever." They confidently assert that you have not offered any evidence to support that declaration, and I need not tell you, Mr. Monahan, that if you fail to prove it, you do not sustain your justification. There certainly is evidence, however, that he called down the curse of God on Mr. John Burke. There is evidence that Mrs. O'Grady was in a tremor——that the scene was an extraordinary and appalling one. The difficulty which you have to contend with, Mr. Monahan, is that portion of the article in which it is asserted that Mr. Gallaher invoked the curse of God on Tobias Burke's head. It certainly appears to me at this stage of the proceedings, that he did not curse both the father and son, although the father's name was introduced into the curse. But you will of course apply yourself to this point.

It appears from the same pamphlet, that Mr. Monahan addressed the Jury after the learned Judge, and in the course of his speech, which occupies pages 57 to 63 of the pamphlet, made the following remark—

To believe the evidence adduced in the rebutting case, you must conclude that all the members of the Burke family, examined here to-day, committed a wilful and corrupt perjury. But how can you deal with the testimony of Mr. Nolan, a gentleman totally unconnected with the Burkes, whom we thought it right to produce. He has substantially borne them out in their view of what did occur. He is no prejudiced or partial witness, yet he swore positively that no qualification was used by the Plaintiff. Gentlemen, if on the other hand, you are inclined to discredit the evidence of the Quins, Cusack, and Ryder—if you believe that our witnesses swore nothing but the truth—what must be your opinion of those who are capable of bringing forward such a defence as has been trumped up on the present occasion? If you place implicit reliance on the evidence of that respectable gentleman and lady examined on behalf of the Defendant, what estimate can you form of the man who paraded before you the wretched things who swore to his bidding? To reconcile the evidence is utterly impossible—TO ACCOUNT FOR THE DISCREPANCIES IN IT ON ANY GROUND BUT THAT OF THE GROSSEST PERJURY, IS WHOLY OUT OF THE QUESTION.

It appears from the same pamphlet, pages 63 to 67, that Mr. Baker addressed the Jury after

Mr. Monahan had sat down, and in the course of his speech is reported to have used the following words—

My friend, Mr. O'Malley, in stating this case to you on yesterday, gentlemen, most aptly remarked that the libels under consideration applied not individually to Mr. Gallaher, but reflected, and were calculated to heap odium and discredit on the venerated ministers of the Church of Rome. From my heart do I repeat the assertion. If Mr. Gallaher, my humble client, had not brought forward this case into a Court of Justice—did he neglect to vindicate his character from the foul aspersions of the malignant Journalist—would not the conclusion be a most natural one, that his Grace the Archbishop of Tuam, the distinguished Prelate who gave evidence here yesterday, sanctioned by his silence and non-interference, the base and unholy conduct attributed to Mr. Gallaher. I ask you, gentlemen, if this clergyman, *under the guidance and control of Doctor M'Hale, were to remain in seclusion and retirement*—neglecting to fling back the foul falsities into the teeth of his maligner—would not *the Roman Catholic Prelate of this district be most fairly presumed to mark with the seal of his approbation the conduct alleged to have been committed by the Plaintiff.* How, then, could my poor client avoid coming here? Was it possible for him to shrink from the searching and scrutinizing ordeal which his conduct has undergone in this public court? The eyes of the world were on him—the Catholic people waited in daily expectation of his vindication. Had my client, then, any course but the one to pursue—could he appeal to a more impartial tribunal for that vindication, than to a Jury of Galway gentlemen? And, gentlemen, while on this subject, allow me to tell you— and I do so with the utmost satisfaction—that if you return a verdict

against my client to-day he is no longer—to the credit of
the Catholic Church be it said—a member of their ministry.
If convicted of the charges preferred against him, he leaves
this court-house, by your solemn recorded opinion, a degraded man, and simply but a man, for his sacerdotal robe
is snatched off his shoulders, and he is pronounced by his
Archbishop an unworthy companion for pure and spotless
men—an improper and unworthy pastor for any flock.
But before you record such a verdict, you will pause and
weigh well the circumstances of the case in all its bearings.

**It appears from the same pamphlet, p. 67,
that after Mr. Monahan had addressed the Jury,
Baron Richards gave his charge to it as follows—**

The case had already occupied much of the public time,
he would not say unnecessarily, for it might have been difficult to shorten the evidence ; but it certainly occurred to
him that a great deal of chaff presented itself which might
now be thrown aside. Three issues would be sent up to the
jury, and it would be for them to say whether the defendant
was guilty or not of the charges contained in the Plaintiff's
declaration—whether he did maliciously and falsely publish a gross and scandalous libel reflecting on the Reverend
Michael Gallaher's conduct as a clergyman—whether he
did commit all the grievances set forth by the Plaintiff.
Two of the issues related to the plea of justification placed
upon the record by the Honourable Mr. Cavendish, who
meets the Plaintiff's case—firstly, by alleging that he is not
guilty of publishing any libel whatsoever ; and secondly,
by avering that whatever he did publish was a true report of the proceedings in the chapel of Islandeady, on the
14th of March last, with fair and *bona fide* editorial com-

ment thereon, published by him in the exercise of his indisputable right as the proprietor of a public journal. Gentlemen, it is right I should inform you, that when justification is pleaded, it is absolutely necessary that all the allegations should be distinctly proved. Now, in one of the defendant's pleas it is averred, that the Rev. Michael Gallaher did invoke the curse of God on the head of Mr. Tobias Burke; the Defendant has failed to prove that fact; and having failed to do so, I must inform you that his justification has not been sustained; and, as the justification goes to the whole of the case, you are bound on this point of law, to find for the Plaintiff on the two last issues. All the rest, gentlemen, remains for you—with it I have little, if anything to do. From the evidence adduced in the course of this investigation the greater part of the expressions attributed to the Plaintiff in the Defendant's journal have been clearly proved, but we have no evidence whatever of his having invoked the curse of God on Mr. Tobias Burke's head. The Defendant, as I before remarked, fails then in his defence, and you must find for the Rev. Plaintiff on the two pleas of justification. To constitute a libel, gentlemen, whether written or printed,—and you have now only to say whether the articles in question were libellous or otherwise—it is necessary to establish the publication by the Defendant in the county where the venue has been laid. There must also be evidence that the Plaintiff was the subject matter of the animadversions. In the present case these two facts have been satisfactorily proved. But, gentlemen, in addition to these two necessary ingredients in the constitution of a libel it must also be shown that the publication was malicious. and on this subject I am of opinion, that if the natural tendency of the words be to vilify, defame, or injure the party animadverted upon, then the publisher must be looked upon as having been actuated by malicious feelings. Gentlemen, it is your province to judge, taking all the circumstances into account, whether the publication is libellous or not—whether it is malicious or not—whether it is defamatory or not. I am not myself called upon to give an opinion with respect to the articles in question. My duty is simply to explain to you the ingredients necessary to constitute a libellous publication, and you are to say whether, from all the facts of the case, you conceive it to come within the definition I have given you. His Lordship then read over the entire evidence from his note-book. Gentlemen, said the learned judge, you will perceive that the publication alleges that Mr. John Burke was cursed on account of his having taken a part in the election of poor law guardians contrary to the wishes of the priest. On the other side it has been asserted that whatever the Plaintiff did was done, not on account of Mr. Burke's interference in this election, but in the discharge of what he conceived to be a *bona fide* duty, in consequence of that gentlemen's immoral conduct. It is important that you should endeavour to make up your minds as to the reality of the case in this respect, and to satisfy yourselves whether the version of the transaction given in the *Mayo Telegraph*, or the version urged by the Plaintiff, be the true and real one ; and it should influence your minds very much indeed.

It appears from the same pamphlet, p. 68, that—

The jury having retired into their room, Mr. Monahan objected to that portion of the Judge's charge in which his Lordship stated that the evidence in support of the justification pleas was not sufficient.

Baron Richards—Draw up your exception to my charge in writing, and I will take it down in my note-book.

Mr. Monahan then handed up to the bench a document, of which the following is a copy ;—" Objection—That the Judge told the Jury there was not sufficient evidence to support the pleas of justification, whereas he should have stated, that the evidence was quite sufficient on these pleas to allow the issue on them to go to the jury."

The jury having remained in their room upwards of one hour, came into court at twenty minutes before eight o'clock, finding for the Plaintiff SIX-PENCE DAMAGES and SIX-PENCE COSTS.

What I have to observe to your Lordship and to the public, on this really " Important Libel Record," as it is termed in the pamphlet from which the above extracts have been made, is this :

I wish not to offer any opinion, whether it was proper in the Editor of the *Telegraph* newspaper, to have taken *any* notice in the columns of that paper, of the evident violation in the Chapel of Islandeady in 1841, of the Resolutions of the Catholic Hierarchy of Ireland in 1830 and 1834. I believe, however, that it is almost the universal wish of the Repeal of the Union party in Ireland, that the Editor had taken no notice of such violation ; but—

1°. I think that *all* the advisers, whether legal or clerical, of the Rev. Mr. Gallaher, who advised him to bring, as Plaintiff, *an action for libel* against the Hon. Frederick Cavendish, on account of the article which appeared in the *Telegraph* newspaper, gave him advice which, *as Catholics*, they had better not have given him. It would have been *much wiser* to have met the accusation, if it had been judged fit to take any notice of it, by a public denial in the same or in any other newspaper, of its truth.

2°. I think that the Editor of the *Telegraph* committed a great mistake in not publishing in his paper the *Irish* words used by the Rev. Mr. Gallaher on the 14th of March, 1841, in the Chapel at Islandeady, in denouncing or " making an *imploration* " against Mr. John Burke, and that the Proprietor, the Hon. Frederick Cavendish, in his plea of justification, committed another great mistake in asserting, that in the article in the *Telegraph*, the Rev. Mr. Gallaher had been justly accused of having cursed Mr. *Tobias* Burke. I think that if the Editor and Proprietor of the *Telegraph* had not committed those two great mistakes, the verdict on the 6th of August, 1831, at the Court of Galway, *might* have been for the Defendant.

But it is of far less importance, as a matter of public import, for the tranquillity of Ireland, or for the credit of the Catholic Religion in Ireland, whether, by the publication of the article in the *Telegraph* newspaper, its Proprietor *committed a mistake* which subjected him to the loss of a law suit under the law of libel, in which the damages being laid at *a thousand pounds*, the Jury return a verdict of *sixpence damages and sixpence costs*, than whether the termination of *such* an action by *such* a verdict can in fact be considered in the light of *an honorable issue to the Plaintiff*, or to the body, from which a verdict in favor of the Defendant would, it seems, (see p. 284) have excluded him. I feel, that the Sligo trial of March 20th and 21st, 1837, is *very strong* proof of the public detriment, which *the system* of Archbishop M'Hale, adopted by him no doubt in full persuasion of its rectitude and propriety, yet in opposition to the wishes and feelings of the Catholic Hierarchy of Ireland, as expressed in the resolutions of 1830 and 1834, is *able* and *likely* to produce to the just reputation which the Roman tribunals, and especially the Sacred Congregation of Propaganda, *ought* to enjoy, and which I certainly wish them to enjoy, in Ireland. I feel that the Galway trial of the 5th and 6th of August, 1841, is *very strong* proof, that *the system* of Archbishop M'Hale, acted upon, I am willing to believe, with a full persuasion of its rectitude and propriety by his followers, yet in opposition to the wishes and feelings of the Catholic Hierarchy in Ireland, as expressed in the resolutions of 1830 and 1834, is *able* and *likely* to produce upon many of the inhabitants of Great Britain as well as of Ireland the impression, that " Catholicity," *under the direction of Archbishop M'Hale,* is "a curse instead of a blessing to Ireland." (*tt*)

It seems to me, that no impartial Christian and loyal subject of Queen Victoria, who has either

(*tt*) See pages 290 and 292, and Appendix No. I. to this Letter, p. 296, l. 29.

T

assisted at the trial at Galway on the 5th and 6th of August, 1841, or read the report of it published in the little pamphlet from which I have presented your Lordship extracts, *and believes that report to be a true one*, can *wish* that such trials should take place. Yet, in my humble opinion, they *must continually take place, and must be attended with similar results*, (*vv*) so long as Archbishop M'Hale *acts upon a system*, evidently in opposition to the FEELINGS of the Catholic Hierarchy in Ireland, as expressed in the Resolutions of 1830 and 1834, which I have felt it my duty, a very painful one, I will admit, to lay before your Lordship and the public. I call it a painful duty, not on account of the Resolutions themselves, which are perfectly— EVEN IN THEIR EXPRESSIONS RESPECTING THE DUKE OF WELLINGTON, TO WHOSE LION-HEARTEDNESS AT VIENNA IN 1815, GREGORY XVI. IS MAINLY IN- DEBTED FOR THE PRESERVATION TO THE PAPAL TIARA OF THE THREE LEGATIONS—in unison with the FEELINGS of Gregory XVI. ; but on account of the proof which that system affords, that there

---

(*vv*) I say this, because such, very properly as I think, is the *National* feeling in Great Britain and Ireland on the Law of Libel, that the result to Plaintiffs in such circumstances as the Plaintiff in the Islandeady case, will generally be *nominal* damages and loss of character ; while the costs will be paid *for* the Defendant *by* public subscription.—See the *Telegraph* of January 19, 1842, article—LAW OF LIBEL, and the list of sub- scribers to the whole amount of the *taxed* costs.

does exist in Ireland, a power which sets at defiance the feelings of Gregory XVI. and of the Catholic Hierarchy in Ireland. That power appears to me TO BE WIELDED BY ARCHBISHOP M'HALE. If it be permitted to Archbishop M'Hale to wield that power much longer, I fear that we shall have Ireland in CIVIL WAR; and what I wish to impress upon your Lordship and upon the public in Great Britain and Ireland, is this impression on my own mind. If the Legislature does not repeal the Law of Elizabeth, it is impossible, as far as I can judge from the result of the communications between Sir Henry Seymour and Count Lutzow, see note (*h*) p. 195 of these letters, and note (*m*) p. 205, or between the Cardinal Lambruschini and the Earl of Shrewsbury, referred to in p. 99 of these letters, to hope, that *any* such "efficient control" to the "irresponsible power" of Archbishop M'Hale, as can secure public tranquillity in Ireland, CAN BE established. No objections drawn from *possible future contingencies,* can have any weight with me, as arguments against a measure which I am convinced is alike necessary for the credit of the Holy See, for the interests of Queen Victoria, and for the tranquillity of Ireland, under *existing* circumstances.

It is *worse* than childish to content ourselves, under existing circumstances, with *merely* saying, that it is *much to be lamented,* that Archbishop M'Hale should have been placed in the unenviable

T 2

position in August, 1841, of answering such questions as that which Baron Richards *stopped him* from answering ; and which if he had answered, might possibly have compromised him as much as his answers to Mr. Blake (not the Chief Remembrancer) have compromised him, in the Sligo trial of March, 1837 ; that it is a *great pity*, the Editor of the *Telegraph* should have noticed the conduct of the Rev. Mr. Gallaher ; that it is a *sad thing* that the Hon. Mr. Cavendish should have subpœnaed Archbishop M'Hale ; but that it can't be helped, and that no more must be said about it ; otherwise scandal will be occasioned. What is this but direct encouragement of *a most vicious system ?* The question is, whether in the present state of agitation in Ireland, and of clerical interference in that agitation, such lamentable occurrences, such great pities, such sad things, must not be expected to be more and more frequent, to the increased disparagement of Catholicity in Ireland, and to the increased ruin of every social sympathy, and of every neighbourly, not to say moral, feeling. When the Catholics of Ireland shall have been persuaded, that their *political* conduct will be a main consideration with their Pastors in their animadversions upon their *moral* conduct ; that the agitator whose moral conduct *is* reprehensible *may be* publicly *laughed at*, and his corporal defects made a subject of merriment, in the House of God during

Divine Service (see p. 237, l. 1, of these Letters);
but that the parishioner who differs in *political* feeling from his parish priest, *will be* publicly
cursed if his moral conduct *has been formerly*
reprehensible, though there be obstinacy in vice
in the agitator, and continued proof of repent-
ance *(ww)* in the non-agitator ; will the interests

(ww) The reader of the report of the trial at Galway, in
August, 1841, will no doubt have observed, that the Rev. Mr.
Henry *swears* (p 264) that it was on account of *the return of
Kitty Blake* to Islandeady, in the beginning of March, 1841,
contrary to his prohibition, and, apparently, contrary to her own
engagement to him not to return, and also on account of *his
having been informed*, in the beginning of March, by Butler
and others, that *she had been visited* by Mr. John Burke *since
her return*, that he had ordered Rev Mr. Gallaher to *denounce*,
and that Rev. Mr. Gallaher *cursed*, Mr. John Burke (not the
girl) from the altar ; but he will also have observed, that Rev.
Mr. Henry *also swears*, that he made no remonstrance, from
the beginning to the 14th of March, to Mr. John Burke, in consequence of the *information* he had received against him since
the girl's return, and that Mr. John Burke *swears* (p. 256) that
he had *renounced all connexion* with the girl since she left his
father's house, previous to Christmas, 1840, and *never visited
her since her return* to Islandeady, where she was living "in the
" very next house to the chapel (p. 265), after she left Mr.
" Burke's house in the family way "—" about the end of August
" or commencement of September, 1840," (says Mr. John Burke,
p. 256,) till *sent away* by Rev. Mr. Henry from *that* house ; in
consequence of which order, she remained at *a distance from the
chapel* till the beginning of March, 1841, when she again returned to live (says Mr. Nolan, p. 254,) "*convenient to the*

either of Christian morality or of public tranquillity in Ireland, be promoted by such a persuasion? I hardly think that Archbishop M'Hale himself, reckless as he has proved himself in his assertions, will maintain the affirmative of *such* a proposition; even though he should continue to declare, and to affect to believe, that they who oppose *his notions* of what is necessary for the advantage of Catholicity in Ireland, however much those notions may be in opposition to the wishes and feelings of Gregory XVI. and of the Catholic Hierarchy of Ireland, as expressed in the resolutions of 1830 and 1834, are the " enemies of " Ireland, screening their enmity, which cannot " be disguised, under the cloak of friendship," which is the accusation published against myself in the *Freeman's Journal* of December 20th, 1841, p. 5, col. 1, and signed " ✝ John, Archbishop of Tuam."

I have the honor to be,
My Lord,
With sincere esteem and respect,
Your Lordship's obedient humble Servant,
CLIFFORD.

" *chapel*,"—" *within one mile* (says Mr. Joseph Burke, p. 252,) " of his father's house," where his brother it seems lived ; while Rev. Mr. Henry, p. 262, states, that he informed his curate, Rev. Mr. Gallaher, when he ordered him to *denounce* Mr. John Burke, that " one of them resided in the *very next house to the* " *girl*."—C.

APPENDIX.

No. I.

·TO THE RIGHT HON. LORD CLIFFORD.

My Lord,

A LETTER has appeared in the *Mayo Telegraph,* calling in
your Lordship's name, on the Proprietor of that journal, to
say whether or no your *respected friend,* the Right Rev. Dr.
O'Finan, brought a criminal action against one priest
Flannelly in 1838.[*] It is with the greatest reluctance I
take leave to address your Lordship on the subject matter
of that document : your Lordship's name has given it an
importance, to which it otherwise would not be entitled.
The high station which your Lordship occupies in society,
the unsullied character of yourself and family, prevent me
entertaining the thought, that your Lordship, in giving that
letter to the public, was actuated by any ungenerous or
unworthy motive. It is, however, painful to the Catholics
to be reminded of the memorable and melancholy confusion,
which for three years covered the diocese of Killala with
disgrace, and the Catholics of Ireland with shame. Your

---

[*] An error of the writer of the Letter, instead of 1837.

Lordship, as a Catholic, would not willingly drag before a lay tribunal the ecclesiastical decisions of the Catholic Hierarchy of Ireland, nor would you subject the wise resolves of Gregory XVI. to an *alien* Parliament.—You, my Lord, whose enlightened mind, free from national prejudice, must not regret that the ecclesiastical affairs of Catholic Ireland are not under the control of the British House of Commons, or the still loftier decisions of that house of which your Lordship is a distinguished member. While the unsubdued fidelity, with which the Catholic people have clung to that religion for which their fathers bled and for which they themselves suffer, may cause your Lordship to drop a tear over the degeneracy of your native land, it may afford you some consolation to find, that the Catholic Hierarchy, entertaining the highest respect for the opinions of Lord Clifford, are subject to the approbation of the Chief Pastor alone. If your Lordship's letter to the *Telegraph* were confined to the columns of that paper, I might not notice it; but having been published in all the Conservative papers of Ireland, and its sentiments made the theme of universal eulogy, I am induced to call your Lordship's attention to the position in which you have placed yourself. Among the many compliments your Lordship's letter has received from the bitterest enemies of Catholic Ireland, permit me to direct your Lordship's attention to one. The *Packet*, that organ of the deepest slander and the foulest abuse of the Catholic people and priesthood of Ireland, says " that if the sentiments contained in your letter were com- " mon to the Catholics of Ireland, Catholicity from being, " as it is, a *curse*, would be a blessing." A compliment coming from that party which calls *Catholicity a curse* must be felt by your Lordship as a keen cutting reproach, for it is to be hoped that even a Catholic Peer of degenerate England, would not willingly undertake the defence of his most valued friend, if that defence proved that his religion was a curse instead of a blessing.*

---

* Though I never have been and probably never shall be officially employed in a diplomatic career, I have lived too long among diplomats, to be provoked to any thing but a *smile* at the exordium of this letter. I cannot indeed expect to continue a favorite with many who have eulogised the two first of these letters, after the publication of the three subsequent ones : and I must confess that if my forebodings on that head should be verified, I shall resign my popularity without a sigh ; but it is precisely in order that some who have *mis-judged Catholicity* in consequence of the Sligo trial and the newspaper productions of " ✠ John, Archbishop of Tuam," may cease to misjudge that *one* Holy Catholic Church, which I profess in the *Apostles'* creed to believe, that I have written and published these letters. Yet there is a deep and important truth, and one which cannot be too sedulously inculcated at the present crisis of Ireland's fate, upon *all* the inhabitants of that long ill-treated Country, *concealed*, if I may so express myself, in the words of the *Packet*, which the writer signing himself " a Roman Catholic Priest of Killala," either does not see, or *affected not to see*, when he penned the words on which I am now commenting. Let that writer take in hand a little work entitled " Substance of Two Speeches delivered in the House of Commons on " May 10th, 1825, and May 9th, 1828, on the Roman Catholic Question, by " Sir Robert Harry Inglis, Bart. London : Hatchard, 1828 ;" and turn to p. 103 of that little work of 174 pages, an afflicting proof of an Anti-Catholic education acting upon a benevolent mind ; and let him say, whether it is wonderful that minds *so* educated, persons who have *so* read history, should call Catholicity *a curse* to Ireland, and in their astonishment at reading in my two first letters to Lord Alvanley, sentiments so utterly repugnant to *their* notions of Catholicity, should exclaim " Such Catholicity as that of the writer " of these two letters, *whoever he may be*, would be *a blessing* to Ireland." The deep and important truth therefore *concealed* in the exclamation of the Editor of the *Packet* is this—Archbishop M'Hale's writings and conduct have not given to the *Protestants* of Ireland *who needed information*, the idea, that the Catholic Church is a *tender Mother*, or that Gregory XVI. is a *tender* Father, however much they may have persuaded either Catholics or Protestants in Ireland, that Archbishop M'Hale is a learned theologian, a classical scholar, a formidable demagogue, or a crafty politician. Such persuasion is far less necessary or advantageous to the Catholics or Protestants in Ireland, than a *deep conviction* that the Catholic Church, of which Gregory XVI. is the head, is a *tender Mother*, and that she requires the obedience in spirituals, and in spirituals *alone*, to *Herself* and *Her* Chief Pastor, and to her *subordinate* Pastors, of *all baptized persons*, not for her

Your Lordship's zeal in defence of your venerable friend
betrays you into indiscretions which your more sober judgment must condemn. Suppose, then, for a moment, that
every word of your Lordship's letter be true, what object
could your Lordship attain by that mischievous production ?
After a good deal of Canon law, which, I think, will puzzle

---

sake but for theirs, since thus only they can enjoy true tranquillity.   I am
willing to hope, that the errors of Archbishop M'Hale as a *political chief*,
may be, like the errors of the anonymous Political Essayist of Maynooth,
errors of judgment rather than of intention ; that he would be the first to
lament the *necessary* consequences of such proceedings, as he recommended
to the Catholics of Ireland, when introduced by Bishop Brown to the Assembly at Galway as " the brightest ornament and lustre of the Catholic
" Clergy of Ireland, and about to speak to that assembly the sentiments of
" its Hierarchy."   But such error of judgment, was the natural consequence
of another, which seems to form the basis of his compositions, especially since
1836 ; namely, the principle of adopting that spirit of *angry invective*, which
always characterizes the productions of seditious and revolutionary writers ;
and of employing *that tone* in advocating what *he conceives* to be advantageous to Catholicity, or in the refutation of the numerous aspersions
and unjust accusations cast upon Catholics by the adversaries of that Holy
Religion.   Violence, whether in words or in action, never *was* the language
or the conduct *approved* by the Catholic Church, and never *ought to have been*
the language or the conduct of her defenders.   " It is certainly," says
S. John Chrysostom, in his 84th homily on the words of the Gospel of *St.
Matthew* x. 16—' Behold I send you as sheep among wolves'—" it is cer-
" tainly a greater and a more admirable thing to change the minds of ad-
" versaries, and to alter their dispositions, than to kill them ; especially as
" they (the Apostles) were only twelve, and the whole world was full of wolves.
" Let us therefore blush, who, acting far otherwise, rush like wolves upon
" our adversaries.   For as long as we shall be sheep, we shall overcome :
" even though a thousand wolves surround us, we *get round* them (perigino-
" metha) and conquer.   But if we will be wolves, we are overcome ; *for then
" recedes from us the assistance of the shepherd*, who does not feed wolves, but
" sheep."
     The Roman Catholic Church appoints this beautifully instructive lesson to
be annually read in her morning office on the feast of S. Barnabas ; and the
passage will be found in the original Greek, in the Protestant edition of
S. John Chrysostom's works, printed at Eton by I. Norton, 1612, vol. II.
p. 225.—C.

the sacred congregation to understand, you say that Dr.
O'Finan is *suspended*, and you also say that he is universally honoured and respected!! Your Lordship is the only
person who doubted either the one or the other. But as
you have thought proper to give your proofs to the world,
it is possible that some evil disposed individuals may *now*
doubt the latter part of your assertion, the first part is
stamped with the eternal seal of the humble fisherman.
" But Dr. O'Finan did not bring an action against a priest
" Flannelly, as impudently represented, but against the pro-
" prietor of the *Telegraph*." Let me then grant your Lordship the full benefit of that assertion also, what end is
gained? Dr. O'Finan was *suspended* , not because he
brought a criminal action against one of his own clergymen,
but in consequence of a series of complaints laid before the
Court of Rome, during the three years his Lordship was,
to use your own phrase, *acting* Bishop of Killala. Thus
you must see, though late, that the cause of your friend
has not been bettered by your zealous but ill-*advised* advocacy. Let me implore your Lordship's best attention
for a moment, and I think you will agree with me, that
your Lordship, and not his Holiness, has been impudently
imposed upon, with regard to the Sligo *criminal* trial, and
that the individual who induced your Lordship to put your
name to that document, should be called by you a *wretched*
man, rather than the translator in whose ability and honesty
the Sacred Congregation reposed their confidence. The
trial at Sligo was instituted in consequence of a letter
signed " Aladensis." That letter, as well as some previous
ones, ascribed the extraordinary conduct of Dr. O'Finan
to the advice and influence of the Rev. Mr. Lyons, appointed by his Lordship Vicar-General of the Diocese.
As his appointment to that important office was supposed
to be the fruitful source of all the evils of Killala, the Court

of Rome relieved the Very Rev. gentleman from his numerous duties, permitting him to enjoy the empty honours of
the Deanship. Thus matters remained. The Dean was
supposed to be the real defendant, as his fitness or unfitness
was supposed to be their chief object of enquiry. For many
months previous to the trial, the *Telegraph,* by its dark
and mysterious insinuations, led the kind-hearted Conservatives of Sligo to believe that nothing less cogent than
proofs positive of conduct unworthy of a clergyman, nay,
of a Christian, would be forthcoming. Under these distressing circumstances the Rev. Mr. Flannelly, accompanied by another clergyman, waited on Dr. O'Finan, and
admitted at once that he was the author of the letter. His
Lordship, however, required a written admission, which
was immediately given, and which his Lordship handed to
his solicitor,* adding that he would be directed by him.
Here then we have a Catholic priest acknowledging to
his lawful superior that he was the author of a letter, which
in law could not be justified. He offers himself as a
peace-offering, he sacrifices himself rather than continue
that scandal which lasted too long. No sooner was it

---

* This is not *quite correct.* Bishop O'Finan observed, that " there was no
" admission made by Rev. Mr. Flannelly of the *untruth* of the statements in
" the Letter signed ' Aladensis,' which the Rev. Mr. Flannelly had assured,
" and *still continued to assure* the Defendant, the Hon. Mr. Cavendish, *were*
" *perfectly true ;* and that consequently, all he could do, was to be directed
" *by his Counsel.*" In law *truth may be a libel.* Bishop O'Finan required,
consequently, of Rev. Mr. Flannelly, *not merely* that he should acknowledge
himself in writing " the *author* of a letter which *in law could not be justified ;*"
but the author of a letter which was *morally unjustifiable* on account of the
untruth and scandalously insubordinate character of its statements. This the
Rev. Mr. Flannelly refused to admit ; and, of course, the Hon. Mr. Cavendish (the Defendant) refused also to admit, feeling confident, that Rev. Mr.
Flannelly, and *they who supported him,* would bear him out in the *truth* of
what he had published under their direction.—C.

known that the authorship of the letter was admitted, than
the Orangemen of Sligo felt all the disappointment of certain anticipated pleasure. But the joy of the Catholic as
well as the regret of the Protestant, was premature. The
trial must go on. The Roman Catholic gentlemen of the
grand jury waited on Dr. O'Finan, requesting his Lordship,
now that the author was in his power, to stop the trial. A
deputation from the Roman Catholics of the town waited on
him for the same purpose, but all in vain. You see, then,
my Lord, that the *Telegraph* in its report was justified in
asserting that the trial was against a Priest Flannelly, and
not against itself. The *Telegraph* states, explicitly and
often, that the trial was against the Reverend Mr. Flannelly. The transaction is then correct. You see, then, my
Lord, you were not justified in calling the translator a
" wretched man, whose object was impudently to impose
" a mischievous calumny on the Pope."* The diocese of
Killala has enjoyed uninterrupted repose these three years,
and still your Lordship regrets to find in your late visit to
the eternal city, that the father of the christian world,
labouring under an unfortunate delusion, refuses, even
at your pressing solicitations, to stir up again the embers

---

* The reason why these words, which the reader by referring to p. 60 of
these letters, will see *are altered*, it is to be feared *intentionally* by the substitution of the words " the Pope " for " those Cardinals," were used by me in
my letter to the Hon. Mr. Cavendish, is, that the translator had represented *the
Priest Flannelly as having cited* Archbishop M'Hale, which the translator
knew not to be the truth. In order to get *the Cardinals* to represent to *the
Pope*, that Archbishop M'Hale was justifiable, or at least excusable, in *appearing* before the Protestant Lay Court, against Bishop O'Finan, it was *necessary* to represent the Archbishop, as appearing *at the request of a Catholic
Priest*, in defence of that Catholic Priest's character, criminally attacked
by his Bishop (O'Finan), who was that Archbishop's suffragan, before that
Court, where the Archbishop, poor artless man ! was *entrapped by the cunning
of the Protestant lawyers* to say things which *he did not mean to say.*—C.

of discord. Your Lordship is supposed by many to be the dupe of two deep designing interested individuals. A letter coming from the proprietor of the *Telegraph* while labouring under the fear of 500*l.* might be looked upon as being doubtful testimony. I have known some very "honourable "men" who would strain a little point for a much smaller sum. As to the other gentleman, the Very Rev. Dean Lyons, whom your Lordship so fortunately met in Dublin, and who is supposed to influence your Lordship to some extent, I shall pass him by. Let me conclude by assuring your Lordship it gives me very great pleasure to find, that your Lordship is the only Catholic Peer of the realm, whose abuse of the professors of your own religion has earned the best thanks of the Orange journals; and that the Very Rev. Dean is the only Catholic priest in Ireland who would be a party to an address to a Lord Lieutenant, whose official adviser would think it better "that Ireland should be barbarous and uncivilized, than Catholic."

I have the honour to be, &c., &c.,
A ROMAN CATHOLIC PRIEST
Of Killala.

P. S.—The writer hopes that it is not unreasonable in him to expect that the Liberal Journals, those faithful guardians of Ireland's rights and liberty, which have given circulation to Lord Clifford's letter, will give insertion to this reply.

ECCLESIASTICAL MISREPRESENTATION.——THE DIOCESE OF KILLALA.

"Fraud will be shamed, and cant and craft must fly,
"And truth stand forth and meet the public eye."

IN the TELEGRAPH of the 8th instant we published a most interesting letter, addressed to the Honourable Mr. Cavendish by the Right Hon. Lord Clifford, an eminent and highly-distinguished Roman Catholic nobleman, on the subject of the removal of Doctor O'Finan from the diocese of Killala. The noble Lord having ascertained with the deepest feelings of regret and surprise, that his Holiness, Gregory XVI., " still laboured under the same delusion " which had been impudently imposed upon him in Novem- " ber, 1838," relative to the state of matters between Dr. O'Finan and his Clergy, called upon Mr. Cavendish to favour him with a declaration of certain facts in his own handwriting, in order to rectify the gross mis-statements forwarded to the eternal city; firmly impressed with the accuracy of which, the Pope suspended Dr. O'Finan, " the " *actual* but not acting bishop of Killala," from exercising the sacred functions of his responsible office, and deprived him of the presidency of that rightful district which his Lordship governed for so long a period. Mr. Cavendish's calm, temperate, and explicit reply appeared in the same post with Lord Clifford's communication ; and we observe, with sincere pleasure, that our cotemporaries—Liberal and Conservative, Radical and Tory—have transfered both into their widely circulated columns.

One syllable of comment on this interesting topic should not, at the present moment, have been penned by us, were it not that in the last number of the *Ballina Advertiser* there appeared a letter bearing the signature, " A Roman " Catholic Priest of Killala," purporting to be a reply to Lord Clifford's communication. In justice to all parties, and actuated with that spirit of fair play which should ever characterize the conduct of public Journalists, we give the precious epistle the benefit of our circulation, although by no means adopting the principle, that it is obligatory on the part of an editor to publish an anonymous communication, in answer to one with a real signature.

Under the style and title of " A Roman Catholic Priest " of Killala," some unknown *literateur* stands forward to champion with the Right Hon. Lord Clifford; but we cannot coerce ourselves into the belief, that any clergyman of that diocese would have the presumption and base hardihood to send before the people of this truth-loving and independent province, knowingly and wilfully, such a terrible tissue of malevolently malicious fabrications, and depraved falsehoods. Generally speaking, the Catholic priesthood, officiating in the diocese of Killala, are incapable of perverting truth. If, however, any member of that enlightened body has so far forgotten the dictates of justice, and overlooked the bounds of veracity—if, in violation of the rules and ordinances which regulate every well-constituted society, he has laboured to vilify the venerable O'Finan, then must he be prepared to stand before the bar of public opinion, and await that condemnation which is ever sure to fall upon the malicious vilifier of purity—the torturer of facts to his own base purposes—and the insiduous slanderer of moral worth, integrity, and independence. Again, before entering into detail, we must express our decided conviction, that the Roman Catholic Priests of Killala had neither hand, act, or part in the concoction of the letter which is now the subject matter of investigation. But we have every well grounded reason to suspect that it is the production of " the " wretched man," who, by himself or his agent, caused the fraud to be practised on his Holiness, by the false translation of the English documents, including the report of the Sligo trial, which led to the suspension of Dr. O'Finan from the performance of his holy functions.

Foremost among the many assertions contained in the letter of " A Roman Catholic Priest of Killala" we find it stated—" Dr. O'Finan was *suspended*, not because he " brought a criminal action against one of his own clergy-

" men, but in consequence of a series of complaints laid
" before the Court of Rome, during the three years his Lord-
" ship was, to use your own phrase, *acting* Bishop of
" Killala." When such reckless averments are recorded
in provincial prints, we see no just reason for objecting to
the old saying, that " Tenterden steeple was the cause of
" Goodwin Sands." Our answer, however, will completely
stamp such a monstrosity with the brand of falsehood.

TEXT CONTINUED.

CORRECTED TEXT.*

Mr. Cavendish, when last he visited the metropolis of Ireland, was favoured with a perusal of the original document drawn up by the Cardinals deputed to inquire into the merits of Dr. O'Finan's case, and addressed to his Lordship by the authority of the sacred congregation of the propaganda, suspending him from exercising the functions of Bishop of Killala, *solely* on the ground of his having brought a criminal accusation against one of his own clergymen before a Protestant lay

Lord Clifford, when Mr. Cavendish last visited the metropolis of Ireland, placed in that gentleman's hands, in presence of the Very Rev. Dean Lyons, the original document in Italian, by which the suspension of Bishop O'Finan was notified to that Prelate by the Cardinal Prefect of Propaganda;† and Lord Clifford also produced to Mr. Cavendish another Italian document‡ in the handwriting of the Secretary of Propaganda, containing certain propositions, the signature of which by the

---

* This corrected text is put along-side of the original text as it appeared without my knowledge in the *Telegraph*, in order that the reader may at once see how the mistake which the Editor of the *Telegraph* has made has occurred, perfectly innocently on his part, but very material as to the proper understanding of the case.—C.

† See p. 156 of these letters.   ‡ p. 158.

U

tribunal in Sligo, instead of referring the ground of complaint to the metropolitan of the diocese, the Most Rev. Dr. M'Hale. This reason, and this *alone*, is assigned by the Cardinals for putting an abrupt termination to the episcopal reign of Dr. O'Finan in the West of Ireland; and with the laudable intention of altogether removing the unfounded impression from the minds of the spiritual authorities at Rome, Lord Clifford addressed the proprietor of this Journal.

Bishop would, in the opinion of the Secretary, entitle the Bishop to return to his diocese of Killala as *acting* Bishop of that See. The sixth of those propositions related to the trial at Sligo. With the laudable intention of altogether removing the unfounded impression from the minds of the spiritual authorities at Rome, which had been produced upon them respecting the nature of the Sligo trial, and the cause of it, Lord Clifford addressed the proprietor of this Journal.

How consistent with truth—how worthy of belief—is this first foul statement of the genius who dubs himself a Roman Catholic Priest? With a pretended display of impassioned earnestness, and a somewhat similar *regard* to truth, the writer declares, " That for many months previous " to the trial, the *Telegraph*, by its dark and mysterious " insinuations, led the kind-hearted Conservatives of Sligo " to believe that nothing less cogent than proofs positive of " conduct unworthy of a clergyman—nay of a Christian, would be forthcoming."* Nothing possibly can be more unfounded or erroneous that the *gravamen* of this paragraph. From commencement to end it is supremely ridiculous, and

---

* Let the reader turn to the note on p. 142 of the second part of these letters. But let him observe that the words there quoted are the words, not of the Editor or Proprietor of the *Telegraph ;* but of Aladensis.——C.

evidently the invention either of a disordered brain or a vicious intellect. No article of a " dark mysterious" character, having the most remote bearing on the subject, can be found in the columns of this Journal, and the reason is obvious. Mr. Cavendish, most judiciously, published not one solitary syllable on the differences which unhappily existed between Dr. O'Finan and his clergymen, unless what was banded to him by the Rev. Mr. Flannelly, accompanied with an explicit undertaking, in writing, that every charge, and every portion of an accusation contained on the records of the court, would be proved to a demonstration, far and away beyond the possibility of a doubt, true, well founded, and authentic.* Nay, more, it was by the direction of this Rev. Mr. Flannelly that the plea of justification was placed upon the records of the court—he having pledged himself, by a written document, to procure witnesses who would justify each and every averment contained in the libellous letters of " Aladensis." Here, then, we have falsehood the second from the self-styled " Roman Catholic Priest of Killala."

" Under these distressing circumstances," continues the *truthful* writer, " the Rev. Mr. Flannelly, accompanied by " another clergyman, waited on Dr. O'Finan, and admitted at " once that he was the author of the letter. His Lordship, " however, required a written admission, which was immedi- " ately given, and which his Lordship handed to his Solici- " tor, adding, that he would be directed by him." Although this paragraph has really no reference whatever to the subject matter of Lord Clifford's queries to the Hon. Mr. Cavendish, it is cunningly dove-tailed into " the pre- " tended reply," with the evident intention of endeavouring to demonstrate that the Rev Mr. Flannelly was the de-

---

* See note on p. 300.

fendant in the action, tried before a Protestant tribunal. The treacherous object will be most expeditiously frustrated by the simple narration of the following facts : The Rev. Mr. Flannelly, it is indisputable, avowed himself to Dr. O'Finan, as the *responsible* author of the letters signed " Aladensis." But let it be clearly understood that this avowal was not made until the eleventh hour, when Dr. O'Finan, without a serious compromise of his own honour and a *bona fide* admission of the charges preferred against him, could not—to use the chaste phraseology of " a Ca- " tholic Priest of Killala"—" drop the trial." On the day previous to that fixed for hearing the record, the author gave himself up ; but, *the pleas of justification* had been entered —Counsel had received instructions therein to justify— witnesses were summoned to support the several aver- ments and allegations. Could Dr. O'Finan, then, we ask—consistently with that character which he boasted was pure and unsullied—attempt to retire from court without adducing evidence to shew that Mr. Cavendish had published in the *Mayo Telegraph* certain reflections on his honour, piety, and probity of conduct, which were without the slightest shadow of a foundation.* Suppose for one instant, that after a surrender of Mr. Flannelly, as the author of " Aladensis's " letters, Dr. O'Finan, with the pleas of justification staring him full in the face, had de- clined proceeding further with his civil action against the

---

* See Rev. Mr. Flannelly's letter, p. 179 of these letters. I have the authority of Bishop O'Finan and of Counsellor West for asserting, that if *at any time* previous to going into Court, Rev. Mr. Flannelly had recognised in writing the *falsehood* of the letters signed " *Aladensis*," the trial would have been abandoned, and I have the authority of the Hon. Mr. Cavendish for asserting, that if Rev. Mr. Flannelly had made the acknowledgment of *falsehood* required by Bishop O'Finan and Mr. West, he would have ac- knowledged the same. In fact, the Hon. Mr. Cavendish repeatedly de- clared that he had no knowledge of his own on the matter.—C.

Proprietor of this Journal, what estimate would have been formed of his moral worth and rectitude? In what light would he be looked upon by the Clergy over whom he exercised control, and the flock whose spiritual welfare he had entrusted to his vigilance? We leave " A Roman " Catholic Priest of Killala" to answer this simple query. What a vast difference it would have caused—how opposite a complexion the entire matter might have assumed —had the Rev. Mr. Flannelly officially communicated to Dr. O'Finan " the secret of his soul," previous to the instituting of the legal preliminary proceedings against Mr. Cavendish, or at all events before the defendant had pleaded justification. Is there a moral doubt on the mind of any rational man, that, if early intimation of this fact had been given to Dr. O'Finan, he would have abandoned the libel prosecution, before " A Protestant Tribunal," against the mere publisher, and, consequently, more innocent party.

The next assertion made by the veritable " Roman " Catholic Priest of Killala" is, that " the *Telegraph*, in its " report, was justified in stating that the trial was against a " Priest Flannelly, and not against itself." Now, we distinctly, and without any equivocation whatsoever, deny that such an absurd and improbable assertion ever appeared in the columns of this journal. If Priest Flannelly was the defendant in the civil action, why were not the damages and costs paid by him? Is it not undeniable that Mr. Cavendish was absolutely incarcerated in his own house for SIXTEEN MONTHS to avoid the Sheriff and Coroner, in whose hands Dr. O'Finan's attorney had placed an execution against the Hon. Gentleman's person for upwards of EIGHT HUNDRED POUNDS damages and costs. Knowing this to be the fact, with what degree of truth has " A " Roman Catholic Priest of Killala " presumed to assert that " the *Telegraph* stated explicitly, and often, that the

" trial was against the Rev. Mr. Flannelly ? " Monstrous calumny ! We dare, we defy, the writer to point out one single line in the *Telegraph* that could be construed, even by the most obtuse and prejudiced mind, into an admission or declaration of such a falsity. Is there a man in Ireland to confirm this audacious fabrication. Such a villainous tirade of falsehood, must prove disgusting—indeed it carries with it its own antidote. We probably may have earned the writer's malignant hostility by exposing his mischievous career—therefore it is that he exercises on the *Telegraph* his capacity for insolent abuse and lying.

During the period of Mr. Cavendish's confinement in his own mansion, his Grace the Archbishop of Tuam not unfrequently corresponded with the Honourable Gentleman, and, on several occasions, honoured him with personal visits. Will it be contended that Dr. M'Hale *ever* insinuated, in Mr. Cavendish's presence, that the action was instituted before " a Protestant Tribunal " against the Rev. Mr. Flannelly ? On the contrary ; did not his Lordship state to Mr. Cavendish, in the presence of several faithworthy persons, that he could *easily* raise the entire amount of the execution issued by Dr. O'Finan's Solicitor ; but that it went against his conscience and the consciences of his clergymen that a single shilling of their money should go either into the pocket of the Right Rev Plaintiff, as payment of the damages, or into that of his Lordship's legal adviser, in discharge of the costs incurred ? Can " A " Roman Catholic Priest of Killala " controvert this hierarchical " peace offering ? " Or will it be denied that Dr. M'Hale suggested to Mr. Cavendish the propriety of allowing himself to be arrested, cast into gaol, and relieved from his responsibilities under the provisions of the Insolvent Debtor's Act—when he would receive from him, not only an amount of money equal to that mentioned in the O'Finan execution, but a further sum for the benefit of his family. Come, speak out " Roman Catholic Priest of Killala " and refute if thou durst, one iota of those seductive offers made to the Proprietor of the *Telegraph* by JOHN of TUAM. And yet, forsooth, the Rev. Mr. Flannelly was the defendant in the *criminal* prosecution brought by Dr. O'Finan before a " Protestant lay tribunal." Wicked, deep-designed, and most malevolent fabrication.

It is almost needless to state that Dr. M'Hale's proposition was indignantly rejected by Mr. Cavendish, and repudiated by every member of his family. The period of his confinement dragged on its slow existence, and he was not released from self-incarceration until Dr. O'Finan most benevolently consented to forgive the £500 damages, provided that his costs, taxed at £328, were discharged. Under these circumstances was he enabled to regain his liberty, and not on the fulfilment of an engagement previously entered into by Dr. M'Hale and the Rev. Mr. Flannelly—an engagement which even up to the present day has not been in any respect perfected—guaranteeing the Proprietor against all pecuniary losses by the publication of the letters bearing the signature " Aladensis."

We should not have entered at such length into the present particulars, had it not been that " A Roman Catholic " Priest of Killala" by his distortion of truth, and assertion of barefaced falsehoods, rendered it indispensably necessary on our part to lay before the public a plain unvarnished statement of facts.

[*From the Telegraph Newspaper, January 5th*, 1842.]

THE SEE OF KILLALA—DOCTOR O'FINAN.

The subjoined letter, from the pen of a "Roman Catholic Priest of Killala," we extract from the congenial columns of a demi-local print, addressed to the *pseudo* Editor :—

SIR,—In endeavouring, through the columns of the public press, to expose the unfounded assertions contained in a letter published in the *Mayo Telegraph*, I expressed my decided belief that Lord Clifford was made the dupe of two deep designing men. The angry effusion poured forth in a recent number of the same journal confirms me in that opinion. The uncompromising defender of the Catholic faith must be assailed—the vigilant and triumphant asserter of her rights and liberties must be calumniated, and the Hon. Proprietor of the *Telegraph*, as well as the ex-vicar-general of Killala, having found from experience, that they themselves long since lost the power to wound—induced his Lordship to give the sanction of his name to charges which from themselves would be quite innocuous. Mr. Cavendish, under pretence of answering the "Roman Catholic Priest of Killala," turns away from that humble individual to pour forth one of his usual ferocious tirades against the Archbishop of Tuam. He, whilst assailing the Hierarchy of Ireland, condescends to compliment the Catholic Clergy of Killala on their habitual love of truth. "The Catholic priesthood," says he, "officiating in that diocese, are incapable of perverting truth." While the Catholic Clergy of Killala shall be proud to secure the approbation of the virtuous and the wise, they must suspect themselves when the betrayer of Mayo's independence and the systematic reviler of the brightest ornament of their religion is made the channel of such approbation.

With the *Telegraph's* attacks on Doctor M'Hale I have

nothing to do; they are foreign to the point at issue. These virulent attacks have been so often repeated, and the fell spirit which dictated them is so well understood, that they injure none except the reckless writer. The Roman Catholic Priest asserted that Doctor O'Finan was suspended, not as Lord Clifford put forth *solely** on account of the Sligo trial, but in consequence of a *series of complaints* laid before the Court of Rome, during the three years he was acting Bishop of Killala. This assertion Mr. Cavendish calls in one of his pet phrases, " a reckless averment—a monstrous falsehood "—and he innocently believes the public will be satisfied with this mere assertion. I will give my facts to that discriminating public—*facts* which are too notorious for *even* Mr. Cavendish's denial; and if the feelings of the Right Rev. Doctor O'Finan must be hurt, I regret it most sincerely, as I am convinced his Lordship is not aware of the officious interference of his *pretended* friends, and that he would be the last person to stir up again the dying embers of religious discord, and let loose the demon of dissention on the diocese of his birth. I have undertaken the unpleasant task of freeing truth from the heap of calumny under which it groaned, and in discharge of that duty, I am forced reluctantly to place before the public *facts* of which they are already cognizant, but which I had hoped might soon be forgotten, and these facts, in my humble opinion, prove to a demonstration that Doctor O'Finan was *suspended*, as I have stated, " in consequence of a *series of complaints* laid before the Court of Rome during the three years be was acting Bishop of Killala." This is the great, indeed, the only point at issue between the writer of this letter on the one hand, and my Lord Clifford with his Lordship's

---

* The reader by referring to the letter here alluded to, which he will find p. 59 of these letters, will see that I make no such assertion as that here imputed to me.—C

protegés on the other. But before stating these facts, as Doctor M'Hale's name has been introduced by the *Telegraph* in connection with these matters, I think it right to premise that it was to Doctor M'Hale's influence Doctor O'Finan was indebted for his elevation to the See of Killala. In proof of this, I shall quote an extract from the Roman document, appointing the Most Rev. Doctor Crolly, Apostolical delegate, to investigate the causes of complaint in the diocese of Killala, which document is dated Rome, June, 1836, and bears the signature of Cardinal Franzoni, Prefect :—

" Denique ut cœtera omittam, summa est animorum discordia inter Episcopum ipsum et Archiepiscopum Tuamensem, quem Episcopus Alladensis sibi infensum esse putat, cum certum sit promotionem ejusdem ad Episcopatum commendationibus Archiepiscopi deberi." In English, thus—

" Finally to omit the other things, there exists the highest state of discordant feelings between the Bishop himself and the Archbishop of Tuam, whom the Bishop of Killala considers to be highly hostile to him, though it is certain that his promotion to the Episcopacy is owing to the recommendations of the Archbishop."

I shall now state the facts to which I have referred.

1st fact.—The first act of Episcopal jurisdiction exercised by Doctor O'Finan—immediately after taking possession of the chair, to which Doctor M'Hale's influence with the Clergy of Killala raised him—was the appointment of the Rev. Mr. Lyons, P.P. Kilmore, Erris, as his Vicar-General. This appointment formed the subject of a complaint to Rome, and the appointment was cancelled.

2nd fact.—The Rev. Mr. Barrett was deprived of the parish of Crossmolina, and suspended. The Rev. Mr. Barrett complains to the Court of Rome, and he is forthwith restored. He did not, however, long survive, and in a few weeks after he was a lifeless corpse. Such was the melancholy fate of that young and amiable clergyman, whose missionary career justified the distinguished literary honours he obtained during a long and laborious academical course— May he rest in peace.

3rd fact.—The Rev. Mr. Conway was suspended and deprived of his parish of Kilfian. The Rev. Mr. Conway complains to Rome, and the Rev. Mr. Conway is restored.

4th fact.—Many of the Clergy of Killala got collations from Doctor M'Hale while Bishop of that diocese.* Doctor O'Finan pronounced such collations null and void. These clergymen, naturally alarmed, complained to Rome, and Rome decided that such collations were canonical and could not be disturbed.†

These are a few of the public *facts* which rest not on my authority. In this state of unprecedented anarchy, that wisdom which has ever marked the character of the successors of St. Peter did not abandon the Roman Pontiff. His Holiness selects the learned successor of St. Patrick— invests him with extraordinary powers—appoints him his apostolical delegate—commissions him to go to Killala to investigate the various complaints of its clergy, to ascertain the causes of those complaints, and report to the Sacred Congregation the result of his enquiry. After a lengthened investigation, during which one would be at a loss whether to admire most the profound knowledge of canon law which he displayed—the unwearied assiduity with which he pro-

---

* On the subject of these collations, here *misrepresented* as conferred by Dr. M'Hale, *Bishop of Killala,* see Counsellor West's accurate statement of the case in pp. 132 and 133 of the second part of these letters, and the other passages referred to in the note on p. 133.—C.

† Rome did no such thing. Dean Lyons had the degree of Doctor conferred upon him at the recommendation of the present Cardinal Mai, then (in 1836) Secretary to Propaganda, in compliment in great measure for the able Exposition of *Canon Law on this subject* which he delivered in to the Sacred Congregation. What is the meaning of the fifth proposition, p. 158 of these letters, *if the collations were valid already* without the confirmation of Bishop O'Finan.—C.

secuted the arduous inquiry—or the unbending impartiality with which he discharged the delicate commission; his Grace of Armagh makes his report, and suggests, as required, the means which appeared to him best calculated to secure permanent peace.

Each and every one of these facts occurred during the three years Doctor O'Finan was acting Bishop of Killala, and though each and every one of those complaints had been decided by the Court of Rome in favor of the appellants—long before the appointment of his Grace of Armagh as a spiritual delegate*—still they were included in the high commission. His Grace of Armagh was, therefore, the official channel of communication; through his prudence and abilities the Sacred Congregation hoped to see peace restored to this distracted diocese—nor were their expectations disappointed. Thus, then, it appears that previous to the Sligo trial, Doctor O'Finan's decisions were reversed—his authority suspended, and himself virtually suspended. Will any individual then dare assert that the Sligo trial was the *sole* cause of his suspension, and not a *series of complaints* laid before the Court of Rome. The second count charges " a wretched man," with falsely representing Mr. Flannelly as the defendant—when Mr. Cavendish was really such. If the suspension of Doctor O'Finan was caused by that translation *solely*, it would be of the utmost importance to Mr. Cavendish to establish the fact. But as I have clearly shown that the suspension was not caused by that trial, it is of no moment to entertain who was the defendant, whether the proprietor of the *Telegraph* or the parish priest of Easkey. On this point Mr. Cavendish seems to place little or no reliance; but it affords him the opportunity which he required for assailing the Archbishop of Tuam.

---

* This assertion is not only untrue in itself, but, I am sorry to say, bears greatly the appearance of a wilful falsehood. See pages 132 and 133 of these letters. I must hope that the prejudices of its writer blinded him.—C.

Mr. Cavendish freely admits that Dr. O'Finan could not be excused in prosecuting the publisher, who was the innocent party, while he had the guilty one in his power, if the admission were made by Mr. Flannelly before the plea of justification was recorded. His Lordship knew from the *best* authority living, six months previous to the trial, that Mr. Flannelly was the author. If his Lordship was merely anxious to free his character from the imputation contained in that letter, his bitterest enemies, as well as his best friends, will easily admit that the author's admission, and his own verdict then pronounced against himself * would, considering the present law of libel, be a prouder testimonial than any verdict the most impartial jury could return. As, then, Mr. Flannelly proffered the most ample satisfaction in open court—it is evident that as regarded man's justification, as far as Mr. Cavendish was concerned, he could not attempt to justify, unassisted by Mr. Flannelly. If Dr. O'Finan had abandoned the trial, and so adopted the course more consistent with the character of a Bishop, his lordship would have gained in public estimation,† and " an innocent family would not be oppressed."

In my letter, as published in the *Telegraph* in juxta-position with Mr. Cavendish's answer, I use the following sentence :—" The Dean (Lyons) was supposed to be the real defendant, as his fitness or unfitness was supposed to be the chief object of inquiry. For many months the *Telegraph*, by its dark and mysterious insinuations, led the kind-hearted Conservatives of Sligo to believe that nothing less cogent than proofs positive of conduct unworthy of a clergyman,

---

* See notes on pp. 300 and 308 of these letters.—C.

† By reference to Counsellor West's letter, p. 147, lines 19, 20, 21 and 22 of these letters, the reader will see that a notable difference of opinion on this point existed between that Honorable gentleman and " A Roman Catholic Priest of Killala."—C.

nay, of a Christian, would be forthcoming." This sentence
Mr. Cavendish applies to Dr. O'Finan, though no allusion
was made to his Lordship in the entire passage. What
confidence can the public have in the assertions of the man
whose unblushing disregard for truth betrays him into so
obvious a perversion—a perversion so easily detected. I
have never, directly or indirectly, imputed blame to his
Lordship*—I have always entertained a high respect for
him; but I have often deplored the fatal course he was
advised to pursue. In taking leave of this subject, and I
hope for ever, I must again express my deep regret that the
imputations contained in Lord Clifford's letter forced me to
lay before the public a statement of the entire transaction.
In doing so, I have endeavoured to avoid wounding the
feelings of any individual—my object being to disabuse the
public mind of the false impressions Lord Clifford's letter
was intended to make; I have done so, I hope, without
resorting to the abuse which Mr. Cavendish has not failed
to employ.

I am, Sir,
Yours, &c. &c.
A ROMAN CATHOLIC PRIEST
OF KILLALA.

---

* From this passage the reader may certainly be *inclined* to conclude that
" Aladensis," quoted in the note on p. 183 of these letters, and " A Roman
Catholic Priest of Killala," are *two distinct personages*, entertaining very
different sentiments of Bishop O'Finan. But before *deciding* upon adopting
such a conclusion, the reader of the foregoing pages may perhaps also be
inclined to suspect, that Dean Lyons or the Honorable Mr. Cavendish, could
give him information which the Roman Catholic Priest of Killala would not
be particularly anxious that he should receive.—C.

The Diocese of Killala.

We are indebted to the *pleasing* and highly *polished* columns of a *ci-devant* Liberal local Journal, for the second letter of " A Roman Catholic Priest of Killala," replete with the usual quantity of *philosophy, enlightened views,* and very *amiable,* as well as *consistent,* writing. In good truth it is a most intellectual *bonne-bouche,* and, if we can credit the pure and argumentative author, conclusive on the subject under consideration, so far at least as he is, was, or has been concerned.

For a two-fold reason we transfer into our present publication " A Roman Catholic Priest's of Killala " second epistle. He has promised to take leave of the subject for ever, having, as he significantly states, " disabused the public mind of the false impressions Lord Clifford's letter was intended to make." This is our first and actuating motive. Secondly—We desire to render ample and perfect justice to all engaged in the controversy on Dr. O'Finan's suspension from the presidency of that rightful diocese which he governed for three years. Having acted thus liberally towards the 'Catholic Priest of Killala,' we feel that we cannot, consistently with our duty, permit his little bantling to reach the hands of our readers without a few editorial observations.

After assailing the *Telegraph* with a burst of the most *gentlemanly* epithets, the " Roman Catholic Priest of Killala," with sparkling and insolent assurance, repeats an oft-denied assertion, "that Lord Clifford has been made the dupe of two deep designing men : " Dean Lyons and Mr. Cavendish. The former Very Reverend and most excellent gentleman is fully able to vindicate triumphantly his character from the foul aspersion sought to be cast upon it ; and we feel assured that he will do so. So far as regards Mr. Cavendish we deny the ribald statement in *toto*. The attack is a meanly scurrile one, which inflicts disgrace and injury on those depraved spirits who presume to make it. Mr. Cavendish, when in Dublin some weeks since, on business totally unconnected with Dr. O'Finan or the diocese of Killala, received a note from Lord Clifford requesting that he would call upon him at his hotel. His Lordship's request was promptly acceded to. The note was the only communication Mr. Cavendish had received from the noble Lord; and the solicited interview afforded him an opportunity of being made acquainted for the first time with the Right Honourable Nobleman. On that occasion, Lord Clifford handed the proprietor of this Journal the important letter which we published on the 8th ult.,* at the same time requesting the favor of a written reply, which was forwarded to Lord Clifford's hotel on the day following.† Now we state in the most distinct manner possible, this to be the entire extent of the intimacy which existed between Lord Clifford and Mr. Cavendish. This display of gross ignorance or wilful misrepresentation in the " Roman Catholic Priest's of Killala," stricture is, in our humble conception, anything but creditable to him.

Again, we find it asserted, " that Mr. Cavendish has assailed the Catholic Hierarchy of Ireland." Like many of the writer's assertions, this statement is untrue, and malevolently false. We defy the self-styled ornament of the Catholic Church to lay his finger on one single syllable either uttered or written by the proprietor of the *Telegraph* that could be tortured, even by the most obtuse and blunted mind, into a demonstration of this wicked averment. But why do we argue with such a stultified scribbler as the " Roman Catholic Priest of Killala?" He has, it seems, a logic peculiarly his own. Its dialectics, however ingenious

---

* See p. 59 of these letters.—C.   † p. 61.—C.

though they may be, will scarcely, we fear, conceal or atone for his forgetfulness or disregard of truth.

We have now another point to settle with the " Priest of Killala." It is with respect to the misquotation of a passage " in our angry effusion which appeared in a recent number of the *Telegraph*." The Killala assailer of Dr. O'Finan will have it that Mr. Cavendish complimented the Catholic clergy of Killala on their *habitual* love of truth in the terms following :—" The Catholic Priesthood officiating in that diocese are incapable of perverting truth." This is a garbled and mis-quoted sentence from our observations ; and when placed in juxta-position with the original one, the difference will at once become perceptible. Our compliment to the Killala priesthood was thus conveyed :—" *Generally speaking*, they are incapable of perverting truth." But most assuredly we did not include all the Killala members in this rather flattering encomium, for had we done so, a grosser libel could not possibly be inflicted on the character of " The Roman Catholic Priest of Killala."

The writer of the epistle under consideration, having worked himself into a most dreadful, but feebly impotent, rage with the *Telegraph*, for " systematically reviling the highest ornament of the Catholic religion," turns his attention to Lord Clifford, whom he charges with stirring up the dying embers of religious discord, and letting loose the demon of dissension on the diocese of Killala. With observations so unjust, and at the same time so irrelevant to the question at issue, we do not consider it within our province to interfere. Should the noble lord, to whom they are directed, deem a reply necessary, he well knows his assailant, and possesses ample materials for his own vindication. But there is a little assertion parenthetically introduced into this tirade which, must not be permitted to escape without notice. " I think it right," says the Roman Catholic Priest of Killala, " to premise that it was to Dr. M'Hale's influence Dr. O'Finan was indebted for his elevation to the See of Killala ; " and in proof of this statement he proceeds to quote an extract from the Roman Catholic document, bearing the signature of Cardinal Franzoni, appointing the Most Rev. Dr. Crolly Apostolical Delegate to investigate the causes of complaint in the diocese of Killala, Far be it from our intention to contradict the *inuendo* conveyed in the Killala priest's averment ; but we cannot refrain from remarking that if it be strictly in accordance with truth, the Lord Archbishop of Tuam has acted most inconsistently ; for it is an indisputable fact, that letters were written by his Grace to the Court at Rome, calling on the Sovereign Pontiff, in the most respectful but artful terms, to cancel Dr. O'Finan's appointment to the presidency of Killala diocese.* Perhaps his Lordship may attempt to palliate this strange incongruity by exclaiming in the words of Ireland's champion :—" Who can blame me for being wiser to-day than I was yesterday."

The ground of Dr. O'Finan's suspension next becomes the subject of the Killala priest's reasoning powers ; but as the falsity of his premises, and the logical absurdity of his conclusions, are so perfectly apparent to every enlightened mind, we shall not enter into any refutation of this portion of

---

* If this were so, I think I must have known it; and in justice to *all* parties I feel myself bound, in re-printing this passage of an article in a newspaper written and published without any communication with me, to declare, that if any *such* communication as that here designated had been made to the Sacred Congregation, its effect would have been to prejudice, not the *object* but the *writer* of such a communication in the estimation of the Holy See. I think that the truth is as I have stated it, p. 327. The *one* letter to which I allude in p. 327, did not call upon the Holy See to *cancel* Bishop O'Finan's election, it only *insinuated* his unfitness, and *I believe that the insinuation was not understood.*—C.

the letter. Ignorance and absurdity, no matter how skil-
fully they may be decorated with sophisms and syllosisms,
can never be mistaken for sound sense and intellectual
capacity.

The enlightened Killala Priest, with genuine swaggering,
next rhodomontades in the following style:—" Mr. Cavendish freely admits that Dr. O'Finan could not be excused in
prosecuting the publisher, who was the innocent party,
while he had the guilty one in his power, if the admission
were made by Mr. Flannelly, before the plea of justification was recorded. His Lordship knew from the *best*
authority living, six months previous to the trial, that Mr.
Flannelly was the author. If his Lordship were merely
anxious to free his character from the imputation contained
in that letter—his bitterest enemies, as well as his best
friends, will easily admit that the author's admission, and
his own verdict then pronounced against himself would, considering the present law of libel, be a prouder testimonial
than any verdict the most impartial Jury could return."
The drift of the writer's laboured argument is evidently to
impress on the public mind that Mr. Flannelly gave himself
up to Dr. O'Finan fully six months before the trial in Sligo.
For who can be *the best authority* unless the responsible
author of the letters reflecting on the Bishop of Killala? That
the statement is totally incorrect there will be little difficulty
in believing, when it is known that Mr. Cavendish has in
his possession at the present moment letters from the Rev.
Patrick Flannelly completely negativing the averment.
But it is unnecessary to resort to such evidence, inasmuch
as " the Roman Catholic Priest of Killala " in his first
letter, which appeared in the *Ballina Advertiser*, distinctly
stated, that " the Rev. Mr. Flannelly, accompanied by
another clergyman, waited on Dr. O'Finan, and admitted
that he was the author of the letter signed ' Aladensis.'

x 2

His Lordship, however, required a written admission, which was given, and which was handed to his Solicitor, adding that he would be directed by him." Now this transaction took place in the town of Sligo, *on the day previous* to that on which the trial commenced. If, then, as is asserted, Mr. Flannelly gave himself up to Dr. O'Finan six months previously, what necessity existed, we should like to know, for a second admission, and a written one too, previous to the Record being called on? The present untruth and the original shuffle are precisely of the same character, and of equal value. Dr. O'Finan knew as much about the author of " Aladensis," until the pleas of justification were placed on the Records of the Court, as the Emperor of China, and no more. But even the " Roman Catholic Priest of Killala " furnishes another proof that it was in Sligo the author " confessed the secret of his soul." Hear the Rev. special pleader soliloquizing in his first letter—"On its being known that the authorship of ' Aladensis' was admitted, the Orangemen of Sligo felt all the disappointment of certain anticipated pleasure. But the joy of the Catholic as well as the regret of the Protestant was premature. The trial must go on. The Roman Catholic gentlemen of the Grand Jury waited on Dr. O'Finan requesting his Lordship—*now that the author was known, and in his power—to stop* the trial. A deputation from the Roman Catholics of the town waited on him for the same purpose : but all in vain." Each and every fact contained in this extract, negatives most conclusively the assertion that " Dr. O'Finan knew from the *best* authority, six months previous to the trial, that Mr. Flannelly was the author."

Unfounded and malevolently malicious as such an affirmation undoubtedly is, unhappily for the character of the *gentleman* dubbing himself " A Roman Catholic Clergyman," he has attached his signature to a *more* infamous and wretched falsity. Hear it, single-hearted men of Mayo!—inhabitants of the Killala diocese—and pity the infatuated being who could lend himself to the promulgation of such a deep designing, and most ribald accusation. " Mr. Flannelly," modestly exclaims the writer, " proffered the most ample satisfaction in open court." Coming from a man who was present during the entire trial we know not in what terms to express our indignation at the publication of such a perversion of truth. Nothing can be more false and infamous. But what else could be expected from the vitiated mind of the proud and presumptive man who penned it ?

Reference to another extract is necessary, and then we shall draw our rather lengthy article to a conclusion. Most complacently, and with a degree of self-sufficiency unparalleled, the Killala Priest asserts that it is of no consequence whether the accusation was a criminal one against Mr. Flannelly, or a civil action against Mr. Cavendish ; nor is it, in his opinion, of any moment to establish the fact whether the translation of the documents were genuine or false. The " Reverend " author of such sentiments must either care little for the difference between right and wrong, or be totally unacquainted with the perpetrator of the gross fraud committed on his Holiness, Pope Gregory XVI.—a fraud deeply plotted and cunningly designed to blight the prospects of Dr. O'Finan, and calculated to bring down upon the individuals who participated in it most lasting disgrace—a fraud infamous in design and most corrupt in execution—a fraud that stamps the man who mis-translated and falsified the report of the Sligo trial with infamy, and brands as a wretched persecutor and characterless moral murderer the other minister of Christ's Gospel who instigated and abetted the fraudulent translation and misrepresentation, that induced the sacred Propaganda at Rome to suspend Dr. O'Finan from exercising his ecclesiastical control over the diocese of Killala. Eternal dishonour be on the heads of these men; but, thank God, the Catholic church, pure and spotless in its principles, has but few similar degraded members.

Our painful task is now completed. We trust we shall have no occasion again to revert to it; but consistently with our duty as public journalists, we could not permit " A Roman Catholic Priest's of Killala " calumnious ribaldry to go before the public without the necessary accompanying observations.

(From the " Telegraph" newspaper, January 19, 1832.)

TO THE HON. FREDERICK CAVENDISH.

HON. AND DEAR SIR,

The able article entitled " The Diocese of Killala," which has appeared in the *Telegraph* of the 5th instant, sets me at liberty to address you thus publicly in a very different manner from that in which I thought it necessary to treat with you, when you did me the favor of calling upon me at Gresham's Hotel about six weeks ago, which, as you very truly observe, was the commencement of our acquaintance. I then foresaw, though I did not think it expedient to tell you so, that it would probably suit the purposes of the writer signing himself " A Roman Catholic Priest of Killala," in the *Telegraph* and another Irish paper, to represent me as *your dupe ;* and I felt it necessary to give you the idea, that I did not wish to claim anything from you, beyond what a perfect stranger had a right to require from an editor of a public newspaper, who had been made the deceived instrument of others, in injuring the reputation of an innocent person. It may, perhaps, be asked, what particular right or pretension I have to come forward, as I have done, in vindication of Bishop O'Finan's character ? My reply is, that I do *not* come forward with the intent of vindicating the character—injured in the estimation of the people of Ireland—of Bishop O'Finan. I come forward to lay before the people of Great Britain and Ireland the truth on a great public question,—on a question of immense importance to public tranquillity in Ireland at the present moment. That question is, whether, notwithstanding all that has occurred in the case of Bishop O'Finan, it is a *safe* policy, leaving morality out of the question, to deceive the Holy See by false statements, calculating upon subsequent impunity on the supposition that such deceit cannot be exposed without bringing discredit on the Holy See. I wish *all Christians* to know, that it is quite possible for those " who ought to know the truth," and whose station in the Catholic Church is such, as to authorise the Holy See to take for granted, that knowing the truth, they *would not* " impugn the known " *truth* " where the weightiest interests of Christianity and social order are at stake, to impose upon the Holy See ; while others, not in such a position as themselves, *could not* do so ; but at the same time I wish *all Christians* to be persuaded of that which every Catholic child learns among the first principles of Christianity, that " to impugn the known truth " is one of the six sins which are called " Sins against the Holy Ghost." (See Abridgment of Christian Doctrine, or First Catechism, p. 49. London : Keating and Brown, Printers to the Vicars Apostolic.) I wish in particular, all Christians in communion with the See of Rome, and who consequently believe that the Bishop of

Rome is the successor of St. Peter, to be persuaded, that though the fate of Ananias and Sapphira may not be the awful and immediate fate of those Catholics who *intentionally* use deceit towards the Holy See, the punishment of their crime either in this world or in the next will not be less severe.

The "Roman Catholic Priest of Killala" says, in his letter which the Editor of the *Telegraph* has republished in his paper of the 5th instant, that Bishop O'Finan " was indebted for his elevation to the See of Killala, to the influence of Archbishop M'Hale." He does not say whether that influence was exerted in Ireland or in Rome. If he means the former, although I do not believe that to be the truth, I have not, though I believe Dean Lyons has, the means of proving the falsehood of the assertion ; therefore, I will not deny it positively; but I do deny positively that Bishop O'Finan was in *any way* indebted for his elevation to the See of Killala, to the influence of Archbishop M'Hale in Rome.

In proof that my venerable friend is so indebted, the " Roman Catholic *Priest* of Killala " cites a letter, bearing the signature of Cardinal Fransoni (Prefect of Propaganda), dated Rome, June, 1836, which contains these words, " It is certain that his (Bishop O'Finan's) promotion to the episcopacy is owing to the recommendations of the Archbishop." Cardinal Fransoni in the above words, wrote what his Eminence *believed to be* the truth—his Eminence is incapable of doing otherwise ; but let the Roman Catholic *Priest* of Killala read the letter (and I know but of one) of Archbishop M'Hale—that is to say, the copy of it, which *he* can easily do—to the Cardinal Prefect, in which that Archbishop gives, as required to do, his opinion of the comparative fitness of the three candidates, O'Finan, Flannelly (Aladensis), and Costello, proposed to the Holy

See by the parish priests of Killala, and see if he can find *one word* of recommendation in favour *of any of the three*. If he can, I will give up my case.

Now for the facts or alleged facts. First—" This appointment (of Dean Lyons) formed the subject of a complaint to Rome, and the appointment was cancelled." I demur to the word "cancelled." They who may read in my fourth letter the evidence of Archbishop M'Hale on this point at the Sligo trial, will see why. But by what means was Cardinal Fransoni induced to believe that the appointment of Dean Lyons—whose character, in consequence of the *still existing autographs* of Bishop Waldron, stands far above the reach of the "Roman Catholic Priest of Killala"—*ought to be* cancelled? I could have read to you, Sir, unhesitatingly, at Gresham's Hotel, from a letter to me, dated Rome, February 9, 1840, proof of the villainy of those means, because I know that the writer of that letter, and that the respectable Ecclesiastic who furnished the writer of that letter with the information to be communicated to me " in confidence," would be the first to wish that the character of Dean Lyons should be cleared from the mass of calumny with which it has been assailed, and you would at once have seen *how* the Holy See has been made to believe, that the appointment of Dean Lyons ought to be cancelled; but I *then* thought it more prudent not to do so without express permission from the writer of that letter. I shall *still* content myself with saying, that I do not recollect having ever met with a greater proof of depravity in any case, than in the case of the totally false accusation, stated to me in that letter as believed at Rome, on account of the reputation enjoyed by the accuser.* But I

---

* Upon subsequent reflection on these words, I think it necessary to observe, that the following would have better expressed my meaning . . . . Rome. If so, it can only be on, &c.—C.

have felt it my duty to let my correspondent know the truth on this detestable calumny ; and he is not likely to be duped a second time by anything coming from the same quarter.

Second—But what am I to think of the reckless and unfeeling audacity which must revolt the feelings of every one, who, knowing the truth of the circumstances stated by the late Mr. West at the Sligo trial, relative to the appointment of the unhappy priest Barrett, to the parish of Crossmolina,* and knowing the circumstances under which the government offer of reward for information on the reported murder of that unhappy priest was withdrawn, would pen these lines, necessarily expressive, to those who know the truth of the melancholy circumstances of the Rev. Mr. Barrett's end, of an awful hardness of heart in the writer.† "The Rev. Mr. Barrett was deprived of the parish of Crossmolina and suspended. The Rev. Mr. Barrett complains to the Court of Rome, and he is forthwith restored. He did not, however, long survive, and in a few weeks after he was a lifeless corpse. Such was the melancholy fate of that young and amiable clergyman, whose missionary career justified the distinguished literary honours he obtained during a long and laborious academical course—May he rest in peace."

Really, Sir, the Holy See would have sunk in my estimation, if it could have supposed the existence in the accusers of Bishop O'Finan, of such heartless depravity, as it must have supposed in them, in order to justify a disbelief in their assertions ; but on the other hand, to all who know, as all at Ballina and Crossmolina *must know*, the

---

* See pages 132 and 133 of these letters.

† These last words after the word "lines" are here substituted for the word "heartless," which preceded that word in the letter I sent to the Honorable Mr. Cavendish.—C.

truth of the circumstances to which I am thus obliged reluctantly to allude in justification of Cardinal Fransoni, the existence of such heartless depravity in those accusers must become, on reading the above lines, a *melancholy certainty*. The painful feelings they *have* excited in my mind would be very inadequately, rather let me say, nowise, expressed, in the concluding words of the " Roman Catholic Priest of Killala," so injuriously applied to yourself, Sir, —" what confidence can the public have in the assertions of the man whose unblushing disregard for truth betrays him into so obvious a perversion—a perversion so easily detected." I did feel some relief to those painful feelings, in reading afterwards these concluding words of the article entitled " Diocese of Killala,"—" Eternal dishonour be on the heads of those men; but, thank God, the Catholic church, pure and spotless in its principles, has but few similarly degraded members."

It is indeed, honourable and dear Sir, consoling to me to read, penned by the Proprietor of the *Telegraph*, these last words, which I firmly believe to be the truth. They form an additional motive for my requesting you to believe me, not only anxious that you should have justice done to you, as I expressed myself in my letter to you of the 26th ult., but desirous also of being considered by you as your sincere friend. CLIFFORD.

No. II.

EXTRACTS FROM "IRELAND; SOCIAL, POLITICAL, AND RELIGIOUS;" BY GUSTAVE DE BEAUMONT; relative to the Union between Great Britain and Ireland. Vol. I.

Consequences of the Insurrection of 1798.—*The Union.*

After the insurrection of 1798, England, holding Ireland under her hand as a vanquished rebel, punished her without reserve or pity. Twenty years before, Ireland had entered into possession of her political liberties. England preserved a better recollection of this success of Ireland, and hastened to profit by abasement to place her again under the yoke.

The Irish parliament, after the recovery of its independence, became a subject of annoyance to England; to become its master, required an endless care of corruption, notwithstanding which, opposition was occasionally experienced; the opportunity seemed favourable for its suppression, and England resolved to abolish it altogether.

At this news poor Ireland was agitated, as a body about to be deprived of life still moves under the irons by which it is mutilated and torn. Out of thirty-two counties, twenty-one protested energetically against the destruction of the Irish parliament. This parliament, from which an act of suicide was demanded, indignantly refused (in 1799), and voted the maintenance of its constitutional existence.

Indignant at the servility demanded from the body of which he formed a part, Grattan vehemently denounced the ministerial proposition. But all resistance was vain.

The only serious obstacle to England was, the reluctance of the Irish parliament to vote its own annihilation. Hitherto its acts were bought, but now its death was to be purchased. Corruption was immediately practised on a large scale ; places, pensions, favours of every kind, peerages and sums of money, were lavishly bestowed ; and the same men who had rejected the Union in 1799, adopted it in 1800 by a majority of 118 to 73. It has been calculated, that out of the 118 votes, 76 were pensioners or placemen.* One of the greatest difficulties arose from the number of boroughs belonging to rich proprietors, who made a lucrative traffic of seats in parliament. To silence these complaints, every rotten borough was valued at 15,000*l.*, and this sum was proffered as an indemnity to all those who by the Act of Union would lose their political privileges.† The engagement was kept, and the total indemity amounted to 1,260,000*l.*

Thus was completed the self-destruction of the Irish parliament, an act imposed by violence and sustained by corruption ; but it was not effected without rousing in Ireland all that remained of national feeling and patriotic sentiment.

When Lord Castlereagh moved " that the bill should be engrossed," Mr. O'Donnell moved as an amendment, " that the bill should be burned" : to which Mr. Tighe also moved as an amendment, " that it should be burned by the hands

---

* Their names are given in Mr. O'Donnell's remarkable amendment, that the Address to the Lord Lieutenant should be presented by the pensioners and placemen. (See Grattan's Speeches, vol. iv. p. 5.)—*Tr.*

† A most extraordinary claim for compensation was made by the Bishop of Ossory ; his petition averred, that his predecessors had got promotion in consequence of their influence in the borough of Canice : he therefore claimed to be remunerated for having his chances of promotion diminished by the disfranchisement of the borough.—*Tr.*

of the common hangman." (But these were vain exhibitions of the "*iræ leonum vincla recusantium.*")

Constitutional and Political Effect of the Union.

Nothing is more common than to mistake the real effect of this measure, and the error arises from taking the word *union* sometimes in a moral sense, and sometimes in too extensive a political sense.

If by *union* we understand the concord and sympathy of two nations formerly divided; we must confess that this term is quite unsuited to the act under consideration; for England and Ireland were, perhaps, never more hostile to each other than after the Union of 1800.

It would also be a great error to suppose that the act of 1800 identified England and Ireland, so as to make this latter a province, subject in all points to the same government, the same police, and the same laws.

Before the act of union, Ireland had its own institutions; it preserved them after the union, with the single exception of its parliament.

When England added Ireland to herself, she did not resolve that Ireland should for the future be governed by the laws and principles of the English constitution; she did not and could not do any such thing. The English constitution is not a charter in a hundred articles which may be granted hastily to a nation in urgent want of a government. It is especially composed of usages, traditions, habits, and a multitude of statutes, connected with the usages from which they cannot be separated, whether they annul or confirm them. Now, though the observance of a law may be prescribed to a people, a usage or custom cannot be so enjoined: a custom is a complex fact, the result of a thousand preceding facts; it is consecrated, not imposed;

were it possible to remove its prescriptions to a people with whom it had not originated, it would be impossible to transfer its spirit. What, then, did England do, when she proclaimed the union with Ireland ? She declared that for the future all laws necessary to the two countries should be made in a common parliament, to which each should send representatives ; but whilst providing for the future, she left the past untouched ; and Ireland, united to England, remained in possession of all her laws and usages, except that which assigned her a separate parliament.*

Thus, after the act of union, there was always *an Ireland;* in the terms of this act, the three kingdoms form a single empire, under the title of the United Kingdom of Great Britain and Ireland. After the union with England, Scotland lost its name, but Ireland kept hers ; and she will still longer keep her national habits and passions.

SECT. VII.—*Corruption of the Irish Parliament.*

Parliamentary reform was rejected, and yet the corruption of parliament was extreme. The Commons were composed of three hundred members ; it would have been a difficult and troublesome task to bribe three hundred independent deputies ; but of this number the greater part were mere creatures of the aristocracy ; more than two hundred were members for rotten boroughs,† belonging

---

* By the eighth Article of the Union, it is enacted, " That all laws in force at the time of the union, and all the courts of civil and ecclesiastical jurisdiction within the respective kingdoms, shall remain now as by law established."

† Some were members for still more rotten corporations, the leaders of which combined to exclude the inhabitants of the towns, whether Protestant or Catholic, from the franchise, so as to enable themselves to sell the representation to some peer who trafficked in boroughs, receiving in return places in the customs or excise for themselves and their children.—*Tr.*

either to peers or rich proprietors, who were also members of the House of Commons; so that it was only necessary to purchase a few in order to have nearly the entire; sometimes a single person could dispose of twenty boroughs, or forty votes.

There were two modes of purchasing members of the House of Commons, by places and pensions. The first was the *honourable* mode of sale; government had a multitude of places at its disposal. When there was not a sufficient number, new places were created; when existing salaries were not sufficient for remuneration, they were augmented.* With regard to the petty offices of judicature and administration, unsuited to the dignity of national representatives, they were publicly sold, and the money thus raised was employed to purchase votes. When places were exhausted, pensions were given out of the Irish revenue;† the money thus employed was that of poor Ireland, who thus paid those that sold her while they sold themselves. Those pensions, which in 1756 were 44,000*l.* rose in 1793 to 120,000*l.* Finally, when places and the fund for pensions were exhausted, the government took what it wanted from the treasury. A viceroy rarely quitted Ireland without leaving an arrear of 200,000*l.*, and sometimes 300,000*l.*

---

* M. de Beaumont deems that his account of the venality and profligacy of the Irish parliament will scarcely be credited; but every one acquainted with the history of the country must be aware that the systematic corruption both of the Irish Lords and Commons is understated. Every body has heard the story of Mr. Hutchinson, founder of the Donoughmore family whose vote, on a particular occasion, was purchased by giving *his daughter* a cornetcy of dragoons.—*Tr.*

† "Infamous pensions to infamous men."—*Grattan's Speeches*, vol. i. p. 23.

This corruption was practised with incredible openness. Grattan * challenged its denial in the midst of the corrupt parliament, and no voice dared to contradict it. Sometimes after a strong opposition had been remarked in parliament, people were surprised to see it suddenly vanish; this happened in 1765, on the bill relating to the exportation of grain. But corruption was actually and openly avowed by the officers of the crown.† During the debate on giving the regency of Ireland to the Prince of Wales, the Irish attorney-general, Mr. Fitzgibbon, afterwards Earl of Clare, said to an astonished house and an indignant nation,—

---

* Mr. Grattan, in the name of the little minority that opposed the destructive and disgraceful system pursued by the Irish administration, used the following pointed and powerful words:—" We charge them publicly, in the face of the country, with making corrupt agreements for the sale of peerages; for doing which, we say they are impeachable. We charge them with corrupt agreements for the disposal of the money arising from the sale to purchase for the servants of the Castle seats in the assembly of the people; for doing which, we say that they are impeachable. We charge them with committing these offences, not in one, nor in two, but in many instances; for which complication of offences we say that they are impeachable—guilty of a systematic endeavour to undermine the constitution, in violation of the laws of the land. We pledge ourselves to convict them; we dare them to go into an inquiry; we do not affect to treat them as any other than public malefactors; we speak to them in a style of the most mortifying and humiliating defiance. We pronounce them to be public criminals. Will they dare to deny the charge? I call upon and dare the ostensible member to rise in his place, and say, on his honour, that he does not believe such corrupt agreements have taken place. I wait for a specific answer."

Major Hobart, the Irish secretary, refused to give any reply, on the ground that an inquiry of the motives of raising persons to the peerage was trenching on the royal prerogative.

† " The threat was proceeded on, the peerage was sold, the caitiffs of corruption were everywhere—in the lobby, in the street, on the steps, and at the door of every parliamentary leader, whose thresholds were worn by the members of the then administration, offering titles to some, amnesty to others, and corruption to all."—*Grattan's Letter to Lord Clare. Miscellaneous Works*, p. 187.

Y

"You have set up a little king of your own; half a million, or more, was expended some years ago to break an opposition, the same or a greater sum may be necessary now."

Their original parliaments were annual; by corruption they became rare, and were gradually protracted during the life of the king. Hence it followed, that if government purchased a majority in the first year, it remained its master, and disposed of it at its pleasure until the accession of a new king. To avoid the evil chance of too short a reign, it was once proposed to vote the supplies for twenty-one years; this was proceeding direct to the object, but the motion failed.*

In the reign of George III. a different system was established; the parliament became octennial, and was obliged to assemble once every two years at the least. The consequence was, that there was a new parliament to purchase every eight years; the members who sold themselves generally disappeared, and were not returned at the new elections; but others, equally venal, came in their stead, and what was regarded as a guarantee of independence, appeared to several a mere increase of expense to the English Government, or rather to Ireland, which had to supply the funds for corruption.

The House of Lords was still more easy to gain. The crown exercised over it that ascendency which a superior necessarily possesses over those who derive from him all they have. Besides, they were almost all a new nobility, and consequently had no root in the country. Occupied with their pleasures in London, or attending on the King of England, they were more eager to pass for English lords

---

* It was lost by a majority of one. The casting vote was given by Col. C. Tottenham, who rode up from the country, and arrived barely in time to turn the contest; hence, "Tottenham in boots" became a popular toast.—*Tr.*

than to be courageous defenders of the interests of their country. The session of the Irish House of Lords was only marked by some interchanges of courtesy with the viceroy;* and every time that these took place, the Irish lords displayed fresh meanness. " Never," says the biographer of Lord Charlemont, " did any nobility equal that of Ireland in varying the forms of obsequiousness and servility."

In truth, the Irish House of Lords neither was nor could be a source of embarrassment to the English government. It was too feeble as a national institution, to render its support valuable; but it offered the British government a resource of another nature which had its value. It sometimes happened that the pension fund was exhausted when money for corruption was wanting; in such a case, peerages were sold to persons who had no claim to nobility, and who were, therefore, eager to become purchasers, and the sums of money derived from this traffic served to purchase the consciences which still remained free. The great merit of the peerage in the eyes of the government consequently was, that the sale of its honours supplied money for bribing the Commons. " Thus," said Grattan, in the Irish parliament, (Feb. 8th, 1791,) " the ministers have sold the prerogatives of the crown to buy the privileges of the people."

The legal agent between England and the two Irish houses of parliament was the viceroy of Ireland. For a long time, this high functionary attended to no part of his office but the emoluments. The charge of viceroy was regarded as a sinecure which the English government bestowed to arrange some political exigency. When a

---

* For several successive days the journals of the Irish House of Lords present the same record. " Met—heard prayers—ordered the judges to be covered—adjourned."—*Tr.*

great lord or borough proprietor demanded some ministerial
employment in spite of his absolute incapacity, he was
named Lord Lieutenant of Ireland ; it was also occasionally
a means for some great person, poor or ruined, to make or
repair his fortune.   The viceroy possessed two magnificent
palaces, one in Dublin, the other in the suburbs, but he did
not reside in either.   Dublin could not compensate him for
London, where he was detained by his habits and his
pleasures.   There were some viceroys who never appeared
in Ireland, such as Lord Weymouth, who was nominated
to the office in 1765.   They generally went over only for
a few months to attend the opening of parliament, after
which they returned to England.   Although his sojourn in
Ireland was so brief, the viceroy derived large profits from
his office.   Lord Wharton, in two years, is said to have
netted 45,000*l*.   So unusual in Ireland was a resident
viceroy, that when Lord Townshend established himself as
such in Dublin (1768) people looked upon the event with
amazement, and seemed almost to doubt such a phenome-
non.

During the absence of the viceroy, the government was
entrusted to three lords justices, selected either from the
privy council, the judges of the four courts, or the dignitaries
of the Anglican church.   These were employed by the
English government to negociate the majority in parliament.

"There were always three or four influential persons in
the Irish parliament," says Dr. Campbell, " whose coalition
necessarily produced a majority on any question whatever,
These were the individuals whom it was important to gain,
and with whom the lords justices treated ; the most immoral
and scandalous transactions followed.   The lords justices
leased out the Irish administration ; they gave up to those
influential members of parliament the disposal of all the

employment and dignities dependent on the executive power, the revenue of Ireland, and the funds for pensions; bargaining that those persons in their turn should carry through parliament all laws desired by the English government. The vile agents thus employed by the English ministers were usually called ' undertakers.' "

In virtue of the powers thus delegated to them, the undertakers appointed to all offices, selecting governors of counties, sheriffs, justices of peace, crown lawyers, collectors of excise and customs, &c. : they could even bestow peerages, or rather, as they never did anything gratuitously, they sold all that was given them. Parliament—justice—administration—everything was venal in Ireland.

The undertakers had every sort of advantage over the viceroy; as they were always on the spot, they knew better than he did the actual state of affairs, and the course of intrigues. Besides, they lent themselves more pliantly than the viceroy to all the base manœuvres in which they were required to act as instruments. The office of viceroyalty was become so degraded, that no viceroy would execute it. All the power being placed in the hands of the undertakers, the viceroyalty was but a nominal dignity; and if a Lord Lieutenant had employed his right to dispose of places and honours, the undertakers would have complained of a breach of contract. In general, the recommendations of the viceroys were utterly disregarded.

Out of twenty viceroys, who, in the course of a century, succeeded each other in Ireland, Lord Townshend was the first who, in 1767, formed the project of administering the government himself. His intentions were pure and honourable; he wished to remove the dominant cabal, and govern Ireland directly without the intervention of the undertakers.

But though the corruptors were removed, all those whom corruption had tainted remained, with the wants and habits they had acquired. Henceforth there were several members of the Irish parliament in both houses, accustomed to live on the pension of England, and whose hostility was to be expected if payment was suspended. Lord Townshend who, above all things, wished to be responsible for Ireland to his own country, had recourse to the only means of success then known. He governed alone, but he governed by bribery, like those whom he had supplanted; but with this difference, that, being a novice in corruption, he submitted to exhorbitant conditions from the consciences he purchased; though he reserved no personal gains for himself, he spent more than the undertakers, who never made a bargain without reserving something for their own share. On the whole, it cost Ireland more to be governed by a man of honour than by a set of political intriguers.* He was honourable, and the system was not. There is not a more ludicrous exhibition in the world than an honest man practising corruption; he understands nothing of the roguery with which he has to deal; vile intrigues should be left to mean minds; in such they are sure to be superior.†

---

* When Lord Townshend left Ireland, the treasury was in an arrear of 265,000*l.*

† When one reflects upon the statements of the above extracts from Mr. De Beaumont's work, and upon the note of his translator, p. 334 of these Letters, and lastly, on these words of Mr. Burke, written in 1792, to Sir Hercules Langrishe—"There never was so much ability, or, I believe, so " much virtue in Ireland,"—who can blame the statesman, who shrinks from the *risk* (God forbid I should say or *think* the certainty) of throwing back— if such is to be, as many apprehend, the consequence of a Repeal of the Legislative Union—England and Ireland into the relative position in which these two component parts of an United Empire stood in 1792?—C.

Section III.—Religious Consequences.

*Legal and official Establishment of Protestant Worship in
the midst of Catholic Ireland—The University and the
Protestant Schools.*

We have seen the influence exercised by the English
and Protestant origin of the Irish aristocracy on civil and
political society; it only remains 'to examine the consequences of the same principle on religious society. Thus,
having considered how this principle affected the mutual
relations of the rich and the poor, governors and subjects,
we are about to consider its influence on the reciprocal
relations of Catholic and Protestant.

We have already noticed under what circumstances
England became Protestant, and how, when she made the
change, she was anxious that Ireland should do the same.
This anxiety was not merely the consequence of a religious
passion, it was also the result of a political principle. No
one in the sixteenth century could comprehend the complete separation of the temporal from the spiritual power;
but, perhaps, in no country was the union of secular government and religious authority more close than in England,
because nowhere else was the head of the state also the
head of the church. It is easy, then, to see why the Eng-
glish, having based their own government on Protestantism,
should have laid a similar foundation for the government of
Ireland. The church and state were then but one. At a
later period, a race of kings was hurled from the throne on
suspicion of Catholicism; it was then required not only to
be Protestant, but Anglican, in order to reign. This
is sufficient to show that the English must have wished
not only to render Ireland Protestant, but Anglican.

In the same way, as it is generally impossible to comprehend the existence of a religion without a system of public worship, the aristocracy could not understand a church without wealth and privileges; it was resolved that the church of Ireland should be wealthy and splendid, and that the aristocracy of Ireland should have an aristocratic church.

In England, the Catholic church was deprived of its lands and rights, which were transferred to the Protestant church. This spoliation might have been unjust, but it was effected for the advantage of a creed accepted by the majority of the nation. In Ireland, the same means for endowing the new church were adopted. It obtained the confiscated church-lands, and a right to the tithe of all Irish produce; but whilst the aristocracy introduced and established the new creed in Ireland, the people of the country clung to the ancient faith; so that a Protestant church was established at great expense in the midst of a Catholic population. Hence arose a forced alliance between the Anglican church and the aristocracy; the latter being naturally attached to the religious system it had founded, and by which it alone profited; the former being entirely devoted to the political power that had created it, and which could alone protect it from the common enemy. We shall hereafter see that the links which united them from their cradle were drawn closer together : although the king ceased not to be the head of the church and state, THE ARISTOCRACY SOON DOMINEERED OVER BOTH; THE RICH MANAGED THE STATE, AND THE BISHOPS THE CHURCH.* Perhaps we may be permitted to see, in this parity of

---

* It is in consequence, possibly, of a conviction in the mind of Lord Roden that such *is* the system of the *Protestant* Hierarchy in Ireland, that he has hastily and erroneously concluded that such *is also* the system of the *Catholic* Hierarchy in Ireland—see note (*g*) on p. 194 of these letters.——C.

origin and precocious confusion of church and state, the germ of a common destiny.

From the time of this union the invasion of Ireland was not simply political, it was also religious. Ireland was not only covered with an army of soldiers and greedy conquerors, but also with a spiritual militia of archbishops, bishops, and Protestant ministers, who came with the avowed intention of changing the national creed; and the people, from the very outset, saw their religion menaced by the pious auxiliaries of those who had taken away their country.

England, which had been, turn about, Catholic and Protestant, at the caprice of Henry VIII., which returned to Catholicism under Mary, became Protestant under Elizabeth, Puritan under the republic, and Anglican after the restoration of Charles II.——England, I say, without doubt believed it sufficient to establish a religious creed in Ireland, supported by the civil law, to effect the conversion of the country. The Anglican church was therefore instituted under the presumption that Ireland would shortly become Protestant. We have already seen the evils that were derived from this delusion; we have seen the persecutions, the massacres, and the cruelties perpetrated by the church and the civil government, in order to convert Ireland to Protestantism. All these rigours have been vain; Ireland has remained Catholic, and it is now a truth established by the irresistible evidence of statistical documents, that the Protestants of Ireland are fewer in proportion to the Catholics than they were two centuries ago. Their ratio to the Catholics in 1672 was as three to eight—at present it does not exceed three to twelve.* Thus Ireland is more Catholic after the persecution than it was before; a consoling

---

* First Report of the Municipal Corporations Inquiry.

result to every one who is the enemy of violence, and superior to the efforts of tyranny.

The age of the religious wars is past; the throats of Papists are no longer cut in Ireland; banishments to Connaught are no longer in force; the penal laws against Catholics have been successively abolished. Persecution has disappeared, but the Anglican church remains. At the present day, as in the first age of the Reformation, there is in Ireland a Protestant militia spread over the whole surface of the country.

The Anglican church envelopes Ireland in a vast administrative net; four provinces, thirty-two dioceses, thirteen hundred and eighty-seven benefices, two thousand four hundred and fifty parishes—such is the religious division of the country. The parish is only an administrative fraction of the benefice which constitutes the smallest ecclesiastical unity; the Protestant worship has establishments everywhere, even where there is no Protestant congregation. Thus, there are in Ireland eighty-two benefices and ninety-eight parishes in which there is not a single member of the Anglican church to be found. The services of the church are not dispensed in the ratio of the Protestant population, but a Catholic country is partitioned in reference to the Anglican church. There are entire dioceses where the population is almost exclusively Catholic, but this does not hinder them from possessing a complete establishment suited to Protestantism. To cite only one example, the diocese of Emly contains ninety-five thousand seven hundred inhabitants, of whom only twelve hundred belong to the Established Church; all the rest, to the amount of more than ninety-four thousand, are Catholics. Nevertheless, the Anglican form of worship has in this diocese fifteen churches, seventy-one benefices, and thirty-one salaried ministers.

The establishment of the Anglican church is naturally divided into the higher and lower clergy; four archbishops,* twenty-two bishops, three hundred and twenty-six dignitaries, such as deans, prebendaries, archdeacons, &c., compose the higher clergy; the inferior or parochial clergy comprises thirteen hundred and thirty-three beneficed ministers, to which must be added seven hundred and fifty-two curates.† A great number of the Anglican ministers possess benefices exclusively tenanted by Catholics, consequently they have nothing to do, and hence are frequently non-resident. It was calculated, in 1830, that out of thirteen hundred and five beneficed clergy, there were three hundred and seventy-seven absent from their posts, and in 1835 there were a hundred and fifty benefices without a resident rector or curate.

The clerical body in Ireland is nevertheless magnificently endowed. Besides its right to tithes, it possesses six hundred and seventy thousand acres of land. On the most moderate and authentic calculation its annual revenues amount to about a million sterling, and all these revenues go to the maintenance of the clergy.‡ The higher clergy, most of whose employments are sinecure, possesses immense wealth,—it takes to itself alone more than 320,000*l.* annually. The Primate or Archbishop of Armagh has over fourteen thousand a year; the revenue of the Dean of Derry is three thousand seven hundred pounds.§

Here, then, is a country where half of the population is annually famishing, and where a million of money is spent every year on the ministers of a creed which is not of that of the people!

Whatever objections may be made to the great wealth of a clerical body, it may still be conceived that a church

---

* First Report of the Municipal Corporations Inquiry.
† Ibid.   ‡ Ibid.   § Ibid.

endowed with large property may be popular and beneficial, when the creed that it represents is that of the entire population.

A religious nation may derive pleasure from surrounding the priests of its faith with splendour and magnificence. The more elevated the notions of the socerdotal office are, the more such a nation desires to aggrandise its ministers. Among a believing people, the priest is the sacred intermediate between God and man. Without him there is no public worship, no solemn devotion. The priest blesses man in his cradle, pronounces the benediction on his union when he takes a companion, stands by him in all the changes of life: he knows nothing of the joys of the rich, but he is never wanting in the hour of misery: the priest hears the first and the last cry of man. It is he who instructs the people in the duties of this life, and the requisites of that which is to come. The people receiving from the priest the knowledge of things human and divine, bestow on him in turn a merited and splendid support.

Besides, there is commonly in the fortunes of the church a principle of charity expressed or understood, which protects them against the apparent scandal of their enormity: this principle is, that the church has only the wardship and distribution of the property entrusted to it. The church is the natural patron of the indigent. It seems as if it could not be made too rich, because its riches are those of the poor. Whatever may be the liberality of political institutions, there is a multitude of individual miseries that escape them, and which charity alone can discover and relieve. A church is religious charity personified. Thus understood, the opulence of the church is easily comprehended, if it be not justified.

But how are we to explain the immense riches of a church which is not that of the people? How are we to understand the immense revenues of a clergy instituted for the cure of souls, as it canons delare, and placed in the midst of a population to which its spiritual aid is odious? What means this charge of instructing the people entrusted to men whose teaching the people rejects? What is the sense of entrusting public charity to a clergy which cannot feel sympathy for the temporal distress of its religious enemies?

The Established Church of Ireland is, in reality, useful only to the small number of Anglican Protestants whose religious wants it supplies, and who pay just so much less for the expence and support of their religion as they compel the entire population, hostile to their creed, to contribute. If the members of the Church of England in Ireland, who amount to about eight hundred thousand, were to support their own church themselves, it would cost each of them, on the average, one pound sterling annually; but, by distributing the charge over six millions and a half of Catholics, and six hundred thousand dissenters, the cost to each member of the Anglican church is only two shillings. What a singular foundation for a church is a system which plunders the poor in order to assist the rich!

A generous or wise aristocracy would endow a church out of its own property, in order that this church, its ally and its friend, might be an intermediate between it and the Pope, and alleviate to the people the injustice and rigours of an aristocracy; but here is an aristocracy seeking its support in a church, useful only to itself, and the burden of which is thrown upon the people.

Such, nevertheless, is the institution with which the fate of the Irish aristocracy is linked.

The bond that unites both, is not only moral, political, and religious, it is also judical; the Protestant ministers have not only the same creed, the same interests, the same passions as the landlords, but they moreover discharge the same administrative and judicial functions.

A great many clergymen of the Church of England are justices of the peace; * that is to say, in other words, the Catholics are placed under the civil jurisdiction of church-men, whose religious jurisdiction they reject. Thus the Irish Catholic, who only knows the Protestant ministers by the tithes he pays them, finds them on the bench, as judges at petty sessions and quarter sessions, meets them at the assizes, sharing in every process, whether civil or criminal where favour prevails over right, where the rich condemn the poor. It is bad, as a general principle, to unite tem-poral and spiritual power in the same hand; it is bad that the voice of the pious minister, which proclaims pardon in the name of the All-merciful, should be charged with the application of a law which does not pardon. And what will be the rule of the priest that is a magistrate? Will he judge crime as a sin, or sin as a crime? Whatever efforts his conscience may make, will he be able to separate one from the other? Will he not condemn, from pious motives, what the law will command him to absolve? and will not christian charity render him indulgent to faults, for which the law prescribes punishment? But, if it is bad to entrust a clergyman with the office of condemning or ab-solving those whom his religious conscience judges differ-ently from his reason as a magistrate, what will be the result if this minister be the pious enemy of those whom he is to punish in the name of the laws,——that is to say, if counsels of severity be found at the very source of charity; if, even without his own knowledge, every legal severity he

---

* Protestants, however, are excluded as well as Catholics.

inflicts on a misdoer flatters the first passion of his heart; if this same man, who, as a Protestant minister, levies tithes on the Catholics, sends them to prison as a justice of the peace? It must follow, that a church so constituted will excite universal hatred, and will have the power of rendering not less odious than itself, every authority of which it is the auxiliary or the friend.

No. III.

Extracts from Minutes of the Committee of Council on Education, with Appendices and Plans of School-houses. 1839-40. London:—Printed by William Clowes and Sons, Stamford Street, (for Her Majesty's Stationery Office.—1840.)

Page 1. —Minutes of the Committee of Council on EDUCATION, relating to the conditions on which the Parliamentary Grant of last Session, for the promotion of Education in Great Britain, is distributed; together with a LIST OF SCHOOLS to which Grants of Money have been made by the Committee up to the present time.

Extract from Minutes of the Committee of Council on Education, 24th September, 1839.

The following regulations will govern the appropriation of the sum entrusted to the superintendence of the Committee for the present year.

THIRD REGULATION.

The right of inspection will be required by the Committee in all cases. Inspectors, authorized by Her Majesty in Council, will be appointed from time to time to visit Schools to be henceforwarded aided by public money: the Inspectors will not interfere with the religious instruction, or discipline, or management of the School, it being their object to collect facts and information, and to report the result of their inspections to the Committee of Council.

Extract from the Minutes of the Committee of Council on Education, 4th January, 1840.

Ordered—That the following Instructions be issued to the Inspectors for their guidance in ENGLAND AND WALES.

(Here follow the ten Instructions.)

INSTRUCTION THE FOURTH.—PAGE 17.

The inspection of schools aided by public grants is, in this respect, a means of co-operation between the Government and the committees and superintendents of schools, by which information respecting all remarkable improvements may be diffused wherever it is sought; you will therefore be careful, at visits of inspection, to communicate with the parochial clergyman, or other minister of religion, connected with the school, and with the school-committee; or, in the absence of a school-committee, with the chief promoters of the school, and will explain to them, that one main object of your visit is, to afford them your assistance in all efforts for improvement in which they may desire your aid; but that you are in no respect to interfere with the instruction, management, or discipline of the school, or to press upon them any suggestions which they may be disinclined to receive.

INSTRUCTION THE SIXTH.

When engaged in the inspection of a School aided by a public grant, a requisition may be presented to you from the promoters of some school, in the same town or village not aided by a public grant, requesting you to visit their school. Whenever the special requirements of the public service permit your compliance with this request, my Lords are

z

of opinion, it is desirable you should visit the school, and should convey to the school-committee or chief promoters (whenever solicited to do so) the results of your experience in school-management and education. You will specially report any such application to this Committee.

My Lords are persuaded that you will meet with much cordial co-operation in the prosecution of the important objects involved in your appointment; and they are equally satisfied that your general bearing and conduct, and the careful avoidance of whatever could impair the just influence or authority of the promoters of Schools or of the Teachers over their Scholars, will conciliate the confidence and good-will of those with whom you will have to communicate; you will thus best fulfil the purposes of your appointment, and prove yourself a fit agent to assist in the execution of HER MAJESTY'S DESIRE, THAT THE YOUTH OF THIS KINGDOM SHOULD BE RELIGIOUSLY BROUGHT UP, AND THAT THE RIGHTS OF CONSCIENCE SHOULD BE RESPECTED.

By order of the
Committee of Council on Education,
JAMES PHILLIPS KAY.

I believe that I am quite correct in asserting, that in these few words of a YOUNG QUEEN of England, have been developed *for the first time* from the throne of England, not to say from any throne, the true principles of national education in a Christian country. It is perfectly in unison with the sentiments of her Majesty's Predecessor, King Ethelbert, as recorded by Bede in his History of the English Church—Life of King Ethelbert

Cæpere plures ad audiendum verbum confluere, ac relicto gentilitatis ritu UNITATI se Sanctæ Christi Ecclesiæ sociare. Quorum fidei et conversioni ita congratulatus esse Rex perhibetur, ut NULLUM TAMEN COGERET AD CHRISTIANISMUM; sed tantummoda credentes arctiore dilectione quasi concives sibi regni cælestis amplecteretur. Didicerat enim a doctoribus auctoribusque suæ salutis, SERVITIUM CHRISTI VOLUNTARIUM NON COACTITIUM ESSE DEBERE.

In Ireland, as the public is but too well aware, the National System of Education, though certainly productive of great public advantage, has also been made an occasion of a very distressing and injudicious public controversy; perhaps on account, in some degree at least, of an original defect in that system, which had for its basis principles less perfect than those LAID DOWN FOR ENGLAND BY QUEEN VICTORIA.

As one principal object of these letters is to do justice to the conduct of the Sacred Congregation of Propaganda at Rome, especially in affairs relating to the dominions of Queen Victoria, not only during the time that my lamented father-in-law, Cardinal Weld, was a member of that Congregation, from 1830 to *April* 1837, when he died, but even afterwards; it is not foreign to that object, but, on the contrary, rather essential to it, that the reader of them should be able to understand *the reasons why* that Sacred Congregation —in disapproving *decidedly* in 1839, 1840, and 1841, of the *newspaper* writings of Archbishop M'Hale on the System of National Education in Ireland and on the conduct of Archbishop Murray; and in *refusing to comply* with the wishes of the *nine* Bishops (two of whom afterwards altered their sentiments upon the case) who took part with that Archbishop against the *other seventeen* took so much time as it did to "investigate the truth or falsehood of the charges" (see p. 105 of these letters) brought against Archbishop Murray in the Irish newspapers, although the representations (or *mis*representations) were "made by parties who *should know* the truth."—*(Ibid.)*

These reasons will sufficiently appear from the two following *publications in Ireland*,—the first of them extracted from the *Dublin Evening Post*, the second from Battersby's Directory for 1841, pages 367, to 371.

Extract from a letter signed " Camillus," published in the Dublin Newspaper, entitled the Weekly Freeman's Journal, page 5, col. 2.—The date of the Newspaper is December 22, 1838.

The Archbishop of Tuam has proved, to the satisfaction of all disinterested men,—and the grasping industry of Athanasius has put it beyond the reach of refutation,—that the rules of this system are in direct opposition to the resolutions framed and circulated in 1826 by the aggregate authority of the bishops; and the slightest inspection of the documents connected with the case will assure the accuracy of their judgment. These resolutions were certainly the result of the deep apprehensions with which the prelates of Ireland viewed the mixed system of education, which the Commissioners of Inquiry were then projecting. The assembled prelates addressed a note to the Commissioners, " praying to know whether a general system of education, " founded on the principles embodied in those resolutions, " would be likely to meet their views, and receive their " approbation." The Commissioners, after a deliberation of three days, retorted their respectful compliments, and said : What?—Is it that the resolutions of the bishops, in synod assembled, were entitled to respect ? Not a word about it.

—That they should be maturely considered, or had been considered at all ? No.—That, in devising a system of education for Catholic Ireland, they felt pained to dissent from the resolutions, and to overlook the authority of all the Archbisohps and Bishops of that country ? Nothing of the kind.—What, then, can you imagine, was their reply ?—This : " As it is the duty of the Commissioners to report their views only to his Majesty, they must abstain from expressing any opinion on the subjects contained in the resolutions, which Dr. Murray (at the request and in the name of the Bishops) has transmitted to them." The Bishops, unawed by the haughty and domineering insolence of this note, re-asserted their determination of consistent and unflinching adherence to their resolutions ; and instructed Dr. Murray to say, in a note to Mr. Franklin Lewis, " that " the Bishops would *not discourage* (a word providentially " cautious) the attendance of Roman Catholic Children at " Schools in which the use of Christian (or scriptural) les- " sons might be required, *provided the regulations of said* " *schools were in accordance with the resolutions of the* " *Bishops.*" Well, perhaps the Commissioners, in the dictatorial note I have just quoted, were straitened by the prudence of official reserve, or wished to surprise the Bishops by an unexpected recognition of all their views in the report submitted to his Majesty. Listen to them once more : ." It is unnecessary for us to state, with respect to the resolution of the Roman Catholic Bishops, bearing date the 21st January, 1826, that we feel it our duty not to suffer them in any way to obstruct or interfere with us in the course we are pursuing."—Vide 9th Report of Education Inquiry, pages 8, 9, 21, 27.

Here, then, is an authentic profession of disregard for the resolutions of the Catholic Bishops, signed and sealed by the framers, and by the Commissioners of the present system.

Extracts from the Complete Catholic Directory, Almanack and Registry, for the year of our Lord, 1841.   Compiled by W. J. B.   *Dublin : sold at 5, Essex Bridge, and by all the Catholic Booksellers in Dublin.*

FEBRUARY, 1840.

10. Letter of ten bishops (including archbishop of Tuam) against certain circulars, sent through their dioceses to their clergy, requesting answers, touching National Education.

—— Annual synod of the Catholic Bishops of Ireland in Dublin.

11to16. Letter of the ten Prelates, concerning circulars on National Education.

12. Meeting and agreement of Catholic Bishops proposed to form a deputation, and present certain resolutions to the Lord Lieutenant, in order to effect an unity amongst all on the principles of National Education.

—— Resolutions of the Bishops' meeting——presentation of said resolutions to the Lord Lieutenant, and his refusal to comply with their unanimous request.

12—15. RESOLUTIONS OF THE CATHOLIC PRELATES ON NATIONAL EDUCATION.——" *At a General Meeting of the Roman Catholic Prelates of Ireland,* held in Dublin, on the 12th of Feb., the Most Rev. Dr. MacHale in the chair.

" It was moved by the Most Rev. Dr. Crolly, and seconded by the Right Rev. Dr. Cantwell, that a committee of three prelates favourable, and of three prelates unfavourable, to the present mixed system of education, be appointed to confer together, for the purpose of making an *arrangement* that would, if possible, establish *unanimity* on the system of combined education, amongst the prelates of Ireland.——THOMAS FEENY, Secretary."

" *At a General Meeting of the Roman Catholic Prelates of Ireland*, held in Dublin, on the 14th of Feb. Most Rev. Dr. Crolly in the chair.

" It was moved by the Right Rev. Dr. Coen, and carried unanimously, that the arrangement which was agreed upon by the above Committee, consisting of the Most. Rev. Dr. Crolly, Right Rev. Dr. Kinsella, and Right Rev. Dr. Ryan, on the one side, and the Most Rev. Dr. MacHale, the Right Rev. Dr. Higgins, and the Right Rev. Dr. Keating, on the other side, be adopted by this meeting, for the purpose of being submitted to his Excellency's consideration.—THOMAS FEENY, Secretary."

Then the following document was laid by four of the prelates before his Excellency.

" *At a General Meeting of the Roman Catholic Prelates of Ireland*, held in Dublin on the 14th of Feb. 1840, the Most Rev. Dr. Crolly in the chair, the following arrangement was proposed and adopted :—

" For the purpose of receiving the *unanimous* co-operation of the Roman Catholic Prelates, in diffusing the advantages of National Education, it was agreed on, that the subsequent regulations be respectfully submitted to the consideration of his Excellency the Lord Lieutenant :—

" 1st. That in every National School for the mixed education of Protestant and Roman Catholic children, the Roman Catholic Bishop of the diocese, the Parish Priest, or the Roman Catholic Curate of the parish in which such school is situated, may be a patron of said school, in order that *he may prevent the appointment of any teacher whose moral or religious conduct should be found objectionable, and, if necessary, direct the dismissal of such teacher from so important a situation.*

" 2nd. *That no book or tract whatsoever, for the religious or moral instruction of the Roman Catholic pupils, shall be admitted into a National School, without the previous approbation of the four Roman Catholic Archbishops of Ireland.*

"3rd. That in every National School where the pupils are all of the Roman Catholic religion, the *Roman Catholic Bishop of that diocese, or the Roman Catholic pastor* in whose parish the school has been established, as patrons of said school, *shall have power to appoint or dismiss the teacher or teachers, whether male or female ;* and that said bishop or pastor shall have access to the school at all times, for the purpose of giving religious or moral instruction to the scholars ; such instruction to be given by the clergy themselves, or by persons appointed by them for that purpose ; and further, that *every book used in the school for the religious or moral instruction of the Roman Catholic pupils shall be composed or selected by the Roman Catholic Bishop of the diocese.*

" 4th. That in future, for the satisfaction of the Roman Catholics, and for the greater security of their religion, the Lord Lieutenant be respectfully requested to select two Lay Roman Catholic members of the Board of National Education from *each of the four ecclesiastical provinces, and that, on the recommendation of the Roman Catholic Bishops of each province,* one of their body be appointed a member of the Board of Commissioners by his Excellency.

"5th. That the Lecturer in the Model Schools, appointed to instruct the Roman Catholic teacher of National schools in the principles of religion, morals, or of history (which is capable of being explained in an irreligious or offensive manner), should be a Roman Catholic, with satisfactory testimonials of religious and moral conduct, *signed by the Roman Catholic Bishop under whose spiritual jurisdiction he previously lived.*

" 6th That it would be very desirable to have *a Model*

School in each of the four provinces, when the funds of the National Board of Education might be found sufficient for that purpose, as such an establishment would inspire the inhabitants of the province with greater confidence in the system of national education.

" W. CROLLY, D.D., Chairman,"

To which his Excellency replied :—

" MOST REVEREND AND RIGHT REVEREND SIRS—I have considered your memorial with the attention which I am always disposed to pay to any representation from your respected body, and with a sincere desire to secure, if I could consistently with what is due to other parties, *the unanimous co-operation of the Roman Catholic prelates* of Ireland, in diffusing the advantages of a national education.

" You must, however, bear in mind, that the diffusion of these advantages, on equal terms, *among all sects and denominations of Christians,* is the fundamental principles of the system administered under the sanction of the legislature by the National Board ; and that any departure from that principle would be a violation of their duty, and a perversion of their trust.

" In conformity to that principle, the National Schools are equally open to Christian children of *all denominations,* and opportunities are equally afforded to their respective pastors to provide them with religious instruction, subject only to the condition of their not attempting to interfere with any, except those of their own church.

" The Board has nothing to do with the selection of patrons, who are locally chosen by those persons whose funds have been subscribed, or whose land has been given for the establishment of the schools.

" With them rest the appointment and dismissal of the masters, over which the Board exercises no control, except

what is absolutely necessary to secure them being morally
as well as intellectually qualified for the duties which they
have to perform.

" No books are allowed to be used in any of the schools
at the time of joint instruction, except such as are *published*
by the Board, or such as have been *sanctioned by their
authority*, in cases where they are provided by local
patrons.

" The model schools at Dublin are *under the immediate
superintendence of the Commissioners, subject to their frequent inspection*, a duty which I well know is not more
assiduously performed by any portion of them than by those
members of your own church whose services have been
devoted to the cause of national education, with such honour
to themselves and such benefit to their country.

" This, surely, ought to be a sufficient security to you,
that the lecturer appointed in these schools to instruct the
Roman Catholic teachers in the principles of religion, or
morals, or history, would never explain them in an irreligious or offensive manner.

" In thus briefly setting before you the manner in which,
on the chief points referred to in your memorial, the Board
have carried out the great principles of the national system,
I cannot but express my regret at the opposition which has
been given to them by some of your body ; and greatly,
indeed, should I rejoice, if that opposition can be removed
by a closer examination, or more intimate knowledge of
their proceedings.

" But, after the best consideration that I can give to the
subject, I am bound distinctly to state to you, that *no
changes such as you desire can, in my opinion*, be made
with advantage to the public, either in the constitution of
that Board, who have hitherto worked so harmoniously
together, or in the general regulations under which they

have acted, and which have enabled them successfully to make head against all obstacles, and to diffuse more and more widely, in each successive year, the blessings of moral and intellectual improvement, *founded on the precepts of divine truth, among all religious denominations* of the people of Ireland."

From these extracts, and from *the time taken* by the Sacred Congregation of Propaganda " to deliberate on the " awful interests " submitted to its decision " with a trem-" bling sense of the obligations which the nature of its office " imposes on it," (see p. 161 of these letters)—may be fairly estimated the truth and justice of the report, certified by Counsellor Fitzgibbon, before a notary public in Dublin (see p. 150 of these letters), to be an accurate report of what was stated *on oath*, before a *Protestant lay*-tribunal in Ireland, on the 20 March, 1837, by Archbishop M'Hale, *respecting the Sacred Congregation of Propaganda*, and afterwards submitted in Judge Perrin's notes, as the statement *on oath* of that Archbishop, to the Court of Exchequer in Dublin, on the appeal which the Hon. Mr. Cavendish *was advised* (Archbishop M'Hale knows by whom) to make, from the decision of the Court at Sligo, to the Court in Dublin. The readers of these letters must also decide for themselves, whether the Sacred Congregation of Propaganda is or is not justly liable to reproach, either for having conferred, *during the life-time* of Cardinal Weld, but *on the recommendation* of the then Secretary of the Sacred Congregation, now Cardinal Mai, the degree of Doctor of Divinity on Dean Lyons, or for having decided,—*after the decease* of Cardinal Weld, but perfectly in unison with his sentiments, as the letter of the Cardinal Prefect of that Sacred Congregation, dated 16th January, 1841, (see pages 34 to 39 of these letters,) shews it to have decided, *in opposition to the wishes* of Archbishop M'Hale, who, on the receipt of that letter of the Cardinal Prefect by the Catholic Hierarchy in Ireland, moved, in a General Synod of that Hierarchy, the resolution which was seconded by Archbishop Murray, and is as follows in p. 171 of the number for March 1841 of " the Catholic Magazine."—London : Booker, Jones, &c.

Resolved,—" That the assembled Prelates do, before they separate, transmit to His Holiness a most dutiful address, tendering to Him the expression of their most profound gratitude for this fresh proof of the Holy Father's paternal solicitude for the spiritual interests of the Roman Catholics of Ireland, and pledging themselves to the most sincere, strenuous, and persevering exertions, in carrying into effect all His Holiness's wishes and instructions."

IV.

Extracts from the Examination of the Reverend PETER KENNY, *late Superior of the Society of Jesus in Ireland, who died at Rome, November* 19, 1841.

Father Kenny appeared on the 7th and 8th December, 1826, before the following Commissioners, nominated and appointed by a commission under the Great Seal, bearing date the 14th day of June, 1824, to enquire into the state of public education in Ireland, and report thereon to Parliament, namely—T. Frankland, Esq., M.P.; J. Leslie Foster, Esq., M.P.; W. Grant, Esq., M.P.; J. Glassford, Esq.; Right Hon. A. R. Blake, Chief Remembrancer. The examination of Father Kenny,—as it appears in the eighth report to the King of the Commissioners, consisting of 461 pages folio, ordered by the House of Commons to be printed 19th June, 1827,—consists of 422 Questions and Answers, occupying from page 381 to page 403 of the Report.

Ques. 1. The Commissioners understand that you were for some time since the Vice-President at the College of Maynooth? I was.

2. In what year did you enter upon that situation? In the year 1812. I think in the month of September, and I left in the following June. I know that the time that I was Vice-President was not longer than one year.

4. Who was the President at that time? Dr. Murray. Were your duties at Maynooth to assist the President? I was his representative when he was absent; and it was my duty to assist him in the general government of the House.

5. Would you be so good as to state what circumstances led to your election to that office? It was Dr. Murray's

own request to me which led to it. He found it rather difficult at the time to get a person to fill that office, and he requested of me to undertake it. My compliance was a great sacrifice of my convenience; but as he was extremely desirous that I should do it, I consented to go, upon the express condition, that I was not to remain longer than a year, if I could remain so long. My acquiescence was entirely a matter of accommodation to meet his wishes.

6. At the time Dr. Murray applied to you to take upon yourself the office of Vice-President of Maynooth, were you a resident in Ireland? I was at that time an officiating priest in Dublin.

7. Are we to understand that you were not a candidate for that office? It was not in any respect that I wished to take that office. It was solely an act of compliance with the wishes of Dr. Murray, and which he was pleased to say he considered an act of condescension on my part.

22. In what seminary were you yourself educated? I studied in Palermo; I studied Theology there. I was also in other seminaries.

23. Be pleased to name them? I was at Carlow seminary; I was afterwards at Stonyhurst, in England; and finished at Palermo in Sicily my course of Theology.

24. Are you a native of Ireland? I am. I am a native of this city.

25. Can you state whether the education given in the College at Palermo is the same, or materially different from that of Maynooth? All the principles of faith and morals are precisely the same.

26. Have you taken the oaths of allegiance appointed for the Roman Catholics of Ireland? I have.

27. Were the principles expressed in those oaths, with respect to the power of the Pope, taught and inculcated at Maynooth when you were there? Most certainly.

28. We understand that since you have left Maynooth, you have been connected with another establishment for the education of the youth of this country? I am connected with an establishment of that nature at Clongowes Wood.

32. Have the goodness to state how long it was after you quitted Maynooth, that you opened the seminary at Clongowes for the reception of pupils? In 1814 the seminary was established at Clongowes; and in the month of July the school commenced.

33. Are you the only individual connected with the establishment at Clongowes Wood, who has at any time held any situation in the College of Maynooth? The only one.

34. Is there an individual in the College at Maynooth who at any time held a situation as an instructor, or in any other way connected with the establishment at Clongowes Wood? Not one.

35. Will you have the goodness to state what number of students have gone from your establishment at Clongowes to Maynooth? I cannot state it with certainty; I have a recollection of two; I think that there was another, but I cannot call his name to mind. There were certainly two who were our pupils when boys, who went to Maynooth after they had left Clongowes Wood.

36. Are there any students at Clongowes whom you know to have the intention of going into the College of Maynooth? No, I cannot say there are : I do not know there is such an intention on the part of any of the students at Clongowes. I might say, as the question is asked, that I was not prepared to be called upon to give any account of the particulars of the establishment at Clongowes Wood. At this moment it has occurred to me, that I have heard that it is the intention of one young boy to go to Maynooth, and that there is some probability of his going thither. I suppose he will go there, because I have heard he purposes

to enter into the secular priesthood, that is all I know of the matter.

37. Do you seek to prevail upon, or to induce young men to go to Maynooth, or dissuade them from doing it? In the matter of ecclesiastical vocations, we never interfere; I mean, we are never the first persons to suggest or introduce it in any way.

38. Does there exist any sort of connection between the establishment of Clongowes Wood and the College of Maynooth? No more than we are priests and Catholics; that is, the clergy of Clongowes Wood are Catholic priests, as well as those who are at Maynooth. There is no connection by which it could be said, that those two houses of Catholic education are more connected than any other two Catholic establishments, which any individuals might please to select.

39. Since you have resigned the situation of Vice-President of the College of Maynooth, have you at any time given instruction within that College? I have.

40. Have the goodness to state on what occasions? On the same occasions on which I gave them before: I have given instruction of the same nature.

41. How often has that occurred? As well as I can now recollect, it cannot be more than three or four times; but I cannot distinctly recollect. I have been very often asked, but declined to accede to the request.

42. On those occasions, we understand you to allude to the spiritual retreats which you have conducted within the college? Yes.

43. And that you gave exhortations and instructions similar to those given by you when Vice-President? Exactly of the same nature.

46. Do you belong to the Order of the Jesuits? I am a Jesuit.

47. Was there any other person in Maynooth, at the time you were Vice-President, belonging to that Order? No, there was not.

48. Is it within your knowledge, that any person at Maynooth has connected himself with that Order? Yes; there are a few who have performed a part of their education at Maynooth.

49. State as nearly as you can, what number they amount to? Three, I distinctly recollect; it seems to my mind, there has been a fourth.

50. Have you reason to be fully assured that there have been no more than four? I am sure—at least, I cannot recollect that there is another; and now I recollect that there has not been a fourth person.

51. During the time you were Vice-President of Maynooth, did you think it your duty to prevail upon any individuals within the college to join your Order, or endeavour to induce them to do it? Never; I never had a conversation or said a word upon the subject, with the exception of one occasion, when a proposition was voluntarily made to me by a young gentleman of that kind, and which I formerly then declined.

52. Had the bull of the late Pope, which authorised the re-establishment of the Jesuits, as an order, in different countries, been issued when you were at Maynooth? No, it had not; it was only in August, 1814, that that bull was issued, and I have already stated, that I left Maynooth in the year 1813.

53. Did the Jesuits, then, in any sense, exist in this country as an Order? They were not recognised as such—they could not be.

54. At what time did you become a member of the Order of the Jesuits? I went to Sicily in the year 1808, or the

beginning of the year 1809 ; I am not quite sure which, but it was at that period.

55. Was the college at Palermo, at that period, under the care of the Jesuits? Yes; there was a partial restoration of the Order, for the kingdom of the two Sicilies, in the year 1804. My studies were performed in that college, which was a college of Jesuits.

56. Did that partial restoration take place through the medium of a bull? It took place by a special brief, as we ·denominate it : this is a different document from the one which I have mentioned before, and which is called a bull.

57. Was that partial restoration, which you say took place in the.year 1804, by the authority of the See of Rome? Yes, it was.

58. Was it a complete restoration, as far as Sicily was concerned? Yes, but confined to the place.

59. It was local? It was.

60. Were you at Stonyhurst after you had been at Palermo? I have been to Stonyhurst since, but not to study there.

61. During the time you were at Maynooth, had you any sort of connection with the individuals connected with the establishment at Stonyhurst? We were friends ; and being upon terms of friendship, I corresponded with them, but never in any manner on the affairs of Maynooth.

150. You have said that your acceptance of the office of Vice-President was attended with a considerable sacrifice of your own convenience ; and that at the time you accepted it, you entertained a doubt whether you could continue at Maynooth so long as a year,—will you explain what you alluded to, when you said it was a sacrifice of your convenience? Of course I gave up my situation in the chapels in town, which I then filled ; I left my own house in Dublin, and exposed myself to all those inconveniences that are at-

tendant on a man relinquishing a situation with which he is pleased, to take one he did not seek nor wished to have; and on leaving his own friends, to live amongst gentlemen who were utter strangers to him.   Other sources of inconvenience might be added, but these are surely sufficient to justify the assertion.

151. Was the purchase of Clongowes Wood effected while you were Vice-President of Maynooth?   No; not until after I had left it.

152. Did you take any measures for collecting your present assistants at Clongowes, or any one to fill those stations in your establishment, while Vice-President of the college at Maynooth?   No.

153. You have said that the Society of Jesuits was restored in Sicily in the year 1804; that is, as we collect, ten years before it was restored generally by the Pope; had it been restored in a partial manner before it had been restored in Sicily?   It had.

154. State where?   In Russia.

159. You must be aware that it has been very generally stated, that the Jesuits continued in fact, though not in name, under the title of Péres de la Foi; are we to understand that this is quite erroneous?   It is quite erroneous.

160. Under what name did they continue to exist in Russia?   Under the name of Jesuits.

161. Was there no interruption to their continuance in Russia?   No interruption.

162. Are they not suppressed at present in Russia? They are not, properly speaking, suppressed; they are exiled from Russia.

180. While you were Vice-President, did you communicate the circumstance of having been appointed to that office to the General of the Order, or to any authority in the Order, intermediate between the General and yourself?   I

never made to him, or received from him, any communication on the subject; and to this moment, I believe that my appointment is utterly unknown in that quarter, as if it had not occurred.

181. If the General of the Order had prescribed the course of conduct to pursue, as Vice-President, in the shape of an order, would you have felt yourself bound to obey it? No, unless such advice were conformable to all my other duties there, and such advice as I would have taken from any other friend.

182. The question is, whether the peculiar duties you were called upon to perform there, as Vice-President, fell under the jurisdiction of the General of your Order, so as to entitle him to interfere if he thought fit? The duties of my office there could not in any way be under his jurisdiction; but he has a right to give me advice on every subject on which he may think right to advise me; but I have no obligation to follow that advice, unless my conscience tells me it is conformable to every other duty I have to discharge.

183. Would you have felt yourself bound to obey implicitly his commands, if those commands did not transgress the rules of your Order? I should not feel myself so bound on every occasion that might possibly occur, because, though the command might not transgress any rule, literally and separately taken, yet it might be in conflict with some other duty.

184. Can you give any instance, as an illustration of what you allude to? The rule of the Order may be supposed to be merely the letter of the law, as contained in the rule. Now that rule does not expressly tell me to honour my father or my mother; there then is a duty not included in the rule, which I am bound to discharge. Now, by possibility, the superior might give an order which would be within the strict letter of the rule of the order, and at the

same time be in conflict with this other duty; and if so, I should not be bound to obey that command: such is the illustration that occurs to me. The rule of the Order, from the beginning to end, does not contain the Lord's Prayer. Now suppose the General were to give me an order not to say the Lord's Prayer,—it might be said, there was nothing in the rule of the Order, literally assumed, to prevent him giving that direction; and yet if he were to give me such an order as that, I should not comply with it, because it would be against a known duty.

185. If he were to give you a command, with respect to which there might be a doubt, whether it was in conflict with any other duty or not,—should you have felt yourself at liberty to resolve that doubt? Most certainly; in such a case it would be on my conscience to apply to the best advice I could procure, in the same way as any discreet person would apply to the best advice he could get in a case of difficulty.

186. Should you in that case be at liberty to apply for advice to any person you please? To any person whom, in my conscience, I thought proper to consult, whether bishop, priest, or layman.

187. Suppose that the General of the Order were to take exception to the oath of allegiance in this country, and desire his inferior in this country not to take it, must he obey—the question supposes that the inferior has not taken the oath at the time he receives the Superior's command? If I had a doubt in my own mind of the propriety of the oath that was to be administered, I should act as I would in the case before-mentioned; if I had no doubt, I would take it; for ALLEGIANCE IS A DUTY WHICH A SUBJECT OWES TO HIS SOVEREIGN, BEFORE ANY OTHER OBLIGATION IS CONTRACTED, WHETHER TO BISHOP OR SUPERIOR, AND HE IS THEREFORE ALREADY BOUND BY THAT PRIOR DUTY.

188. Suppose the General of the Order were to admit

the principle—that allegiance was due by the inferior in this country to the Sovereign ; but to take objection to the particular form of the oath of allegiance,—he having been apprized of the form of oath, not through any application made to him by his inferior for advice, but from other sources,—the question is, in that state of things, were he to think proper to issue his command to his inferior, not to take that particular form of oath, would the inferior, in the case put, be at liberty to take it ? He would be perfectly at liberty to take it, if he had sufficient grounds to believe that the oath was otherwise lawful. The way he is to ascertain whether there are just grounds for admitting a particular form of oath is, not by applying to his religious superior, who is not the proper tribunal for deciding on the lawfulness or unlawfulness of an oath, he should go to the proper tribunal, which is the judgment of the bishops. No religious superior in the Catholic Church, who is not a bishop, is a judge in matters relating to faith and morals.] The inferior should then apply to the bishop, and if he tells him that such oath is consonant to the principles of Catholic faith, or rather to be more explicit, that it contains nothing repugnant to the truths of divine revelation, as held in the Catholic Church ; —then such religious inferior would not only be justified in taking that oath, but be bound to do it when the laws of his country required it.*

---

* From this and the preceding answer, and from the answers to questions 4 and 5, the reader of these pages will easily understand, why my lamented father-in-law, Cardinal Weld, attached so much importance to the circumstance of the selection by Gregory XVI. of Father Robert S. Leger, who, besides having had the advantage of being personally acquainted with Lord William Bentinck in Sicily, when he was a member of the Jesuits' College there in 1811, was, in 1833, a member of Clongowes' Wood College, of which he is now Superior, to be Superior of the Roman Catholic mission in Bengal. See his Pastoral Letter among the Papers laid on the table of the House of Lords, October 4, 1841, No. 6, in my letters on East India affairs. London : Jones, 63, Paternoster-row, 1841.—Pages 53 to 59.

NOTICE TO THE PUBLIC.

As repeated intimations have been made to me during this and the preceding month, that the course I am pursuing respecting some of the parties concerned in the trial at Sligo, of March 20 and 21, 1837, is nowise calculated to be of service to the reputation of my venerable friend Bishop O'Finan; but directly calculated to produce public scandal, and likely to draw down upon him and upon myself the censures of the Catholic Church, I hereby declare, that I alone am responsible for every word contained in these letters; and that I submit them entirely, in every thing appertaining to faith, morals, or whatsoever is within the jurisdiction of the Catholic Church, to the judgment and decision of the Holy See, to which I engage to conform myself in all such matters in the spirit of perfect obedience.

CLIFFORD.

London, January 18,
Feast of S. Peter's Chair at Rome, 1842.

F I N I S.

W. Davy, Printer.
8, Gilbert-st. Oxford-st.

Check Out More Titles From HardPress Classics Series In this collection we are offering thousands of classic and hard to find books. This series spans a vast array of subjects – so you are bound to find something of interest to enjoy reading and learning about.

Subjects:
Architecture
Art
Biography & Autobiography
Body, Mind &Spirit
Children & Young Adult
Dramas
Education
Fiction
History
Language Arts & Disciplines
Law
Literary Collections
Music
Poetry
Psychology
Science
…and many more.

Visit us at www.hardpress.net

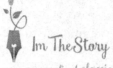

CPSIA information can be obtained
at www.ICGtesting.com
Printed in the USA
BVHW081612120819
555665BV00014B/1287/P